Teacher's Book

A RESOURCE FOR PLANNING AND TEACHING

Level 3.1 Enjoy

Introductory Selection:	**Miss Nelson Is Missing!**
Theme 1	**Oink, Oink, Oink**
Theme 2	**Community Ties**
Theme 3	**Disaster!**
Theme 4	**What's Cooking?**
Theme 5	**Weather Watch**
Theme 6	**What a Day!**

Senior Authors

J. David Cooper
John J. Pikulski

Authors

Kathryn H. Au
Margarita Calderón
Jacqueline C. Comas
Marjorie Y. Lipson
J. Sabrina Mims
Susan E. Page
Sheila W. Valencia
MaryEllen Vogt

Consultants

Dolores Malcolm
Tina Saldivar
Shane Templeton

INVITATIONS
TO LITERACY

Houghton Mifflin Company • Boston

Atlanta • Dallas • Geneva, Illinois • Palo Alto • Princeton

Literature Reviewers

Librarians: **Consuelo Harris,** Public Library of Cincinnati, Cincinnati, Ohio; **Sarah Jones,** Elko County Library, Elko, Nevada; **Maeve Visser Knoth,** Cambridge Public Library, Cambridge, Massachusetts; **Valerie Lennox,** Highlands Branch Library, Jacksonville, Florida; **Margaret Miles,** Central Library, Sacramento, California; **Danilta Nichols,** Fordham Library, New York, New York; **Patricia O'Malley,** Hartford Public Library, Hartford, Connecticut; **Rob Reid,** L.E. Phillips Memorial Public Library, Eau Claire, Wisconsin; **Mary Calletto Rife,** Kalamazoo Public Library, Kalamazoo, Michigan

Teachers: **Debora Adam,** South Dover Elementary School, Dover, Delaware; **Linda Chick,** Paloma School, San Marcos, California; **Bea Garcia,** Kolfax Elementary School, Denver, Colorado; **Flavia Gordon-Gunther,** Morningside Elementary School, Atlanta, Georgia; **Linda Macy,** Washington Elementary School, Wichita, Kansas; **Paul Warnke,** Onate Elementary School, Albuquerque, New Mexico; **Margaret White,** Hilton Head Elementary School, Hilton Head, South Carolina

Program Reviewers

Debora Adam, South Dover Elementary School, Dover, Delaware; **Sue Bradley,** Ardmore Elementary School, Bellevue, Washington; **Marsha Kiefer,** Truman Elementary School, Rolla, Missouri; **Paul Warnke,** Onate Elementary School, Albuquerque, New Mexico

Be a Writer Feature

Special thanks to the following teachers whose students' compositions are included in the Be a Writer features in this level:

David Burton, Blake Lower School, Hopkins, Minnesota; **Linda Chick,** Paloma Elementary School, San Marcos, California; **Debora Adam,** South Dover Elementary School, Dover, Delaware

Credits

Photography: Tracey Wheeler Studio, pp. 6A, 34D, 34G, 34H, 60A, 60K, 60L, 60O, 88A, 88N, 114A, 114C, 114H, 114K, 114M, 114N, 117B, 117E, 119A, 119C

Banta Digital Group, pp. 34C, 35B, 60K, 60N, 88C, 88O, 114N, 114O, 117E, 119C

Harry Allard, p. 8A; F. Damm (ZEFA/The Stock Market), p. 67D; Francois Gohier (Photo Researchers Inc.), p. 88N; Ross Humphreys, p. 67A; Don King (The Image Bank), p. 114M; Stephen J. Krasemann (DRK Photo), p. 67D; Charles Krebs (Tony Stone Images), p. 67D; Glenn Kremer, p. 34H; Donivee Martin Laird, p. 91A; Renee Lynn (Tony Stone Images), p. 35F; Roy Morsch (The Stock Market), p. 67D; Marc Romanelli (The Image Bank) p. 99M; Eugene Trivizas, p. 35C; Art Wolfe (Tony Stone Images), p. 60M, 88N

Illustration: James Marshall, Title Page

Acknowledgments

Special thanks to David E. Freeman and Yvonne S. Freeman for their contribution to the development of the instructional support for students acquiring English.

Grateful acknowledgment is made for permission to reprint copyrighted material as follows:

"August," by Sandra Liatsos. Copyright © 1990 by Sandra Liatsos. Reprinted by permission of Marian Reiner for the author.

Launching the Program

with

Miss Nelson Is Missing!

INTRODUCTORY SELECTION

INVITATIONS
TO LITERACY

Launching the Program

Managing Instruction

Grouping

Use a variety of group sizes to meet individual needs.

- **Whole class** for concepts all students need to learn.

- **Small groups** of three or more for meeting special needs.

- **Cooperative groups** with partners for completing a common task.

- **Individual activities** for focusing on a special need or individual choice.

Previewing the Literature

Cooperative Learning

Ask students to look through their anthologies and to work with partners to complete the graphic organizer. Discuss students' responses.

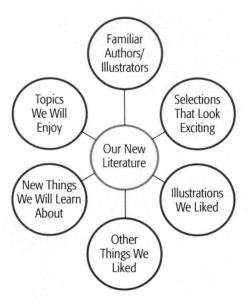

Discussing Themes

Direct students to the table of contents of their anthologies and point out that the literature is organized in groups that go together called themes—**Oink, Oink, Oink, Community Ties,** etc. Ask volunteers to read the theme titles. Have the class select one theme to preview. Divide the class into small groups. As students look through the theme, bring out the following points in discussion:

- Each theme has different types of literature—stories, information, poems.

- There are activities for responding to the literature.

- Author/illustrator information is given.

- **Be a Writer** is a place where student writers share their work.

Making a Collage About Me

Invite students to make a collage that tells about themselves by gluing pictures on a piece of paper. Suggest that they cut out pictures that show:

- what they like to do for fun
- their favorite foods
- how they feel
- things they would like to learn
- their interests

Put names on the backs of collages and display them for others to see. You may want to make and display your own collage. As everyone gets to know each other, have students guess which collage belongs to which student.

Materials
- magazines
- safety scissors
- construction paper
- markers or crayons
- glue

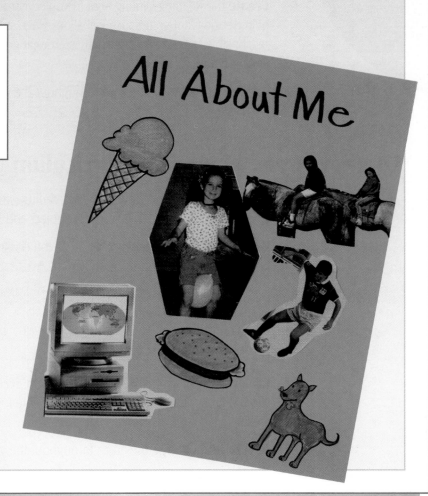

Portfolio Opportunity

Save students' collages for a record of their interests and favorite activities.

A Literacy-Centered Classroom

A Reading-Writing Area

Discuss with students the importance of having a place in the classroom where reading and writing get special attention.

Brainstorm with students a list of things the Reading-Writing area might have:

- books to check out
- comfortable chairs and pillows
- a rug or carpet
- a bulletin board to display things written about books students have read and student-written books
- tables

- writing materials—paper, pencils, pens, markers
- magazines and newspapers
- a checkout system for books
- a plant or other things to make the area attractive
- posters

Create the Reading-Writing area in your classroom by having students help decide what your space will allow. Have students sign up to be responsible for certain tasks such as arranging book displays, organizing writing materials, etc.

Add to and change the area throughout the year.

Literacy Areas Across the Curriculum

Discuss with students how they use reading, writing, listening, speaking, viewing, and thinking skills in every subject and in everyday life.

Brainstorm with students other areas the classroom might include to help them become more literate:

- a listening area
- a display area for science and social studies activities
- a math manipulatives table

- an area for painting and other art projects
- a computer area

Create other areas by having students help decide what the class needs. Have small groups of students be responsible for helping to arrange the area.

Add to and change the areas throughout the year.

Making an Independent Reading-Writing Chart

Explain to students that there will be time each day for independent reading as well as independent writing. Ask students to share their ideas about what everyone should do during these times. Record responses on a chart to display in the classroom.

Reading	Writing
• Everyone reads during reading time.	• Everyone writes during writing time.
• Select reading materials before the special time.	• Write stories, letters, cartoons, and other things.
• The teacher may talk and read with the students.	• There may be teacher/student conferences.
• Keep a record of books read.	• Have a folder to keep writing.
• Share with a friend what has been read.	• Share your writing with a friend.

Managing Instruction

Independent Reading and Writing

Schedule daily time for independent reading and independent writing. Build time up to 15–20 minutes per day for each.

Give these times special names:

- DIRT, Daily Independent Reading Time
- WART, Writing and Reading Time
- DEAR, Drop Everything and Read

 # Making a Journal

Discuss with students that a journal is a place for them to keep their thoughts, questions, and feelings about what they have read. Journals may also include a list of new words, things they have written, and a list of stories they would like to read independently.

Materials
- writing paper
- construction paper or notebooks
- stapler
- yarn
- markers or crayons

Invite students to create their own journals and decorate the covers. Have them divide their journals into sections:

- Reading
- Vocabulary
- Writing
- Independent Reading

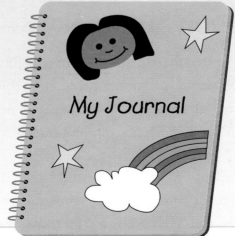

Managing Instruction

Journals

There are many different ways to use journals. Encourage students to:

- record thoughts and feelings about what they read
- write or draw responses
- keep a list of new/interesting words
- write predictions or questions about their reading

Read students' journals and write responses to their entries.

Have students read a partner's journal and write a response.

INTRODUCTORY SELECTION:

Miss Nelson Is Missing!

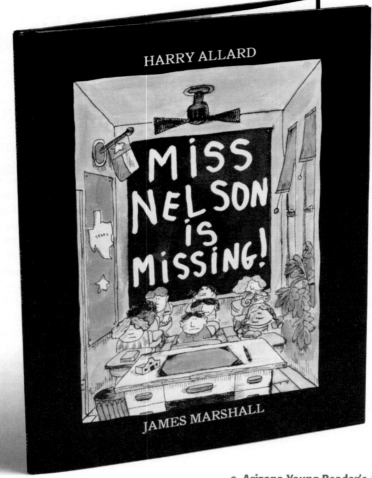

HARRY ALLARD

JAMES MARSHALL

AWARD WINNER

- **Arizona Young Reader's Award**
- **California Young Reader Medal**
- **Georgia Children's Picture Storybook Award**

by Harry Allard

Other Books by the Author

Miss Nelson Is Back
The Stupids Step Out
The Stupids Take Off

Selection Summary

The kids in Room 207 are the worst-behaved class in the school. Their teacher, Miss Nelson, decides that something must be done. One day the students are greeted by a new teacher in an ugly black dress—Miss Viola Swamp. Miss Swamp scares them into behaving and loads them down with work.

The students want Miss Nelson back! Just as they are losing hope, Miss Nelson returns to school. The students are overjoyed and, of course, behave like angels. But Miss Nelson won't say where she has been. And when she returns home that night, she hangs up her coat beside an ugly black dress.

Lesson Planning Guide

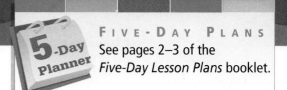

FIVE-DAY PLANS
See pages 2–3 of the
Five-Day Lesson Plans booklet.

	Skill/Strategy Instruction	Meeting Individual Needs	Lesson Resources
1 **Introduce** *the* **Literature** *Pacing: 1 day*	**Preparing to Read and Write** Introducing a Reading Strategy, 10A Prior Knowledge/Building Background, 10A **Selection Vocabulary**, 11A • misbehaving • detective • worst-behaved • change • act up • rapped • secret	**Other Choices for Building Background**, 11A	*Literacy Activity Book,* Reading Strategies, p. 1; Vocabulary, p. 2 **Transparency**, Vocabulary, IS–1
2 **Interact** *with* **Literature** *Pacing: 1–3 days*	**Reading Strategies** Predict/Infer, 13 Think About Words, 17 Self-Question, 19 Monitor, 21 Evaluate, 23 Summarize, 27	**Choices for Reading**, 12 **Students Acquiring English**, 13 **Extra Support**, 15 **Challenge**, 29 **Minilessons** Predict/Infer, 13 Think About Words, 17 Self-Question, 19 Monitor, 21 Evaluate, 23 Summarize, 27	**Reading-Writing Workshop,** 29D-30B *Literacy Activity Book:* Comprehension, p. 3; Prewriting, pp. 4–5; Revising, p. 6 The Learning Company's Ultimate Writing & Creativity Center software
Reading- Writing Workshop *Pacing: 3 days*	About the Workshop, 29B Prewriting, 29C–29D Drafting, 29E Revising, 29E–29F Proofreading, 29G Publishing and Sharing, 29G–30A	**Students Acquiring English**, 29E Minilessons Prewriting, 29D Drafting, 29E Revising, 29E–29F Proofreading, 29G Publishing and Sharing, 29G–30A	*Literacy Activity Book:* Prewriting, pp. 4–5; Revising, p. 6 The Learning Company's Ultimate Writing & Creativity Center software

The **Introductory Selection** provides an opportunity for students to settle into a new school year in a literacy-centered environment. This is also a time for teachers to get to know students through informal observations of reading and writing.

Formal instruction begins with the first selection of the theme Oink, Oink, Oink. See page 35D.

1

Introduce *the* Literature

Preparing to Read and Write

Literacy Activity Book, p. 1

My Reading Strategy Guide

As I read, do **predict/infer** by . . .

Looking for important information?	☐
Looking at illustrations?	☐
Thinking about what I know?	☐
Thinking about what will happen next or what I want to learn?	☐

As I read, do **self-question** by . . .

Asking questions to answer for myself as I go along?	☐

As I read, do I **think about words** by . . .

Figuring out words by using context, sounds and word parts?	☐

As I read, do I **monitor** by asking . . .

Does this make sense to me?	☐
Does it help me meet my purpose?	☐
Do I try fix-ups:	
• Reread	☐
• Read ahead	☐
• Look at illustrations	☐
• Ask for help?	☐

Do I **summarize**, both while I read and after reading by . . .

Thinking about story parts?	☐
Thinking about main ideas and important details?	☐

As I read, do I **evaluate** by . . .

Asking myself how I feel about what I read?	☐
Asking myself if this could really happen?	☐

Introductory Selection ①

Managing Instruction

Reading Strategies

- At the beginning of and throughout each selection, students will be directed in thinking about each of the reading strategies.

- In this selection, minilessons are provided to give practice with each strategy. Use these as needed to help students learn the strategies.

Introducing a Reading Strategy

Have students work with a partner to brainstorm what they think good readers do as they read. Share and discuss students' ideas.

Direct partners to compare their ideas to the checklist on *Literacy Activity Book* page 1. As students review the checklist, bring out the following points.

- Good readers use these strategies whenever they read.

- Different strategies are used before, during, and after reading.

- As readers are learning to use strategies, they must think about how each strategy will help them.

Ask students to read the points under each strategy and discuss what they mean. Suggest that students use this checklist as they read.

Prior Knowledge/Building Background

Key Concept

Understanding how students behave in class

Reproduce the chart below. Ask students to work with a partner to suggest ways they should behave in school. Then construct a class chart by having students share ideas. Invite students to predict what might happen if students did not behave properly in school.

How We Should Act in School

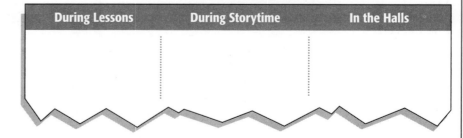

During Lessons	During Storytime	In the Halls

Other Choices for Building Background

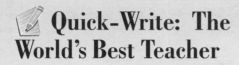 Quick-Write: The World's Best Teacher

Ask students to think about what the "best teacher in the world" might be like. Invite them to write a short description of this teacher in their journal. Have volunteers share their answers.

Teacher Read Aloud

Students Acquiring English Read aloud page 13 of *Miss Nelson Is Missing!* Have students use the illustration to describe the things that the "worst-behaved class in the whole school" might do.

INTERACTIVE LEARNING

Selection Vocabulary

Key Words

- misbehaving
- worst-behaved
- detective
- change
- act up
- rapped
- secret

Display Transparency IS–1. Read it aloud and then have students take turns reading it aloud with partners. Encourage students to use the context and their own knowledge to discuss the meanings of the underlined words.

You may wish to check students' understanding of the Key Words by asking these questions:

What word means information you don't want someone else to know?	secret
Who has a job of finding out other people's secrets?	detective
What words have to do with people acting bad or improperly?	misbehaving, worst-behaved, act up
What word means hit or struck sharply?	rapped
What would a bad person have to do to turn into a good person?	change

Vocabulary Practice Have students complete *Literacy Activity Book* page 2.

Interact
with
Literature

Reading Strategies

► **Predict/Infer**
Monitor
Think About Words
Self-Question
Evaluate
Summarize

Teacher/Modeling Have students look back at their Reading Strategy Guide on *Literacy Activity Book* page 1. Discuss how these strategies can be used together as students read. Model the process with a Think Aloud.

Think Aloud

First, I'll look at the pictures and predict what I think will happen. As I read I will monitor my predictions and change them as I get new information. I may have questions that I want to answer as I read. I'll think about words I don't know. Can I sound them out? As I read and after I read I'll summarize the story and evaluate how I feel about it.

Predicting/Purpose Setting

Invite students to look at the pictures on the cover and on page 13. Ask them to predict what they think will happen in the story.

HARRY ALLARD

MISS NELSON IS MISSING!

JAMES MARSHALL

12

Choices for Reading

Independent **Reading**	**Cooperative** **Reading**
Guided **Reading**	**Teacher** **Read Aloud**

The kids in Room 207 were misbehaving again. Spitballs stuck to the ceiling. Paper planes whizzed through the air. They were the worst-behaved class in the whole school.

13

Predict/Infer

Teach/Model

Discuss with students whether they try to figure out what might happen next in a story. Point out that good readers use pictures and other details to predict what might happen and to infer, or figure out, things that the author doesn't say directly. Model this with a Think Aloud.

Think Aloud

As I read the title of the book, look at the pictures, and read the first page, I can tell the teacher is having a tough time. The kids are awful. I can infer that this is Miss Nelson. I predict that she is going to leave.

Practice/Apply

Ask students to read pages 14–15, look at the pictures, and predict what will happen next. Have volunteers tell what clues they used to make their predictions.

 Journal

Have students write predictions in their journals. Encourage them to check and revise their predictions as they continue reading.

 MEETING INDIVIDUAL NEEDS
Students Acquiring English

Encourage students to use the illustrations to tell the story in small groups. Students might also write speech balloons for the characters in the illustrations.

Interact
with
Literature

"Now settle down," said Miss Nelson in a sweet voice.

But the class would *not* settle down. They whispered and giggled. They squirmed and made faces. They were even rude during story hour. And they always refused to do their lessons.

"Something will have to be done," said Miss Nelson.

14

QuickREFERENCE

MEETING INDIVIDUAL NEEDS
Students Acquiring English

To further comprehension, invite students to role-play both the kids and Miss Nelson in the scene.

The next morning Miss Nelson did not come to school. "Wow!" yelled the kids. "Now we can *really* act up!" They began to make more spitballs and paper planes. "Today let's be just terrible!" they said.
"Not so fast!" hissed an unpleasant voice.

15

Multicultural Link

Schools Have students who have attended schools in other countries share their experiences with the class.

 Extra Support
MEETING INDIVIDUAL NEEDS

Vocabulary Some students may need help with the words *squirmed* and *hissed*. Have volunteers demonstrate how the kids *squirmed*. Read aloud the line that is *hissed* by an unpleasant voice.

Interact
with
Literature

A woman in an ugly black dress stood before them. "I am your new teacher, Miss Viola Swamp." And she rapped the desk with her ruler.

"Where is Miss Nelson?" asked the kids.

"Never mind that!" snapped Miss Swamp. "Open those arithmetic books!" Miss Nelson's kids did as they were told.

16

Informal Assessment

As students read, make notes about how well they stick to the task and whether they seem to be enjoying the story. If any students are reading aloud, note how well they decode difficult words.

Think About Words

Teach/Model

Point out that readers always come across new words. Good readers use clues to figure out how to say the word and what it means. Discuss these hints:

Find out what makes sense.
Read to the end of the sentence or paragraph to see if this helps. Sometimes the words around a new word can help you.

Sound out letters or word parts. How does the word begin? How does the word end? What word parts do you know?

Look for other clues. Look at pictures or think of other words that look like the new word.

Think Aloud

As I read page 16, I come to the word *rapped,* a word that I don't know. I read to the end of the sentence. I know what a ruler is. What could Miss Swamp do to the desk with a ruler? She could hit it to make a noise. *Rapped* must be another word for *hit*. And it makes sense when I reread the sentence.

Practice/Apply

Have students work with partners to select another word in the story and tell how they could figure out what it means and how to pronounce it.

QuickREFERENCE

Students Acquiring English

Have students begin a profile of Miss Viola Swamp by creating a word web of words related to her. Students can start by describing details in the illustration on page 17. Encourage them to add to their webs as they read.

They could see that Miss Swamp was a real witch.
She meant business.

Right away she put them to work. And she loaded
them down with homework.

18

Self-Assessment

Ask students how they are helping
themselves with their reading. Encourage
them to ask themselves:

- Am I understanding the story?
- Am I thinking about words and
making predictions?
- How do I feel about the story so far?

Quick**REFERENCE**

Math Link

Sums Encourage students to work
out the sums pictured on the chalkboard to see if Miss Nelson's kids
arrived at the correct answers.

Self-Question

Teach/Model

Ask students what questions they have about the story so far. Record responses on the board. Explain that good readers ask questions as they read, and they keep reading to find the answers.

Practice/Apply

Ask volunteers to tell what questions they want to have answered as they read more of the story. Examples might include

- Where is Miss Nelson?

- Who is Miss Swamp?

"We'll have no story hour today," said Miss Swamp.

"Keep your mouths shut," said Miss Swamp.

"Sit perfectly still," said Miss Swamp.

"And if you misbehave, you'll be sorry," said Miss Swamp.

The kids in Room 207 had *never* worked so hard.

Days went by and there was no sign of Miss Nelson. The kids *missed* Miss Nelson!

19

Interact
with
Literature

"Maybe we should try to find her," they said.
Some of them went to the police.

Detective McSmogg was assigned to the case.
He listened to their story. He scratched his chin.
"Hmmmm," he said. "Hmmm. I think Miss Nelson is
missing."

Detective McSmogg would not be much help.

20

Informal Assessment

If you notice that students reading independently are having difficulty, suggest
that they complete their reading cooperatively. Have partners take turns reading
pages aloud.

Other kids went to Miss Nelson's house. The shades were tightly drawn, and no one answered the door. In fact, the only person they *did* see was the wicked Miss Viola Swamp, coming up the street.

"If she sees us, she'll give us more homework." They got away just in time.

21

Monitor

Teach/Model

Explain that when you monitor something, you keep watch over it. Readers monitor their reading to make sure they understand what they read. Discuss with students how rereading, finding answers to questions, checking predictions, and reading further can help readers understand a selection.

Think Aloud

As I first read page 20, I don't understand why Detective McSmogg won't be much help. After I reread the page and think about what I already know, I realize that he only tells the kids what they already know.

Practice/Apply

Ask students to work with partners to read page 21 and discuss things that might not make sense to them. Have them tell how they could monitor their reading to clear up what they don't understand.

Interact
with
Literature

Maybe something *terrible* happened to Miss
Nelson! "Maybe she was gobbled up by a shark!" said
one of the kids. But that didn't seem likely.

22

"Maybe Miss Nelson went to Mars!" said another kid. But that didn't seem likely either.

23

Evaluate

Teach/Model

Ask a volunteer how he or she feels about the story so far. Then explain that the student has just evaluated the story. Good readers evaluate what they read by asking questions such as:

- How do I feel about this story? Why?

- Do I believe this could really happen?

Practice/Apply

Ask students to read pages 22–23. Then ask volunteers what they think of the kids' ideas. Could these things really happen? Would the story be as interesting if the kids had come up with more everyday ideas?

Science Link

Mars Invite students to tell what they know about Mars. Share these facts:

- It is the fourth planet from the sun.

- It was named after the Roman god of war, *Mars*, because of its reddish color.

- A Martian year is equal to 687 Earth days.

- The mean temperature on Mars is -23 degrees C (-9.4 degrees F).

- It has the largest known volcano in the solar system, Olympus Mons, which is 375 miles (600 kilometers) in diameter and over 65,600 feet (20,000 meters) high.

Interact
with
Literature

"I know!" exclaimed one know-it-all. "Maybe Miss Nelson's car was carried off by a swarm of angry butterflies!" But that was the least likely of all.

24

The kids in Room 207 became very discouraged. It seemed that Miss Nelson was never coming back. And they would be stuck with Miss Viola Swamp forever.

They heard footsteps in the hall. "Here comes the witch," they whispered.

"Hello, children," someone said in a sweet voice.

25

Interact
with
Literature

It was Miss Nelson! "Did you miss me?" she asked.

"We certainly did!" cried all the kids. "Where were you?"

"That's my little secret," said Miss Nelson. "How about a story hour?"

"Oh, yes!" cried the kids.

Miss Nelson noticed that during story hour no one was rude or silly. "What brought about this lovely change?" she asked.

"That's *our* little secret," said the kids.

26

Self-Assessment

Reflecting Ask students to talk about reading the story. Have them answer questions about the experience:

- Did I think the story was easy or difficult? What made it easy/difficult?
- What parts did I like best? Why?

Back home Miss Nelson took off her coat and hung it in the closet (right next to an ugly black dress).

When it was time for bed she sang a little song. "I'll never tell," she said to herself with a smile.

P. S. Detective McSmogg is working on a new case. He is *now* looking for Miss Viola Swamp.

27

Summarizing

Teach/Model

Explain that a summary tells the main points of a selection. To summarize a story like *Miss Nelson Is Missing!*, a reader thinks about story parts. Draw the chart below and use a Think Aloud to help students begin to fill it in. Have students complete the chart on their own. Then ask volunteers to summarize the story.

Characters
Setting
Problem
Events
Ending

Think Aloud

I know that Miss Nelson, Miss Viola Swamp, and the students are main characters. The story takes place at school. The problem is that the students behave badly in class, and Miss Nelson doesn't know what to do.

Practice/Apply

Have students work with partners to complete a chart on a well-known story. Have pairs share their summaries with the class.

Interact *with* Literature

More About the Author

Harry Allard

When you read a book by Harry Allard, don't look for the message. "I hate anything with a message," says Allard. His children's books are strictly for fun.

Allard's first book, *The Stupids Step Out*, was inspired by the drawings of James Marshall. *The Stupids* and the *Miss Nelson* series are among the many popular books Allard and Marshall created together.

More About the Illustrator

James Marshall

James Marshall had a gift for seeing the ridiculous—especially in his own life. The evil Miss Viola Swamp was inspired by his second grade teacher, who squelched his budding interest in art. It was only by accident—literally—that Marshall rediscovered his talent. He was studying the viola (from which Miss Swamp got her name) when a hand injury ended his plans for a career in music. He became a teacher instead and began drawing for fun in his free time. At a friend's urging, Marshall showed his drawings to a publisher. Some of them were only sketches on paper napkins—but they sparked a career that soon had millions of readers giggling over characters like George and Martha, the Stupids, Miss Nelson, Fox, and the Cut-Ups.

Meet the Author
Harry Allard

Harry Allard is always writing something. He keeps a diary. He writes a lot of letters. And, of course, he writes books. When Allard gets an idea for a story, he just begins writing. Even if it's three in the morning.

Meet the Illustrator
James Marshall

How would you like to have Miss Viola Swamp for a teacher? James Marshall once said that he had a second grade teacher like her. In fact, when he drew Miss Swamp, he kept his teacher in mind.

Harry Allard and James Marshall were a team for almost twenty years. Two other popular books by them are The Stupids Step Out and Miss Nelson Is Back.

28

Investigating the Story

 RESPONDING

Put On a Puppet Show
Settle Down, Class!
What might Miss Nelson and Miss Swamp say to *your* class? Make puppets of them. Then, with a partner, make up things for them to say.

Make a Poster
Wanted: Miss Viola Swamp
Help Detective McSmogg find Miss Viola Swamp. Create a "Wanted" poster. Be sure to include a picture of her and a description of the way she acts.

29

Responding Activities

Personal Response
Have students write about and/or draw their favorite part of the story.

Anthology Activities
Students can choose one of the activities on page 29 to do alone or with a partner.

Student Acquiring English
Invite students to use the puppets made in "Settle Down, Class!" to retell the story.

QuickREFERENCE

 Home Connection
Have students interview someone older at home to find out who their best teacher was and what he or she was like. Encourage students to share and discuss their findings.

Informal Assessment
Use students' responses to assess general understanding of the story. If you need more information about each student's comprehension, have them individually retell the story. See the *Teacher's Assessment Handbook.*

2

Interact *with* Literature

Responding

Comprehension Check

Use *Literacy Activity Book* page 3 and/or the following questions to check comprehension:

1. Who comes to take Miss Nelson's place? (Miss Viola Swamp)

2. Why did someone come to take Miss Nelson's place? (The class was misbehaving and they didn't appreciate Miss Nelson.)

3. Who do you think Miss Swamp was? Why? (Sample: Miss Nelson. She had an ugly black dress and a wig in her closet.)

Literacy Activity Book, p. 3

Where Did She Go?

Complete the story map about *Miss Nelson Is Missing!*

Setting: Where did the story take place?

Main Characters: Who were the main characters?

Problem: What was the big problem in the story?

Events: List at least three main things that happened.

Ending: How did the story end?

Introductory Selection 3

Portfolio Opportunity

- For a record of selection comprehension, save *Literacy Activity Book* page 3.

- For a writing sample, save students' personal response.

More Choices for Responding

Literature Discussion

- What surprised you in the story?

- What do you think the boys and girls learned from their encounter with Miss Viola Swamp?

- Have you ever had a teacher like Miss Nelson? Have you had one like Miss Viola Swamp? Describe them.

- What other things could Miss Nelson have tried to get her class to behave better? If you were a student in her class, what could you have done to get your classmates to behave better?

Making a Mural

Invite interested students to make "before and after" murals depicting scenes from the story. You might suggest murals showing

- the kids in Room 207 before and after Miss Viola Swamp's visit

- Miss Nelson before and after transforming herself into Miss Viola Swamp

Students Acquiring English Students can refer to the murals to help them retell the story orally.

Putting On a Skit

Have students work in small groups to develop and perform a skit for *Miss Nelson Is Missing!* Encourage students to practice their skits several times. They might want to invite another class to view their performances.

The Return of Miss Viola Swamp

Invite students to write and illustrate a sequel to *Miss Nelson Is Missing!* If students have difficulty getting started, you might propose the following scenarios:

- Detective McSmogg is missing and Miss Viola Swamp takes over his job.

- Miss Viola Swamp becomes principal at the school.

Afterward, students may enjoy reading the two sequels produced by the team of Harry Allard and James Marshall, *Miss Nelson Is Back* and *Miss Nelson Has a Field Day*.

Reading-Writing Workshop

About the Workshop

The Reading-Writing Workshops throughout *Invitations to Literacy* are designed to help you guide students through a writing project, using the writing process. Within the guidelines of each workshop, students can develop writing on topics of their own choosing. Minilessons offer brief, point-of-use instruction on specific writing techniques or elements. In this introductory workshop, students write and publish a class book about themselves. The minilessons focus on the stages of the writing process to build background on the process approach.

In this and other workshops, keep these points in mind:

• Writing Process
Encourage students to use the writing process as a guide, not as a rigid sequence of steps.

• Selecting Topics
Give students freedom to select their own topics. Each workshop suggests ways for them to think of topics they want to write about.

• Switching Topics
Allow students to abandon an unsatisfying or frustrating piece and begin again, switching topics or using a different technique.

• Work Environment
Provide a comfortable atmosphere for students to work at their own pace.

• Minilessons
Use minilessons as needed for whole-class or small-group instruction.

• Peer Support
Encourage students to help each other throughout the process, especially in peer conferences.

• Publishing
Celebrate students' writing by providing many different opportunities for publishing and sharing.

• Independent Writing
Provide time each day for students to write independently, as well as time to continue their workshop activities.

Connecting to *Miss Nelson Is Missing!*

Ask students what new children in school might have thought of Miss Nelson's class at the beginning of the story. Have them list ways that students new to a school can get to know their classmates. What suggestions do they have for ways that all students in a class can get to know each other and their teacher at the start of a new school year?

Reading-Writing Workshop
A Class Book

Warm-Up

Shared Writing

Brainstorm with students a list of things they would like to know about each other and about you. Suggestions may include such things as names, birthdays, interests, favorite things, and after-school activities. Record responses on the chalkboard. Guide students to see that writing a class book would be a good way to put all the information together.

Prewriting

LAB, pp. 4, 5

Choose a Topic

Students narrow their topic choices and select their own topics.

- **Narrow the Choices** Using the brainstorm list, discuss parts students will include on their page. Then invite students to choose one additional topic. Encourage them to choose a topic that they think is important for others to know about them.

- **Talk and Think About It** Have partners explore their topic choices, answering these questions about each one: Why do I want to write about this topic? Is this important for others to know about me?

- **Settle on a Topic** Bring the class back together to finalize their choices.

Help with Topics

Class Clown?

Encourage students to think about whether they will tell something funny or something serious about themselves. Discuss how this might affect what they write.

Topics for Two

Students Acquiring English
Some students may benefit from working with a partner to gain needed vocabulary to write about particular topics.

Students can use The Learning Company's new elementary writing center to brainstorm and organize their ideas.

Prewriting (continued)

Plan Your Writing

Students plan their page of the book, listing and organizing their ideas.

- **Main Ideas and Details** Encourage students to jot down their main ideas, leaving plenty of space between them. Under each idea, have them note smaller ideas that go with it — reasons, examples, and details.

Help with Planning

Cut and Paste

Students can cut their lists apart and tape them in a new order.

 TECH TIPS Students using a word processor can use the Cut and Paste features to reorganize ideas.

What Order Works?

Help students think of how to put their ideas in the best order. For example, talk about how they might organize a description of themselves or a family member.

Literacy Activity Book, p. 4

The Writing Process

Prewriting
- Choose a topic.
- Plan your writing.

Drafting
- Write a first draft.
- Get your ideas down.
- Don't worry about mistakes.

Revising
- Read your draft thoughtfully.
- Make your ideas clear.
- Check the order.
- Think of strong words.

Proofreading
- Read your draft carefully again.
- Use proofreading marks.
- Correct spelling mistakes.
- Check capital letters and punctuation.

Publishing and Sharing
- Think of a good title.
- Make a clean copy and check it over.
- Find ways to share your writing.

4 Introductory Selection

Literacy Activity Book, p. 5

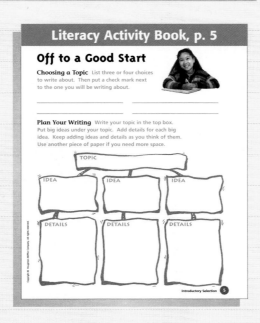

Off to a Good Start

Choosing a Topic List three or four choices to write about. Then put a check mark next to the one you will be writing about.

_____

Plan Your Writing Write your topic in the top box. Put big ideas under your topic. Add details for each big idea. Keep adding ideas and details as you think of them. Use another piece of paper if you need more space.

TOPIC

IDEA   IDEA   IDEA

DETAILS   DETAILS   DETAILS

Introductory Selection 5

Prewriting

LAB, p. 4

Use *Literacy Activity Book* page 4 to review the writing process with students. Encourage them to use this page as a reminder not to try to do everything at once.

Now have students discuss how to get started writing. Elicit that a good topic is one you're interested in, know something about, or want to learn about. Ask how to get topic ideas:

- brainstorm
- make lists
- look at journal or photo album
- answer a partner's questions
- make a cluster or web of experiences and interests

You may want to model one of the prewriting strategies for your page of the class book.

Next, discuss what to do with a topic once it's chosen.

- list ideas and details
- make a cluster or web
- think about a good order
- draw a picture

Continue modeling your own prewriting. Emphasize to students that there isn't a right or wrong method. Encourage them to try different ways to see what works best for them and their topic.

Reading-Writing Workshop *(continued)*
A Class Book

MINILESSON

Drafting

Ask students to compare two ways of taking a trip: (1) using a map and knowing where you're headed; and (2) just starting off, with no map or plan. Compare prewriting with planning a trip. With a plan, writing a first draft should go smoothly.

Be sure students understand the term *first draft.* Emphasize the word *first* and that drafting is simply getting ideas into words and onto paper. Assure them they'll have plenty of time to make changes and corrections later.

Give students these guidelines for writing a first draft:

- Think about your purpose and who your readers will be.
- Write down your ideas as quickly as you can.
- Don't worry if your paper is messy.
- Don't worry about spelling or punctuation. You can fix them later.

Discuss with students what to do if they get stuck during drafting. Remind them to do more prewriting for additional ideas or details.

Self-Assessment

Have students evaluate their book page, using the Revising Checklist on *Literacy Activity Book* page 6.

Drafting

Students use their prewriting notes to write a first draft.

- **Getting Ideas Down** Remind students that the purpose of a first draft is to get ideas on paper. They shouldn't worry about mistakes now.

Help with Drafting

Tips for Drafting

Urge students to write on every other line. Writing on only one side of their paper will allow them to cut and paste during revising, if they wish.

Keep On Writing!

Students Acquiring English Encourage students to keep writing, even if they're unsure about how to say something. Invite them to ask questions when they need to.

Revising
LAB, p. 6

Students revise their drafts and discuss them in writing conferences.

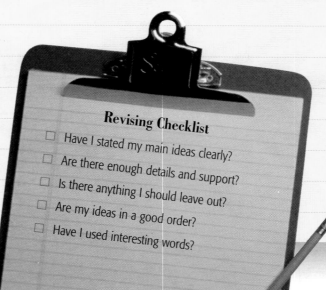

Revising Checklist
- ☐ Have I stated my main ideas clearly?
- ☐ Are there enough details and support?
- ☐ Is there anything I should leave out?
- ☐ Are my ideas in a good order?
- ☐ Have I used interesting words?

Revising (continued)

Writing Conference

Cooperative Learning Have students read aloud their revised draft and discuss it with you or a classmate. When they've listened to a partner's writing, they can use questions such as these, which appear on *Literacy Activity Book* page 6. You may need to modify the questions so that they are specific to the writing your students are doing.

Questions for a Writing Conference

- What is the best thing about this piece?
- Does it stay on the topic?
- Does it seem well organized?
- Does it help me get to know this person?
- What additional information would a new friend like to have?
- Does it end in a strong way?

Help with Revising

Mark It Up!

Ask students to cross out and write new words in the space above instead of erasing.

TECH TIPS Students writing at a computer may find it helpful to read their draft on a printout. They can cut and paste either on paper or on the computer.

Conference Cues

Remind students to be positive and helpful in their writing conferences. Encourage them to ask one another questions and make suggestions.

Revising

Provide a sample of writing from your own draft page for the class book. Be sure that your sample is in first draft form, with obvious need for revision.

Ask volunteers to suggest ways you could revise your writing. Model how to use questions from the revising checklist as you work through the sample. Encourage students to think of interesting words and to point out where additional details would help.

Using students' suggestions, model how to revise by using arrows and crossing out words. Have a volunteer read the revision aloud. Elicit that the writing is clearer. Discuss that revising is a way to help readers know what the writer really means.

Literacy Activity Book, p. 6

Revising Your Writing

Reread and revise your page of the class book. Use the Revising Checklist as a guide. Then have a writing conference with a classmate. Use the Questions for a Writing Conference to help your partner.

• Revising Checklist •

- ☐ Have I stated my main ideas clearly?
- ☐ Are there enough details and support?
- ☐ Is there anything I should leave out?
- ☐ Are my ideas in a good order?
- ☐ Have I used interesting words?

Questions for a Writing Conference
- What is the best thing about this piece of writing?
- Does it stay on the topic?
- Does it seem well organized?
- Does it help me get to know this person?
- What additional information would a new friend like to have?
- Does it end in a strong way?

Write notes to help you remember ideas from your writing conference.

My Notes

6 Introductory Selection

Reading-Writing Workshop (continued)
A Class Book

Proofreading

Congratulate students on their revised drafts. Tell them that now is the time to check for mistakes in spelling, capital letters, and punctuation marks. Elicit that correcting mistakes will make their reader's job easier and more pleasant.

Review proofreading marks with students. They can refer to the list in the Handbook at the back of the *Literacy Activity Book*. Write these marks on the chalkboard:

⌐⌐ Indent new paragraph
∧ Add something
℘ Take out something
≡ Capitalize
/ Make lowercase letter

Next, write these sentences on the chalkboard without the corrections.

i enjoy teching because I make so many knew Friends.

Then ask volunteers to use proofreading marks and make corrections at the board.

Proofreading

Students proofread their revised drafts, correcting errors in spelling, capitalization, and punctuation.

Grammar and Spelling Connections

- **Checking Sentences** Remind students to be sure each sentence begins with a capital letter and ends with the right punctuation.

- **Special Nouns** Have students check that special names of people and places begin with capital letters.

- **Spelling** Have them check each word for spelling, especially words with *-ed* and *-ing* endings.

Help with Proofreading

Proofreading Marks

Refer students to the proofreading marks in the Handbook at the back of the *Literacy Activity Book*. They may need to practice making paragraph symbols and delete marks.

Using a Checklist

A proofreading checklist is in the Handbook at the back of the *Literacy Activity Book*. Encourage students to add to the checklist as they find mistakes in their own writing.

Checking It Twice

Urge students to proofread their writing more than once to be sure of catching everything that needs correction.

Publishing and Sharing

Students make a clean copy of their writing and combine pieces to form a class book.

- Have the class decide on a title and discuss how they want their finished book to appear.
- *Cooperative Learning* Invite volunteers to form teams to create a cover design, write a table of contents, and make illustrations for the book.
- Discuss ways of making the book available to new students, classroom visitors, and parents.

Ideas for Publishing and Sharing

Making Copies

Elicit suggestions and volunteers for making multiple copies of the book. Volunteers might photocopy the inside pages and have each student make a cover for one of the copies.

Showing It Off

Have students suggest ways to share their book with readers beyond their own classroom.

Open House

If your school holds a parents night or an open house, copies of the class book might be distributed.

MINILESSON

Publishing and Sharing

- Ask a volunteer what the word *publish* means. Invite students to list things that are published. Use the classroom as a starting point, but also include real-world publications, such as newspapers, magazines, newsletters, posters, brochures, and calendars, along with many kinds of books.

- Review with students the list of people who might use their class book. Remind them that all their hard work has a purpose when they share it.

- Invite students to suggest other kinds of writing they may do this year and the ways they can share their writing with readers beyond the classroom.

Portfolio Opportunity

You may wish to save students' writing as an example of their written work early in the year. You might attach their notes and drafts to indicate their use of the writing process.

Selection Wrap-Up

ASSESSMENT

Managing Assessment

Portfolios

Question: How can I get students interested in portfolios?

Answer: Try these suggestions:

- If possible, share an example of a portfolio from another class or a previous year. Model for students how you might evaluate the contents:

  1. Compare two pieces of writing from different times during the year. Point out ways in which the student's work improved over time.
  2. Discuss a piece of work the student selected for inclusion in the portfolio. Point out what it shows about the student's interests and strengths.

- Explain that a portfolio includes many different samples of a student's work. Discuss how a variety of work samples provides a better picture of student's growth than, for example, a single test score.

- Note that during the first theme students will make collection folders to hold all their work, and that later they will take part in selecting samples of their work to be put in their portfolios.

Reflecting/Self-Assessment

Ask students how well they did during the reading of *Miss Nelson Is Missing!* Use prompts such as these to help them think about their work:

- How well did you understand the story?
- How did you use strategies to help your reading?
- What worked well in your writing? What worked less well?
- How much did you take part in class discussions?

Have students copy and fill in the graphic organizer below. Help individuals identify strengths and areas for improvement.

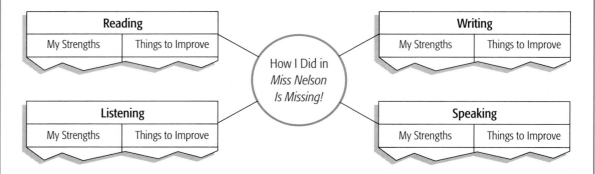

Discussing Literacy Assessment

Explain to students that during the year you and they will use many ways to evaluate their growth as readers, writers, speakers, and listeners. List some of these ways on the board:

- Observing daily work in class
- Checking *Literacy Activity Book* pages
- Listening as students read aloud
- Listening during class discussions and speaking activities
- Checking written work, especially from Reading-Writing Workshops

- Comparing examples of past and present work
- Meeting with students to discuss their work
- Assigning Performance Assessment activities
- Giving tests

Note that they will be saving samples of their work throughout the year. Invite them to save one piece of work they did during *Miss Nelson Is Missing!* Talk with students about creating collection folders and portfolios to hold their work. (See Managing Assessment note on left.)

Oink, Oink, Oink

Three Little Pigs' House

Table of Contents

THEME: Oink, Oink, Oink

Watch Me Read   *PRACTICE OF HIGH-FREQUENCY WORDS AND CUMULATIVE PHONICS SKILLS*

Goldie Bear and the Three Locks by Jed Mannheimer
Ham and Eggs for Jack by Andrew Clements
Red Riding Hood and Gray Wolf by Rob Hale

LITERATURE FOR SMALL-GROUP INSTRUCTION

PAPERBACK PLUS

PAPERBACK PLUS

SOAR TO SUCCESS!

EASY

Sidney Rella and the Glass Sneaker

by Bernice Myers

In the same book . . .
• a version of the original "Cinderella"
• a matching game about shoes

AVERAGE/CHALLENGING

Sleeping Ugly

by Jane Yolen

In the same book . . .
• a version of the original "Sleeping Beauty"
• sleep jokes
• facts about dreams

THE INTERMEDIATE INTERVENTION PROGRAM

Level 3 Books

A collection of books with teacher support for small-group intervention

Bibliography
Books for Independent Reading

 Multicultural

 Science/Health

 Math

 Social Studies

 Music

 Art

VERY EASY

Pig
 by Mary Ling
Dorling 1993 (24p)
The growth of a pig from birth to adulthood.

Poppleton
by Cynthia Rylant
Blue Sky 1997 (56p) paper
Poppleton, a big-city pig, moves to a small town and makes friends with his new neighbors.

Pigs from 1 to 10
by Arthur Geisert
Houghton 1992 (32p)
Readers search for hidden numerals in this story about ten piglet brothers.

Pigs from A to Z
by Arthur Geisert
Houghton 1986 (32p); also paper
Readers must find the letters hidden in Geisert's illustrations.

Smart, Clean Pigs
by Allan Fowler
Childrens 1993 (32p) paper
How and where pigs live and why they behave as they do. **Available in Spanish as *Los limpios e inteligentes cerdos.***

Somebody and the Three Blairs
by Marilyn Tolhurst
Orchard 1991 (32p); 1994 paper
In a reversal of roles, a bear visits the home of three humans.

EASY

All Pigs Are Beautiful
by Dick King-Smith
Candlewick 1993 (32p); also paper
A famous author tells why he loves pigs.

Pigs Will Be Pigs
by Amy Axelrod
Four Winds 1994 (32p)
The Pigs search their house for money to eat out. Menu and prices included.

The Fourth Little Pig
by Teresa Celsi
Raintree 1990 (24p) paper
A visit from their sister changes the three little pigs' attitude.

The Great Pig Escape
by Eileen Christelow
Clarion 1994 (32p); also paper
Pigs on their way to market escape to Florida.

Pigs Aplenty, Pigs Galore!
by David McPhail
Dutton 1993 (32p); Puffin paper
As the narrator tries to read, several pigs wreak havoc in his home. **Available in Spanish as *¡Cerdos a montones, cerdos a granel!***

Mrs. Goat and Her Seven Little Kids
by Tony Ross
Atheneum 1990 (32p)
A cheerful, satirical updating of the well-known Grimm classic.

Cinder Edna
by Ellen Jackson
Lothrop 1994 (32p)
Cinderella could learn something from her feisty neighbor, Cinder Edna.

Piggie Pie
by Margie Palatini
Clarion 1995 (32p); also paper
Clever pigs impersonate other animals to avoid becoming Piggie Pie.

Pigsty
by Mark Teague
Scholastic 1994 (32p)
Wendell Fultz's room looks like a pigsty, so several pigs move in.

The Gruff Brothers
by William Hooks
Bantam 1990 (32p) paper
A new twist to "The Three Billy Goats Gruff."

The Pigs' Wedding
by Helme Heine
McElderry 1988 (32p); 1991 paper
Curlytail and Porker get married and have a wild wedding reception.

Los tres lobitos y el cochino feroz (The Three Little Wolves and the Big Bad Pig)
by Eugene Trivizas
Text in Spanish.

AVERAGE

The True Story of the Three Little Pigs
by Jon Scieszka
Viking 1991 (32p)
A. Wolf gives his version of what really happened in the famous tale. **Available in Spanish as *La verdadera historia de los tres cerditos.***

The Tortoise and the Jackrabbit
by Susan Lowell
Chronicle 1994 (32p)
A humorous retelling set in the Southwest.

Princess Furball
by Charlotte Huck
Greenwillow 1989 (40p); also paper
A strong-willed princess overcomes many obstacles in this Cinderella variant.

Tales of Amanda Pig
by Jean Van Leeuwen
Dial 1982 (56p); Puffin 1994 paper
Five stories about Amanda Pig and her brother Oliver. **Available in Spanish as *Cuentos de la cerdita Amanda.*** See others in series.

Piggins
by Jane Yolen
Harcourt 1987 (32p); 1992 paper
Piggins, the very proper butler, keeps things running smoothly. See others in series.

The Frog Prince, Continued
by Jon Scieszka
Viking 1991 (32p); Puffin 1994 paper
The honeymoon is over for the princess and the frog.

The Amazing Bone
by William Steig
Farrar 1983 (32p); 1993 paper
Pearl the pig needs help outwitting
robbers *and* a hungry fox.
**Available in Spanish as *El
hueso prodigioso.***

Wild Boars
*by Daniel Nicholson
Carolrhoda 1987 (48p)*
A photo essay about the pig's
wild relative.

The Three Little Pigs
and the Fox
by William Hooks
Macmillan 1989 (32p)
Appalachian variant.

Garth Pig Steals the
Show
*by Mary Rayner
Dutton 1993 (32p)*
More hilarious adventures of
Garth Pig and the Pig family
band. See others in series.

Cinder-Elly
by Frances Minters
Viking 1994 (32p)
Cinder-Elly stays
home while her
sisters attend a basketball
game in this urban retelling.

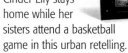

Parents in the Pigpen,
Pigs in the Tub
by Amy Ehrlich
Dial 1993 (40p)
When the pasture gate is left open,
farm animals move into the house.

Piggies, Piggies, Piggies:
A Treasury of Stories,
Songs, and Poems
*by Walter Retan
Simon 1993 (96p)*
An assortment of selections,
some illustrated, about pigs.

Peeping Beauty
*by Mary Jane Auch
Holiday 1993 (32p)*
Poulette Pig wants to become a bal-
lerina, but the fox has other ideas.

Hog Eye
by Susan Meddaugh
Houghton 1995 (32p)
When a young pig is captured by a
wolf, she uses her ability to read to
foil his plans to make soup of her.

Hooray for the Golly Sisters
by Betsy Byars
Harper 1990 (64p); also paper
Sisters May-May and Rose
share adventures that include
disappearing pigs.

Dear Peter Rabbit
by Alma Flor Ada
Atheneum 1994 (32p)
Peter Rabbit, Goldilocks, Red Riding
Hood, and friends exchange letters.
**Available in Spanish as
*Querido Pedrín.***

Chester the Worldly Pig
by Bill Peet
Houghton 1978 paper
When Chester joins the circus,
he quickly learns that farm life
isn't so bad.

CHALLENGING

Quentin Corn
by Mary Stolz
Godine 1985 (128p)
Learning he will soon become a
meal, Quentin disguises himself
and runs away.

King Emmett the Second
by Mary Stolz
Greenwillow 1991 (56p)
Emmett Murphy moves from New
York to Ohio and misses his friends,
especially his pet pig.

Pigs Might Fly
by Dick King-Smith
Viking 1982 (158p); Puffin paper
Daggie Dogfoot, a runt piglet with
a deformity, becomes the hero of
the farm.

Farmer Palmer's Wagon Ride
by William Steig
Farrar 1974 (32p); 1992 paper
Farmer Palmer's return trip from the
market is full of obstacles.

Technology Resources

Software

Great Start™ Macintosh or Windows CD-ROM software.
Includes story summaries, background building, and
vocabulary support for each selection in the theme.
Houghton Mifflin Company.

Spelling Spree™ Macintosh or Windows CD-ROM
software. Includes spelling, vocabulary, and proofreading
practice. Houghton Mifflin Company.

Channel R.E.A.D. Videodiscs "License to Drive" and
"The Ordinary Princess." Houghton Mifflin Company.

Internet: Education Place (www.eduplace.com)
Visit the Reading/Language Arts Center in the Teachers'
Center to find projects, games, and theme-related links
and activities. Houghton Mifflin Company.

Teacher's Resource Disk Macintosh or Windows software. Houghton Mifflin Company.

Writing Software The Learning Company's Ultimate
Writing & Creativity Center. Macintosh or Windows
software. The Learning Company®.

Video Cassettes

Princess Furball by Charlotte Huck. Weston Woods

The Three Little Pigs by James Marshall. Weston
Woods

The Pigs' Wedding by Helme Heine. Weston Woods

The Pigs' Picnic by Keiko Kasza. Amer. Sch. Pub.

The Amazing Bone by William Steig. Weston Woods

Audio Cassettes

Princess Furball by Charlotte Huck. Weston Woods

The Three Little Pigs by James Marshall. Weston
Woods

The Pigs' Wedding by Helme Heine. Weston Woods

The True Story of the Three Little Pigs by Jon
Scieszka. Viking

Audio Tapes for "Oink, Oink, Oink." Houghton Mifflin
Company

AV addresses are on pages H7–H8.

Books for Teacher Read Aloud

Zeke Pippin
*by William Steig
Harper 1994 (32p)*
When Zeke the
pig plays his har-
monica, everyone
falls asleep.

That Extraordinary Pig of Paris
by Roni Schotter
Philomel 1994 (32p)
Monsieur Cochôn, a pig in Paris, has
quite a day when he gets too close
to a pastry shop.

Mrs. Pig Gets Cross
by Mary Rayner
Dutton 1986 (64p); Puffin paper
Seven short stories about Mr. and
Mrs. Pig and their ten children.

Theme at a Glance

Selections	Reading		Writing and Language Arts	
	Comprehension Skills and Strategies	Word Skills	Responding	Writing
The Three Little Wolves and the Big Bad Pig	✓ Genre: Fantasy, 41 Summarizing: Story Structure, 45, 60B–60C Making Judgments, 47 Fantasy/Realism, 57 Reading Strategies, 38, 44, 48, 50	✓ Base Words, 60F–60G Short Vowels, 60G	Personal Response, 60 Anthology Activities, 60 Home Connection, 60 Literature Discussion, 60A Selection Connection, 60A	Character Role Reversal, 59 ✓ Writing a Sentence, 60D
What's Up, Pup?	Making Comparisons, 60P			Narrative Nonfiction, 61
This Little Piggy!	Predict/Infer, 64		Home Connection, 66	
The Three Little Javelinas	✓ Compare and Contrast, 75, 88B–88C Predicting Outcomes, 79 Summarizing: Story Structure, 83 Reading Strategies, 70, 72, 76, 78, 80, 84	✓ Inflected Endings -ed and -ing, 88F–88G Long Vowel Pairs and Vowel-Consonant -e, 88G	Personal Response, 88 Anthology Activities, 88 Home Connection, 88 Literature Discussion, 88A Selection Connection, 88A	Setting, 85 Writing a Book Report, 88D
My Hairy Neighbors	K-W-L Chart, 88P Photo Essay, 89		Home Connection, 89, 91 Literature Discussion, 90	Author's Voice, 89
The Three Little Hawaiian Pigs and the Magic Shark	✓ Fantasy/Realism, 95, 114B–114C Compare and Contrast, 103 Sequence, 107 Reading Strategies, 94, 98, 100, 108	✓ Using Context, 114F–114G Alphabetical Order, 114G	Personal Response, 114 Anthology Activities, 114 Home Connection, 114 Literature Discussion, 114A Selection Connection, 114A	Anthropomorphism, 97 ✓ Combining Sentences: Compound Sentences, 114D
Pigs	Reading a Poem, 114P		Home Connection, 115	
Reading-Writing Workshop **Be a Writer: Surprise, Surprise**				**Reading-Writing Workshop** A Story, 116–117F; Workshop Minilessons: Characters and Setting, 117A; Beginning, Middle, and End, 117B; Dialogue, 117C
The Wild Boar & the Fox	Genre: Plays, 119			

✓ *Indicates Tested Skills.* See page 34F for assessment options.

Theme Concept

Traditional stories can be retold in a variety of humorous, altered versions.

Pacing

This theme is designed to take 4 to 6 weeks, depending on your students' needs.

Multi-Age Classroom

Related theme from:
Grade 2 – Tell Me a Tale
Grade 4 – Super Sleuths

Cross-Curricular

Spelling*	Grammar, Usage and Mechanics	Listening and Speaking	Viewing	Study Skills	Content Area
✔ Short Vowels, 60I	✔ Subjects and Predicates, 60J–60K	Storytelling, 60L Interviewing the Big Bad Pig, 60L	Watching a Video, 60M Using Facial Expressions and Body Language, 60M Examining Real Wolves and Pigs, 60M		**Science:** Careers in Construction, Tools of the Trade, Building Your School, Looking at Blueprints, 60N **Math:** Playing a Huff and Puff Game, 60O **Dance:** Dancing the Tarantella, 60O
				✔ Taking Notes, 63	
				K-W-L, 65	**Science:** Animal Myths, 67 **Health:** Staying Cool, 67 **Social Studies:** Finding Habitats, 67
✔ Vowel-Consonant -e, 88I	✔ Correcting Run-on Sentences, 88J–88K	Listening to a Poetic Picture, 88L Building a Language Tree, 88L Hearing a Range of Sounds, 88M	Watching a Video of Desert Life, 88M Taking a Walking Tour, 88M		**Science:** Making a Desert Terrarium, Exploring the Saguaro Cactus, 88N **Art:** Designing Outfits, 88O **Math:** Graphing Desert Weather, 88O
					Math: A Javelina's Height, 91 **Science:** Omnivorous Animals, 91
✔ Long *a* and Long *e*, 114I	✔ Kinds of Sentences, 114J–114K	Literature Discussion Guidelines, 114L Hawaiian Music, 114L	A Game of Disguise, 114M Let's Visit Hawaii, 114M Hula Hands, 114M		**Social Studies:** Discovering Tropical Fruits, Making a Relief Map of Hawaii, 114N **Science:** Collecting Shark Facts, Making a Food Chain Mobile, 114O
		Reading a Poem, 114P			
Words Often Misspelled, 117E					**Social Studies:** Symbols, 115; **Music:** Song, 115 **Art:** Class Book, 115
Theme Assessment Wrap-Up: Spelling Review, 119B		Reading a Play, 118			

Additional spelling lists with practice, Literacy Activity Book, pp. 139–148 (optional)

Meeting Individual Needs

 Students Acquiring English
Activities and notes offer strategies to help students' comprehension.

 Challenge
Challenge activities and notes stimulate critical and creative thinking.

 Extra Support
Activities and notes offer strategies to help students experience success.

Through Literature...

Instructional Reading

Anthology
Level 3.1, pp. 30–119

Teacher's Book
Oink, Oink, Oink

Supported/Independent Reading

Watch Me Read Books
Goldie Bear and the Three Locks
Ham and Eggs for Jack
Red Riding Hood and Gray Wolf

Easy Paperback Plus
Sidney Rella and the Glass Sneaker
by Bernice Myers

Average/Challenging Paperback Plus
Sleeping Ugly
by Jane Yolen

Bibliography
Teacher's Book, pp. 34A–34B

Extra Support/Students Acquiring English

 Great Start™ CD-ROM software
Oink, Oink, Oink

Audio Tapes
for Oink, Oink, Oink

 SOAR TO SUCCESS
The Intermediate Intervention Program

Extra Support Handbook
Levels 3.1–3.2,
pp. 11–23, 96–103

Students Acquiring English Handbook
Levels 3.1–3.2,
pp. 56–81, 224–331

Language Resources:
Chinese, Hmong, Cambodian, Vietnamese

Extension/Challenge

Teacher's Book
• Theme Projects
• Communication Activities
• Cross-Curricular Activities

Home/Community Connections
Levels 3.1–3.2

Internet:
Education Place
www.eduplace.com

Through Instruction...

Teaching Choices Reading, Writing, Language Arts, Cross-Curricular

Teacher's Book
Choose among skill Minilessons, Interactive Learning Lessons, and Reteaching Lessons and activities to meet students' needs.

Literacy Activity Book
Level 3.1, pp. 7–43

Extra Support/Students Acquiring English

Extra Support Handbook
Levels 3.1–3.2,
pp. 11–23, 96–103

Students Acquiring English Handbook
Levels 3.1–3.2,
pp. 56–81, 224–331

 Channel R.E.A.D. Videodiscs
• "License to Drive"
• "The Ordinary Princess"

Extension/Challenge

Teacher's Book
• Spelling Challenge Words
• Performance Assessment

Internet:
Education Place
www.eduplace.com

 Spelling Spree CD-ROM

 The Learning Company's Ultimate Writing & Creativity Center software

Planning for Assessment

Performance Standards During this theme, all students will learn to

- *Recognize when and how a story can be altered for humorous effect*
- *Write a story*
- *Summarize fiction stories*

- *Compare fiction selections by completing a chart*
- *Edit writing, with an emphasis on sentence variety*

Informal Assessment

Informal Assessment Checklist, pp. H5–H6

- Reading and Responding
- Summarizing: Story Structure, Compare and Contrast, Fantasy/Realism
- Writing Sentences, Comparison/ Contrast Paragraphs
- Word Skills and Strategies
- Grammar
- Attitudes and Habits

Literacy Activity Book

- Selection Connections, p. 34G
- Comprehension Check, pp. 60A, 88A, 114A
- Comprehension Skills, pp. 60C, 88C, 114C
- Writing Skills, pp. 60E, 88E, 114E
- Word Skills, pp. 60F, 88F, 114F

Reading–Writing Workshop

- Writing a Story, p. 116
- Scoring Rubric, p. 117F

Performance Assessment

- Creating a Story Strip, p. 119A
- Scoring Rubric, p. 119A

Retellings–Oral/Written

- *Teacher's Assessment Handbook*

Formal Assessment

Integrated Theme Test

Test applies the following theme skills to a new reading selection:

- Reading Strategies
- Summarizing: Story Structure, Compare and Contrast, Fantasy/Realism
- Word Skills and Strategies
- Writing Fluency
- Grammar and Spelling (optional)
- Self-Assessment

Theme Skills Test

- Summarizing: Story Structure, Compare and Contrast, Fantasy/Realism
- Base Words, Inflected Endings -ed and -ing, Context
- Writing Skills
- Study Skills
- Spelling
- Grammar

Benchmark Progress Test

- Give a Benchmark Progress Test two or three times a year to measure student growth in reading and writing.

Managing Assessment

Theme Checklists

Question: How can I best use the Informal Assessment Checklist?

Answer: The Informal Assessment Checklist can help you keep track of informal observations you make throughout the theme. These tips can keep it simple to use:

- The Checklist has individual and group forms. Use the group form to monitor most students. Use the individual form for students who are a focus of concern.
- Don't try to check all categories for all students. For many students, occasional checks during a theme will be sufficient to document their progress or to note any difficulties in particular areas. For students needing more support, plan more observations, focused on the categories of concern.
- Some teachers keep the Checklist on a clipboard and make notes as they teach. Others take a moment at the end of the day or week to reflect and record their observations. Experiment to find the way that works for you.

For more information on this and other topics, see the *Teacher's Assessment Handbook*.

Portfolio Assessment

The portfolio icon signals portfolio opportunities throughout the theme.

Additional Portfolio tips:

- Introducing Portfolios to the Class, p. 119B
- Selecting Materials for the Portfolio, p. 119B
- Grading Work in Portfolios, p. 119B

Launching the Theme

Selection Connections

Discuss with students the Selection Connections on *Literacy Activity Book* page 8. Students should note that they will return to the chart after each selection and at the end of the theme.

See the Houghton Mifflin **Internet** resources for additional activities.

See the **Teacher's Resource Disk** for theme-related support material.

INTERACTIVE LEARNING

Theme Concept Traditional stories can be retold in a variety of humorous, altered versions.

Setting the Scene

Teacher Read Aloud

Ask students if they are familiar with "The Three Little Pigs." Read aloud one of the popular versions of the story (such as James Marshall's), or use the version that appears on page 35A. Note: The story is also available in Spanish (*Tres cerditos,* Addison Wesley 1989; *Tres cochinitos,* Western 1993).

Fractured Tales

Note that the stories in "Oink, Oink, Oink" are versions of "The Three Little Pigs" that have been fractured to make them funny. Explain that *fractured* is another word for *broken.* Speculate how a story might be fractured. Have students complete *Literacy Activity Book* page 7.

Students Acquiring English Make sure students know that *oink* is the English word for the sound that pigs make.

Dramatizing a Tale

Let students bring the original version of "The Three Little Pigs" to life by creating and performing their own play version. Then encourage them to fracture the title of that story and improvise the play that results. Suggest such titles as "The Three Enormous Pigs" or "The Three Little Pigs and the Hyena."

Students Acquiring English Give parts with repetitive lines to students acquiring English and allow them to rehearse.

Interactive Bulletin Board

Help students to recall folktales they know or to make up new ones. Invite them to write or draw these stories and post them. During the theme, encourage students to create fractured versions of these stories and add them to the bulletin board.

Choices for Projects

Building Your Own House
Cooperative Learning

Each of the three little pigs used a different material to build his house. Students may enjoy making their own houses out of readily available materials, such as packing peanuts, buttons, or popsicle sticks. Have groups of three choose one material and use it to build a house. Later, students can compare their projects and explain their choice of material.

Materials
- packing peanuts, buttons, or popsicle sticks
- cardboard
- glue or two-sided sticky paper
- scissors

- Glue together a cardboard frame of a house, with the windows and door already cut.
- Cover the house with glue, or apply two-sided sticky paper.
- Attach materials to the house.

Making a Fractured Flip Book

2 Collect the pictures into a book. Add a cover and secure with staples across the top.

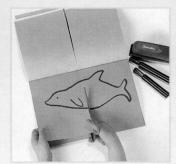

1 Hold sheets of paper horizontally and fold them in half, side to side. Unfold them. Then on each sheet draw a picture of a favorite animal, making sure the fold runs down the center of the drawing.

3 Cut the pages in half along the folds. Flip through the pages to create funny new combination animals.

Encourage discussion about why these unusual pairings are silly. Challenge volunteers to make up stories about some of the fractured animals.

Materials
- markers or crayons
- paper
- stapler
- scissors

Independent Reading and Writing

One fun way to foster independent reading and writing each day is to have a Drop-Everything break. All other work stops for a specified time so that individuals can read and/or write on their own. For independent reading, invite students to go to the library and select their own books, provide books from the Bibliography on pages 34A–34B, or encourage students to read one of the Paperback Plus books for this theme.

Easy reading: *Sidney Rella and the Glass Sneaker* by Bernice Myers

Average/challenging reading: *Sleeping Ugly* by Jane Yolen.

For independent writing, encourage students to choose their own activities. For those who need help getting started, suggest one or more of the activities on pages 60E, 88E, and 114E.

 See the *Home/Community Connections Booklet* for materials related to this theme.

Portfolio Opportunity

- Save *Literacy Activity Book* page 8 to show students' ability to compare selections.
- The Portfolio Assessment icon highlights other portfolio opportunities throughout the theme.

THE CLASSIC TALE

The Three Little Pigs

Teacher Read Aloud

Once upon a time, there were three little pigs, who lived with their mother in a cottage in the woods. Although she struggled to make ends meet, the pigs' mother grew poorer and poorer. And so one morning she sent the three little pigs out into the world to make their own way. As she kissed them good-bye, she said, "Watch out for the Big Bad Wolf. He eats little piggies like you!"

Now the First Little Pig hadn't gone very far when he met a man carrying a bundle of straw. He asked the man for some straw so that he could build a house. The man agreed. The First Little Pig built his house quickly, and then he went out to play. He played all morning, and so by lunchtime he was very hungry. As he was fixing himself something to eat, he heard a knock at the door. The First Little Pig peeked out the window, and lo and behold there stood the Big Bad Wolf.

"Little Pig, Little Pig, let me come in," said the wolf.

Remembering his mother's warning, the pig said, "Not by the hair of my chinny-chin-chin."

"Then I'll huff and I'll puff and I'll BLOW your house in," said the wolf.

And that is exactly what he did. After which, he ate the First Little Pig all up.

The Second Little Pig hadn't gone very far when he met a man with a cartload of sticks. The Second Little Pig asked for some sticks so he could build himself a house. The man agreed, and before long the Second Little Pig had a fine stick house. Then he went out to play. He played all day, and so he was very hungry by suppertime. As he was fixing his dinner, he heard a knock at the door. When he peeked out the window, who do you think he saw? The Big Bad Wolf!

"Little Pig, Little Pig, let me come in," said the wolf.

"Not by the hair of my chinny-chin-chin," said the pig.

"Then I'll huff and I'll puff and I'll BLOW your house in," said the wolf.

The wolf blew down the house and ate up the Second Little Pig.

The Third Little Pig met a man with a wagonload of bricks. He asked the man for some bricks so that he could build himself a house. The man agreed, and so the Third Little Pig got to work building himself the best house he could. He worked long and hard, and by the end of the day he was very tired. He was just crawling into bed, when he heard a knock at the door. And he heard a voice that said, "Little Pig, Little Pig, let me come in."

The Third Little Pig looked out his bedroom window and saw the Big Bad Wolf at his doorstep.

"Oh, no," said the pig. "Not by the hair of my chinny-chin-chin."

"Then I'll huff and I'll puff and I'll BLOW your house in," said the wolf.

The Big Bad Wolf huffed and puffed, but he couldn't blow the brick house down. So he crawled up onto the roof, intending to go down the chimney to get that third little piggy. But the pig heard the wolf pawing around on his roof, and he guessed what the wolf had in mind. He put a big kettle of water in the fireplace, and he lit a fire under it. When the wolf came down the chimney, he landed with a HOWL in the boiling water.

That was the end of the Big Bad Wolf. The Third Little Pig lived happily ever after.

bricks

straw

sticks

SELECTION:

The Three Little Wolves and the Big Bad Pig

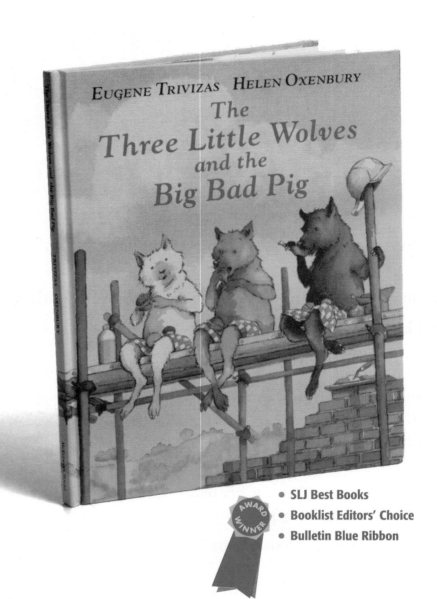

EUGENE TRIVIZAS   HELEN OXENBURY

The Three Little Wolves and the Big Bad Pig

- SLJ Best Books
- Booklist Editors' Choice
- Bulletin Blue Ribbon

AWARD WINNER

by Eugene Trivizas

Selection Summary

A mother wolf sends her three little wolves out into the world with this warning: Beware of the big bad pig!

The wolves build a house of brick that is demolished by the sledge-hammer-wielding big bad pig. The little wolves build again and again, each time with stronger materials, but the pig always finds a way to destroy their work.

Finally, they build a house of flowers. When the pig inhales its beautiful scent, he has a change of heart and mends his ways. Seeing that the pig has changed, the wolves invite him in for tea, and he becomes a member of the family.

Lesson Planning Guide

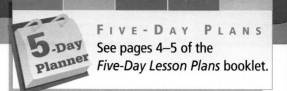
FIVE-DAY PLANS
See pages 4–5 of the
Five-Day Lesson Plans booklet.

	Skill/Strategy Instruction	Meeting Individual Needs	Lesson Resources
1 **Introduce** *the* **Literature** *Pacing: 1 day*	**Preparing to Read and Write** Prior Knowledge/Building Background, 35E **Selection Vocabulary,** 35F • prowling • grunted • crumbled • trembling • scorched **Spelling Pretest,** 60I • ask • next • mix • smell • black • shut • lock • truck	**Support in Advance,** 35E **Students Acquiring English,** 35E **Other Choices for Building Background,** 35E **Spelling Challenge Words:** • knock • scent • plenty • fetch	*Literacy Activity Book* Vocabulary, p. 9 **Transparency:** Vocabulary, 1–1 **Great Start** CD-ROM software, "Oink, Oink, Oink" CD
2 **Interact** *with* **Literature** *Pacing: 1–3 days*	**Reading Strategies:** Monitor, 38, 44 Predict/Infer, 38, 48 Think About Words, 48 **Minilessons:** Fantasy, 41 ✓ Summarizing: Story Structure, 45 Making Judgments, 47 Fantasy/Realism, 57 Writer's Craft: Role Reversal, 59	**Choices for Reading,** 38 **Guided Reading,** 38 Comprehension/Critical Thinking, 42, 46, 52, 58 **Students Acquiring English,** 39, 41, 43, 46, 49, 55, 56, 60 **Extra Support,** 38, 40, 49, 55, 59 **Challenge,** 48, 54, 57	**Reading-Writing Workshop** A Story, 116–117F *Literacy Activity Book,* pp. 40–42 The Learning Company's Ultimate Writing & Creativity Center software
3 **Instruct** *and* **Integrate** *Pacing: 1–3 days*	✓ **Comprehension:** Summarizing: Story Structure, 60B ✓ **Writing:** Writing a Sentence, 60D **Word Skills and Strategies:** ✓ Structural Analysis: Base Words, 60F Phonics Review: Short Vowels, 60G **Building Vocabulary:** Vocabulary Activities, 60H ✓ **Spelling:** Short Vowels, 60I ✓ **Grammar:** Subjects and Predicates, 60J–60K **Communication Activities:** Listening and Speaking, 60L; Viewing, 60M **Cross-Curricular Activities:** Science, 60N; Math, 60O; Dance, 60O	**Reteaching:** Summarizing: Story Structure, 60C **Activity Choices:** Shared Writing: A Reversed Tale, 60E; Write a Song, 60E; Give Directions, 60E **Reteaching:** Base Words, 60G **Activity Choices:** Synonyms for *big* and *bad*, Classifying/Categorizing, 60H **Challenge Words Practice,** 60I **Reteaching:** Subjects and Predicates, 60K **Activity Choices:** Listening and Speaking, 60L; Viewing, 60M **Activity Choices:** Science, 60N; Math, 60O; Dance, 60O	**Watch Me Read:** *Goldie Bear and the Three Locks* **Reading-Writing Workshop** A Story, 116–117F **Transparencies:** Comprehension, 1–2; Writing, 1–3; Grammar, 1–4 *Literacy Activity Book* Comprehension, p. 11; Writing, p. 12; Word Skills, p. 13; Building Vocabulary, p. 14; Spelling, pp. 15–16; Grammar, pp. 17, 19 **Spelling Spree** CD-ROM **Channel R.E.A.D.** videodisc: "License to Drive" **Audio Tape** for Oink, Oink, Oink: *The Three Little Wolves and the Big Bad Pig* The Learning Company's Ultimate Writing & Creativity Center software

✓ *Indicates Tested Skills. See page 34F for assessment options.*

Introduce *the* Literature

Preparing to Read and Write

Support in Advance

Use this activity for students who need extra support before participating in the whole-class activity.

Animal Characterizations Discuss how different animals are depicted as good and evil in stories. Ask students to give examples from their own reading and TV viewing.

 Management Tip
Students not participating in Support in Advance can engage in self-selected writing or silent reading.

Students Acquiring English
Begin a wall chart of words about building and construction. Invite students to contribute words they know. As students read, add words such as these from the story: *bricks, concrete, sledgehammer, barbed wire, padlocks,* and *Plexiglas.*

Note: Some terms, such as *padlocks* and *barbed wire,* may be distressing for children from war-torn areas.

INTERACTIVE LEARNING

Prior Knowledge/Building Background

Key Concept
Wolves vs. Pigs

Semantic Chart Discuss how the wolf and the pig are depicted in "The Three Little Pigs."

Wolf	• big and bad	• sneaky	• hunts alone
Three Pigs	• cute and fun-loving	• clever	• work together

Tell students that the next selection turns the original folktale upside down: in this story, it's a pig who's the villain and three little wolves who are being chased. Explain that folktales that have been turned around like this are called *fractured tales.*

Key Concept
Being Bad

Semantic Map Discuss with students the meaning of the word *bad* as it is used in the phrase *big bad pig.* You may wish to use a semantic map like the following for this purpose.

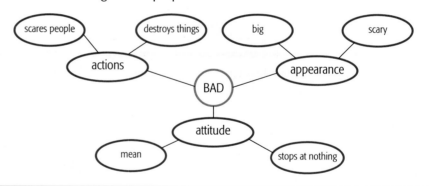

Other Choices for Building Background

Quick Writing

Challenge Ask students to write about how "The Three Little Pigs" might have turned out if the big bad wolf had been a big *good* wolf.

Describing Words
Cooperative Learning

Ask students to make lists of words that describe both friendly animals (soft, fluffy) and fierce animals (mean, angry).

Great Start
For students needing extra support with key concepts and vocabulary, use the "Oink, Oink, Oink" CD.

INTERACTIVE LEARNING

Selection Vocabulary

Key Words

prowling

grunted

crumbled

trembling

Display Transparency 1–1. Note that students will encounter the underlined words in the story. Have students read each sentence aloud and substitute their own words and phrases for the underlined words. If necessary, discuss the meaning of the underlined words. For example:

> The three little pigs felt safe in their new house. But then the big bad wolf came **prowling** down the road.
>
> But then the big bad wolf came creeping down the road.

Students can continue the story in their journals. Or, as they read the selection, they can jot down other words they would like to study. Later, these can be added to their journals, together with definitions.

Students Acquiring English You might wish to introduce these additional words: *escape, secure, strong,* and *fragile.*

Vocabulary Practice Have students work independently or in pairs to complete the activity on page 9 of the *Literacy Activity Book.*

Transparency 1–1

Big Bad Words

The three little pigs felt safe in their new house. But then the big bad wolf came prowling down the road.

The first pig saw the wolf coming and locked the front door. The second pig hid behind a plant. He was trembling so hard that the leaves on the plant shook. The third pig backed away from the door and right into the fireplace. He burned his curly little tail.

The wolf pounded on the door. "Little pigs, little pigs, let me in," he grunted.

Soon they heard someone kicking in the chimney and saw that chunks of ash had crumbled to the ground.

Suddenly the little pigs had a terrific idea...

Science

Teacher FactFile

Wolves: did you know. . .

The expression "to eat like a wolf" derives from the fact that an adult wolf can eat 20 pounds of meat at one feeding.

Wolves helped primitive people track down fleet-footed animals. For their reward they received leftover bones and meat scraps.

Wolves hunt everything from moose to mice. They sometimes travel 40 to 50 miles a day looking for food.

Wolves share responsibility for raising their pups. Adult wolves will take turns bringing food to the pups.

Literacy Activity Book, p. 9

Get the Message?

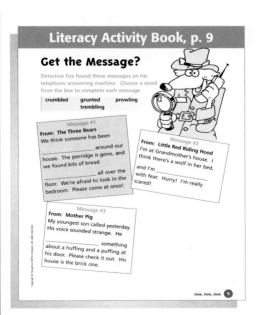

Detective Fox found these messages on his telephone answering machine. Choose a word from the box to complete each message.

| crumbled | grunted | prowling |
| trembling | | |

Message #1
From: **The Three Bears**
We think someone has been _____ around our house. The porridge is gone, and we found bits of bread _____ all over the floor. We're afraid to look in the bedroom. Please come at once!

Message #2
From: **Little Red Riding Hood**
I'm at Grandmother's house. I think there's a wolf in her bed, and I'm _____ with fear. Hurry! I'm really scared!

Message #3
From: **Mother Pig**
My youngest son called yesterday. His voice sounded strange. He _____ something about a huffing and a puffing at his door. Please check it out. His house is the brick one.

Oink, Oink, Oink 9

Interact
with
Literature

More About the Author

Eugene Trivizas

Eugene Trivizas is a leading writer for children in Greece. In that country his books have been the inspiration for comics, television series, and plays. He has won numerous prizes for his work, including a diploma awarded by IBBY (International Board on Books for Young People) for excellence in writing. *The Three Little Wolves and the Big Bad Pig* is the first story he has written in English.

Dr. Trivizas also teaches criminology and has served as an honorary advisor to the Minister of Justice in Greece. He is the author of papers on subjects as diverse as football, hooliganism, censorship, and the effect of diet on criminal behavior.

About the Author

Eugene Trivizas

has written many books — but in Greek. *The Three Little Wolves and the Big Bad Pig* is the first book he wrote in English. Eugene lives part of the year in Greece and part of the year in England. He has written about many subjects, including football and crime.

About the Illustrator

Helen Oxenbury

has always loved to draw and paint. She once had a job drawing pictures for birthday cards and other greeting cards you buy in stores. Now she lives with her family in London, England, and illustrates books for children.

36

EUGENE TRIVIZAS HELEN OXENBURY

The Three Little Wolves and the Big Bad Pig

37

More About the Illustrator

Helen Oxenbury

British illustrator Helen Oxenbury had a background in theater design before she began illustrating children's books. Her main inspiration for entering the field was "the fact that I [as a young mother] couldn't find any books to show my baby."

She quickly became known for picture books but, as her children grew, she became interested in doing books for older children who "can appreciate things like atmosphere and detail."

No matter what age group Oxenbury aims to reach, she respects her audience. "I believe children to be very canny people who immediately sense if adults talk, write, or illustrate down to them," she says.

Interact *with* Literature

Reading Strategies

▶ **Predict/Infer**
  Monitor

Teacher Modeling Discuss how good readers pay attention while reading and make adjustments if they need to. Model the use of strategies using a Think Aloud.

Think Aloud

The title says the pig is big and bad, and in the picture the three little wolves look friendly. That's the opposite of the story I know. I can predict that a lot of things in this story will be backwards. I'll have to monitor, or pay attention, as I read, so I won't get confused.

Predicting/Purpose Setting

Have students predict what will happen to the three wolves. Then suggest that they read and check if their predictions are correct.

Choices for Reading

Independent Reading	Cooperative Reading
Guided Reading	Teacher Read Aloud

Guided Reading

Have students using the Guided Reading option read to the end of page 43. Use the questions on page 42 to check comprehension.

Once upon a time, there were three cuddly little wolves with soft fur and fluffy tails who lived with their mother. The first was black, the second was gray, and the third was white.

One day the mother called the three little wolves around her and said, "My children, it is time for you to go out into the world. Go and build a house for yourselves. But beware of the big bad pig."

"Don't worry, Mother, we will watch out for him," said the three little wolves, and they set off.

38

QuickREFERENCE

Math Link

Calculating Ages Young wolves are usually cared for by their mothers until they're two months old. Ask students to estimate the ages of these little wolves in weeks (eight) and days (sixty).

Extra Support

Story Review If students do not know "The Three Little Pigs," you may wish to
- read the story aloud on pages 35A–35B
- play a videotape of the story
- have other students tell the story

Soon they met a kangaroo who was pushing a wheelbarrow full of red and yellow bricks.

"Please, will you give us some of your bricks?" asked the three little wolves.

"Certainly," said the kangaroo, and she gave them lots of red and yellow bricks.

So the three little wolves built themselves a house of bricks.

39

Interact
with
Literature

The very next day the big bad pig came <u>prowling</u> down the road and saw the house of bricks that the little wolves had built.

The three little wolves were playing croquet in the garden. When they saw the big bad pig coming, they ran inside the house and locked the door.

40

QuickREFERENCE

★★★ Multicultural Link

Games Often games vary from culture to culture. For example, the English "London Bridge" is known as "The Hen Runs" in Chile or "The Fountain" in Cuba. Ask students to share information about games they know.

Extra Support

Croquet Explain that croquet players use a mallet—originally a *crochet*, or "crooked stick" in French—to hit a ball through wire rungs, or wickets. Have students who have played croquet demonstrate how it is played.

41

Genre

Fantasy

Teach/Model

Remind students that *The Three Little Wolves and the Big Bad Pig* is a fantasy. Discuss what parts of the story are make-believe.

Explain that there are many different kinds of fantasies. Model by putting this chart on the board.

Three Kinds of Fantasies
With Animal Characters:
Goldilocks and the Three Bears   *Charlotte's Web*
With Toys or Dolls:
Pinocchio   *Winnie the Pooh*
With Characters That Have Special Powers:
Mary Poppins   *Pippi Longstocking*

Other types of fantasies that you might want to add to the list include ones with tiny characters (such as *The Borrowers*) and ones involving time travel.

Practice/Apply

Invite students to copy the chart and add additional categories and stories from their own reading.

Students Acquiring English

MEETING INDIVIDUAL NEEDS

To help students keep track of the narrative, suggest that they make a chart with these two headings: *Type of House* and *What Happens?* Each time the wolves build a new house, have students paraphrase what happens and then fill in the chart.

Visual Literacy

Dimension Have students name figures in the foreground of the illustration (the gray and black wolves) and the background (the white wolf, the pig). Discuss how the figures get smaller from the foreground to the background.

Interact
with
Literature

 Guided Reading

Comprehension/Critical Thinking

1. How is the story different from the original tale of "The Three Little Pigs"? (Roles are reversed; three little wolves must watch out for a big bad pig; also, the three wolves stick together instead of going their separate ways.)

2. Why do you think the big bad pig is so dangerous? (He is much bigger and stronger than the wolves. He will stop at nothing to try to catch them.)

3. What else could the wolves do to try to stop the pig? (Sample answer: Perhaps build a fence around the house, or get a watchdog.)

Predicting/Purpose Setting

Discuss with students whether their earlier predictions were accurate. Then ask them to predict what the big bad pig will do next. Have students read pages 44–47 to find out if their predictions are correct.

The pig knocked on the door and <u>grunted</u>, "Little wolves, little wolves, let me come in!"

"No, no, no," said the three little wolves. "By the hair on our chinny-chin-chins, we will not let you in, not for all the tea leaves in our china teapot!"

42

Informal Assessment

If students' responses indicate that they understand that the pig is the villain in this story, have them finish reading the story independently or cooperatively.

QuickREFERENCE

★★★ Multicultural Link

Wolves Although the wolf is seen as evil in many folktales, there are exceptions, such as the Sarcee legend "How the Indians Obtained Dogs," in which a wolf helps feed a family. Ask students to explain how their cultures view wolves.

"Then I'll huff and I'll puff and I'll blow your house down!" said the pig.

So he huffed and he puffed and he puffed and he huffed, but the house didn't fall down.

43

MEETING INDIVIDUAL NEEDS

Students Acquiring English

Encourage students to practice reciting the wolves' response *("No, no, no . . .")* and the pig's threat *("Then I'll huff . . .")* on pages 42–43. Then have them repeat the exchange each time it subsequently appears (pages 46, 51, and 55).

Interact with Literature

Reading Strategies

▶ **Monitor**

Use a Think Aloud such as the following to model how readers monitor their reading.

Think Aloud

In this part of the story I was confused because I thought brick and concrete were equally hard. I couldn't understand how the wolves were improving their situation. But then I thought about concrete slabs. They are much larger and heavier than bricks. You can hold bricks in your hand, and they can crack if they're thrown on concrete. So concrete is a more solid material.

But the pig wasn't called big and bad for nothing. He went and fetched his sledgehammer, and he knocked the house down.

The three little wolves only just managed to escape before the bricks crumbled, and they were very frightened indeed.

"We shall have to build a stronger house," they said.

Just then they saw a beaver who was mixing concrete in a concrete mixer.

"Please, will you give us some of your concrete?" asked the three little wolves.

44

Informal Assessment

Oral Reading To check oral reading fluency, have individual students read pages 44–45 aloud.

Students should be allowed to first read the pages silently. Use the Oral Reading Checklist in the *Teacher's Assessment Handbook* as a guide for assessment.

QuickREFERENCE

Background: FYI

Concrete vs. Cement The words *cement* and *concrete* are often misused. For example, a sidewalk is concrete, not cement. Cement is a powder that is mixed with water, sand or gravel, and pebbles to make concrete. Concrete is fireproof, watertight, and relatively inexpensive. If you have concrete walls in your class, invite students to test the strength and examine the texture of them.

"Certainly," said the beaver, and he gave them buckets and buckets full of messy, slurry concrete.

So the three little wolves built themselves a house of concrete.

45

 QuickREFERENCE

 Home Connection

Public Works Is road work being done in your area? Suggest that students go with family members on a field trip to these sights. Students acquiring English may want to make a list of the tools and equipment being used.

Summarizing: Story Structure

Teach/Model

TESTED SKILL

Explain that a story's structure can be used to summarize, or retell, it.

Begin reviewing story elements using this chart.

Characters	*who* is in the story
Setting	*where* or *when* the story happens
Problem	*what* needs to be solved
Events	*what* happens
Ending	*how* the problem is solved

Practice/Apply

Have students use the chart as a guide for summarizing a story they have read recently. You may wish to model with this example.

"The Three Little Pigs" is about three little pigs and a big bad wolf. The wolf wants to eat the pigs, so the pigs try to build strong houses to avoid him. He easily destroys their houses of straw and sticks but, when he can't get into their brick house, he slips down the chimney. The pigs are ready for him, though. The wolf falls into boiling water and is no longer a danger to the pigs.

Afterward, discuss the details that were excluded from the summary and why you left them out.

SKILL FINDER

Full lesson/Reteaching, pp. 60B–60C

Minilessons, p. 83; Theme 2, p. 207

Interact with Literature

Guided Reading

Comprehension/Critical Thinking

1. How did the big bad pig destroy the house of bricks? (with a sledgehammer)

2. Why did the wolves build a concrete house? (Concrete is stronger than brick; the wolves knew they needed a safer house.)

3. Do you think the wolves would have been better off if they had split up and built separate houses? (Have students support their answers by listing reasons.)

Predicting/Purpose Setting

Allow students to discuss whether any of their predictions were correct. Then ask what they think the pig will do next and how the wolves will counteract. Have them read pages 48–51.

No sooner had they finished than the big bad pig came prowling down the road and saw the house of concrete that the little wolves had built.

They were playing battledore and shuttlecock in the garden, and when they saw the big bad pig coming, they ran inside their house and shut the door.

The pig rang the bell and said, "Little frightened wolves, let me come in!"

"No, no, no," said the three little wolves. "By the hair on our chinny-chin-chins, we will not let you in, not for all the tea leaves in our china teapot."

"Then I'll huff and I'll puff and I'll blow your house down!" said the pig.

So he huffed and he puffed and he puffed and he huffed, but the house didn't fall down.

46

QuickREFERENCE

★★★ Multicultural Link

Badminton Battledore and shuttlecock, a British game, is an early form of badminton. A *battledore* is the paddle, and *shuttlecock* is the birdie. Ask students who have played badminton to describe the game briefly.

Students Acquiring English

Students may enjoy role-playing the scene on pages 46–48 between the wolves and the pig. Encourage them to make up additional dialogue to show what the characters are thinking and feeling.

Making Judgments

REVIEW & MAINTAIN

Teach/Model

Explain that readers make judgments based upon the evidence—what the characters do and say. Model with this Think Aloud.

Think Aloud

It's easy to make the judgment that the pig is big and bad. But I'm interested in collecting evidence to learn just how big and bad he is. I'll review what he's said and done.

Big Bad Pig	
Words	• threatened wolves
Actions	• prowled
	• destroyed houses

Discuss how this evidence leads to the judgment that the pig is "bad" in the sense of being menacing.

Practice/Apply

Cooperative Learning In small groups, have students use a chart to judge how well the little wolves defended themselves.

Little Wolves	
Words	• refused to come out
Actions	• received help
	• built several solid houses
	• escaped from pig
	• built flower house

SKILL FINDER

Full lesson/Reteaching, Theme 6, pp. 255C–255D

Minilessons, Theme 4, p. 27; Theme 6, pp. 239, 285

Visual Literacy

Discuss the illustration on page 47. Ask students to point out features of the concrete house that would seemingly protect the wolves without fail. Discuss how each wolf's posture indicates whether he is aware of the pig's presence.

Interact *with* Literature

Reading Strategies

▶ **Think About Words**

Use these questions to prompt students to think about what *Plexiglas* is (a transparent, weather-resistant plastic).

- What common word is "hidden" in the word *Plexiglas*? *(glass)*

- How do you know Plexiglas must be strong? (It is being used with iron bars, padlocks, and other strong material.)

- Why is the first letter in *Plexiglas* capitalized? (It is a proper noun, like the brand name *Kleenex*.)

Reading Strategies

▶ **Predict/Infer**

Use these questions to prompt students to make inferences and predictions.

- Will it be easier or more difficult for the pig to destroy the wolves' new house? Why? (more difficult; wolves are using barbed wire and armor plates)

- If the pig had to use a pneumatic drill the last time, what do you think he will use now? (Answers will vary, but should show an understanding that a more powerful tool is required.)

But the pig wasn't called big and bad for nothing. He went and fetched his pneumatic drill and smashed the house down.

The three little wolves managed to escape, but their chinny-chin-chins were <u>trembling</u> and trembling and trembling.

"We shall build an even stronger house," they said, because they were very determined. Just then they saw a truck coming along the road carrying barbed wire, iron bars, armor plates, and heavy metal padlocks.

"Please, will you give us some of your barbed wire, a few iron bars and armor plates, and some heavy metal padlocks?" they said to the rhinoceros who was driving the truck.

"Sure," said the rhinoceros, and he gave them plenty of barbed wire, iron bars, armor plates, and heavy metal padlocks. He also gave them some Plexiglas and some reinforced steel chains, because he was a generous and kind-hearted rhinoceros.

48

QuickREFERENCE

Vocabulary

Silent Letters Explain that the letter *p* in the word *pneumatic* is silent. Ask different students to pronounce the word (noo–MA–tik).

 Challenge

Analogies A pneumatic drill is run by compressed air. Challenge students to draw analogies among *pneumatic* and *pneumonia* (a lung disease) and *automatic* (self-operating). How are these words related to *pneumatic*?

 Extra Support

Oral Reading To check fluency, ask students to read aloud the last three paragraphs on page 48. Allow students to first reread these paragraphs silently. Students acquiring English may benefit from reading with a strong reader in English.

 Journal

Categorizing Suggest that students list words they come across in the story that can be categorized under the following headings: animals, games, flowers.

 Students Acquiring English

Word Meaning Students can use the illustration on page 49 to identify the following words and add them to the vocabulary wall chart: *barbed wire, iron bars, armor plates, metal padlocks,* and *reinforced steel chains*.

Interact *with* Literature

Guided Reading

Comprehension/Critical Thinking

1. How did the pig destroy the concrete house? (with a pneumatic drill)

2. What kind of house did the wolves build next? (a house with iron bars, armor plates, metal padlocks, and barbed wire)

3. What did the pig do this time to prove he wasn't called *big and bad for nothing?* (He used a crane with a wrecking ball.)

4. If the iron bars and armor plates fail, what material do you think the wolves should try next? Why? (Accept responses that show an understanding of the wolves' predicament.)

Predicting/Purpose Setting

Have students review and modify their predictions if necessary. Ask what they think will happen next. Then have students read to the end of the story (page 59).

Self-Assessment

Reflecting Invite students to reflect on their reading with questions such as

• How has making predictions helped me understand the story?

• Have I been thinking about the story's structure?

• Have I thought of ways to figure out the meanings of words I don't know?

• What makes this story funny?

So the three little wolves built themselves an extremely strong house. It was the strongest, securest house one could possibly imagine. They felt absolutely safe.

The next day the big bad pig came prowling along the road as usual. The three little wolves were playing hopscotch in the garden. When they saw the big bad pig coming, they ran inside their house, bolted the door, and locked all the thirty-seven padlocks.

The pig dialed the video entrance phone and said, "Little frightened wolves with the trembling chins, let me come in!"

50

QuickREFERENCE

Vocabulary

Have students reread aloud the sentences describing the wolves' new house. Ask them to point to words containing the *-est* ending. Discuss how one can use the ending to figure out the words' meanings. (the *most* strong, the *most* secure)

Multicultural Link

Hopscotch is played all over the world. An ancient hopscotch diagram can be found in the Forum in Rome. Students might describe how they play this game or a similar game. (Variations: the shape of the board; the way players hop.)

"No, no, no!" said the little wolves. "By the hair on our chinny-chin-chins, we will not let you in, not for all the tea leaves in our china teapot."

"Then I'll huff and I'll puff and I'll blow your house down!" said the pig.

So he huffed and he puffed and he puffed and he huffed, but the house didn't fall down.

But the pig wasn't called big and bad for nothing. He rented a crane, drove it to the house, swung the wrecking ball as high as it could go, and . . .

51

Technology Link

Video Entrance Phones By use of a hidden camera, a video entrance phone enables people to observe who is at their door. Ask students to name places where they have seen these phones in use.

Interact
with
Literature

he demolished the house. The three little wolves just managed to escape with their fluffy tails flattened.

"Something must be wrong with our building materials," they said. "We have to try something different. But *what?*"

At that moment they saw a flamingo coming along pushing a wheelbarrow full of flowers.

"Please, will you give us some flowers?" asked the little wolves.

"With pleasure," said the flamingo, and he gave them lots of flowers. So the three little wolves built themselves a house of flowers.

52

QuickREFERENCE

Home Connection

Students may enjoy sharing both the original story of "The Three Little Pigs" and this new version with their families. Students might also ask family members if they know any other versions of the story.

53

Art Link

Flower Houses Making a flower house is a fun project for students. They can

- use pictures of flowers cut from magazines or nursery catalogs
- make three-dimensional models, using colored tissue paper

Visual Literacy

Ask a volunteer to reread the first paragraph on page 54 aloud while the rest of the class studies the illustration on page 53. Have students point out each of the flowers mentioned, and discuss how the frame of the house was constructed.

One wall was of marigolds, one of daffodils, one of pink roses, and one of cherry blossoms. The ceiling was made of sunflowers, and the floor was a carpet of daisies. They had water lilies in their bathtub, and buttercups in their refrigerator. It was a rather fragile house and it swayed in the wind, but it was very beautiful.

Next day the big bad pig came prowling down the road and saw the house of flowers that the three little wolves had built.

54

QuickREFERENCE

MEETING INDIVIDUAL NEEDS **Challenge**

Researching Flowers Invite students to research other varieties of flowers and recommend additional flowers for the wolves' new house. Students might want to draw pictures of their flowers to share with their classmates.

He rang the bluebell at the door and said, "Little frightened wolves with the trembling chins and the flattened tails, let me come in!"

"No, no, no," said the three little wolves. "By the hair on our chinny-chin-chins, we will not let you in, not for all the tea leaves in our china teapot!"

"Then I'll huff and I'll puff and I'll blow your house down!" said the pig.

But as he took a deep breath, ready to huff and puff, he smelled the soft scent of the flowers. It was fantastic. And because the scent was so lovely, the pig took another breath and then another. Instead of huffing and puffing, he began to sniff.

He sniffed deeper and deeper until he was quite filled with the fragrant scent. His heart grew tender, and he realized how horrible he had been. Right then he decided to become a big *good* pig.

He started to sing and to dance the tarantella.

56

57

MINILESSON

Fantasy/Realism

REVIEW & MAINTAIN

Teach/Model

Discuss how fantasy has both real and make-believe elements in it. For example, in this selection the fact that there are wolves building a house is fantasy, but the materials they use are real.

Practice/Apply

Invite students to pick out other story elements and events that are real and fantasy. You might list their responses in a chart.

Real	Fantasy
wheelbarrow	kangaroo talking
croquet	wolves playing it
sledgehammer	pig demolishing house
wire, iron bars	wolves building house
crane	wolves escape

End by discussing how mixing fantasy with realistic elements adds to the humor of the story.

SKILL FINDER

Full lesson/Reteaching, pp. 114B–114C

Minilessons, p. 95;
Theme 5, p. 211

Challenge

MEETING INDIVIDUAL NEEDS

The Tarantella Explain that the tarantella is from southern Italy. A person dancing it would be whirling and spinning. Challenge students to learn the origin of this word, especially as it relates to *tarantism* (an uncontrollable urge to dance).

Interact
with
Literature

Guided Reading

Comprehension/Critical Thinking

1. What kind of house did the wolves build next? Why? (They built a house of flowers; they needed a different solution to their problem with the pig.)

2. Was the house of flowers strong? Describe this house. (Students might paraphrase page 54: *It was a rather fragile house and it swayed in the wind, but it was very beautiful.*)

3. What happened when the pig tried to blow down the house? (The scent of the flowers made his heart grow tender. He began to dance.)

4. What if the house of flowers *hadn't* worked? What do you think the wolves could have done next? (Answers should show an awareness of the difficulties of the wolves' predicament.)

Self-Assessment

Ask students to assess their reading using these questions:

• How did monitoring my thinking while reading help me better understand this story?

• How well did I predict and infer actions and events in the story?

• How did knowing the original version of "The Three Little Pigs" help me predict events in this story?

• Would the story still be funny without the role reversals?

At first the three little wolves were a bit worried. It might be a trick. But soon they realized that the pig had truly changed, so they came running out of the house.

They started playing games with him.

First they played pig-pog and then piggy-in-the-middle, and when they were all tired, they invited him into the house.

58

QuickREFERENCE

Health Link

Sports Croquet, battledore and shuttlecock (badminton), hopscotch, and piggy-(monkey)-in-the-middle are games that the three little wolves enjoy playing. Ask students what game they think the characters are playing on pages 58 and 59.

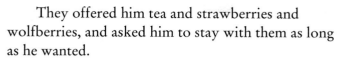
They offered him tea and strawberries and wolfberries, and asked him to stay with them as long as he wanted.

The pig accepted, and they all lived happily together ever after.

59

MINILESSON

Writer's Craft

Character Role Reversal

Teach/Model

Discuss how author Eugene Trivizas has enlivened a familiar tale by reversing the roles of the main characters and giving it a contemporary setting.

Practice/Apply

Recall with students details from the traditional tale that have been altered in the modern version. You may wish to place responses in a chart like the following.

Little Pigs	Big Bad Pig
small ⟶	large
sweet ⟶	mean
leave mother ⟶	no mother

Big Bad Wolf	Little Wolves
menacing ⟶	fun-loving
eats pigs ⟶	drink tea
will stop at nothing ⟶	want peace

Discuss how other familiar folk or fairy tales could be altered in a similar way.

SKILL FINDER

Writing Activities: A Reversed Tale, p. 60E

Reading-Writing Workshop, pp. 116–117F

MEETING INDIVIDUAL NEEDS

Extra Support

Rereading You may wish to have students reread all or part of the selection in order to understand the twist in this story. Students gaining proficiency in English may benefit from working with a strong English reader.

Interact
with
Literature

Responding Activities

Personal Response

Invite students to write or tell their feelings about the story's ending. Were they glad that the big bad pig, unlike the big bad wolf, was not hurt?

Anthology Activities

Choose, or have students choose, a response activity from page 60. For students acquiring English, discuss why the second activity is called "Twice Upon a Time." Also explain the idea of turning something *inside out.* Relate it to the concept of role reversal.

Informal Assessment

Check students' responses for a general understanding of the selection and how it relates to the original story of "The Three Little Pigs."

Additional Support:

- Use Guided Reading questions or the Summarizing: Story Structure minilesson to review.
- Have students work cooperatively to complete a Venn diagram comparing this story with the traditional tale.

RESPONDING

Building on the Story

Design a House
Home, Sweet Home

What else other than flowers could turn a big bad pig into a big *good* pig? With a partner, design a new house made out of something that looks, smells, or tastes really good.

Tell a Story
Twice Upon a Time

Think of another story you can turn inside out. Maybe the Three Bears pay a visit to Goldilocks' house or Little Red Riding Hood dresses like the wolf's granny.

60

QuickREFERENCE

MEETING INDIVIDUAL NEEDS
Students Acquiring English

The "Home, Sweet Home" activity on page 60 is appropriate for most students acquiring English. You may wish to bring in a book or magazine with pictures of different houses to help get students thinking.

🏠 Home Connection

Animal Contractors Suggest that students work with family members to brainstorm a list of animals and the kinds of homes they build. (beavers/dams, spiders/webs, birds/nests, and so on)

More Choices for Responding

Materials
- construction paper
- scissors
- stapler
- markers or crayons

Thank-You Notes

As the three little wolves, students can write notes to the other story characters to thank them for the building supplies and to tell what happened to the homes the wolves built.

1 Have students use 2 pieces of paper together to cut out flower shapes.

2 Have students staple the flower shapes together.

3 Then have students write their messages inside.

Share Favorite Things

In their response to the pig, the wolves always say *"not for all the tea leaves in our china teapot."* Ask students to think of a favorite thing they own that they would never want to give up. Students could bring their valued objects in and share why these objects are so important to them.

Selection Connections
LAB, p. 8

Have students complete the portion of the chart relating to *The Three Little Wolves and the Big Bad Pig.*

Literature Discussion

- Tell about a time that you met someone who, like the big bad pig, was unfriendly at first but later became your friend. What happened that turned you into friends?

- What do you think the wolves' mother would say if she visited the flower house and saw her children living with the pig?

- How long do you think the big bad pig will stay and live with the three little wolves? What could he do for the wolves to show them that he has changed for good?

Comprehension Check

To check selection comprehension, use the following questions and/or have students complete *Literacy Activity Book* page 10.

1. What does the pig do in this story to prove that he is big and bad? (He demolishes three houses in his tireless pursuit of the little wolves.)

2. Why do you think the wolves didn't try to hurt the big bad pig? Was this a good idea or not? (It only would have made the pig madder and provided him with a reason to continue to attack them.)

Literacy Activity Book, p. 10

What a Week!

The Big Bad Pig wrote a letter to his brother. Complete the letter to tell what happened in the story.

Dear Hammond,

I had an incredible week. It began when I came upon a _____ built by these three wolves. At first I tried _____, but then I decided to use a sledgehammer to _____. Soon after, they built a house of _____. It was a bit more work, but my _____ smashed that house down. Then they collected _____ and built their strongest house. I needed _____ to demolish that one. Their last house was the best, though. It was made of sweet-smelling _____. I decided this is where I'd love to live! So now I play games like _____ with my furry friends. Come visit sometime!

Sincerely,

10 Oink, Oink, Oink

Portfolio Opportunity

- Selection comprehension: Save *Literacy Activity Book* page 10.
- Writing samples: Save thank-you notes or responses to other writing activities.

3

Instruct *and* Integrate

Comprehension

Transparency 1–2

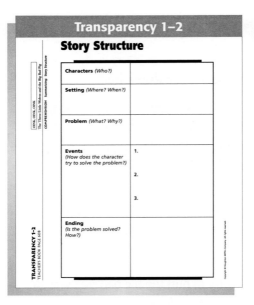

Story Structure

Characters (Who?)	
Setting (Where? When?)	
Problem (What? Why?)	
Events (How does the character try to solve the problem?)	1. 2. 3.
Ending (Is the problem solved? How?)	

TRANSPARENCY 1-2
TEACHER'S BOOK PAGE 60B

Literacy Activity Book, p. 11

Winter Dance

Read the fable. Then complete the chart.

One winter day, some ants were hard at work in a field. A grasshopper came along and asked if the ants could give him a few grains of corn. "Please," said the grasshopper, "for I am starving."
"What did you do all last summer while we gathered food?" the ants asked.
The grasshopper replied, "I was busy singing."
"Then you can dance all winter," said the ants.

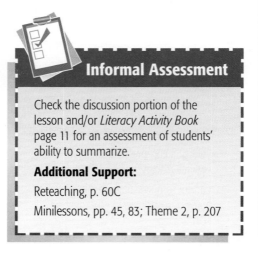

Setting	
Characters	
Problem	
Events	
Ending	

Oink, Oink, Oink **11**

Informal Assessment

Check the discussion portion of the lesson and/or *Literacy Activity Book* page 11 for an assessment of students' ability to summarize.

Additional Support:

Reteaching, p. 60C

Minilessons, pp. 45, 83; Theme 2, p. 207

INTERACTIVE LEARNING

 TESTED SKILL

Summarizing: Story Structure

LAB, p. 11

Teach/Model

Discuss how focusing on the following elements of a story can help readers organize their thoughts when they want to summarize.

- **Characters:** the main people (or animals) in the story
- **Setting:** where and when the story takes place
- **Problem:** what the main character sets out to do
- **Events:** what the character does to solve his/her problem
- **Ending:** how the problem is (or is not) solved

Display Transparency 1–2. Work with students to fill in the chart. Then ask volunteers to use the chart to summarize the story in their own words. If necessary, model with this summary.

Think Aloud

This version of "The Three Little Pigs" is about three little wolves and a big bad pig. The pig in this story does more than huff and puff. He uses different tools to smash the wolves' houses. The wolves finally decide to build a house of flowers, and it works: the pig loves flowers, and he becomes their friend.

Characters	3 wolves, a pig
Setting	a wooded area, Once Upon a Time
Problem	Wolves must avoid Big Bad Pig.
Events	1. Wolves build brick house, but pig hammers it down.
	2. Wolves try cement house, but pig uses pneumatic drill.
	3. Wolves build secure house, but pig uses a crane.
Ending	Wolves build a house of flowers, and pig, who loves flowers, becomes their friend.

Practice/Apply

- Have students complete *Literacy Activity Book* page 11.
- Have students summarize another story they know well.

SKILL FINDER   Minilessons, pp. 45, 83; Theme 2, p. 207

Summarizing: Story Structure

MEETING INDIVIDUAL NEEDS

Cooperative Learning

Read the classic version of "The Three Little Pigs" on pages 35A–35B. Divide students into four small groups and assign a story element to each group. Have students listen carefully and draw every element except the problem (which can be stated in a sentence or two). You may wish to reuse Transparency 1–2 for this activity or make a chart on the bulletin board. Tape students' pictures in the appropriate rows and discuss how each artist chose to capture a story element.

Students can use the **Channel R.E.A.D.** videodisc "License to Drive" for additional support with Summarizing: Story Structure.

Setting

Characters

Problem

Pigs must make their own way in the world.

Events

Ending

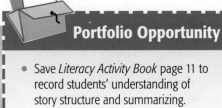

Portfolio Opportunity

- Save *Literacy Activity Book* page 11 to record students' understanding of story structure and summarizing.

Instruct *and* **Integrate**

Writing Skills and Activities

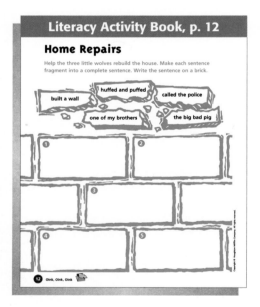

Transparency 1–3

Writing a Sentence

The wolves played croquet.
The big bad pig.
Built a house of bricks.

1. One of the wolves.

2. Came crashing down.

3. Swayed in the wind.

4. The pig's new friends.

Literacy Activity Book, p. 12

Home Repairs

Help the three little wolves rebuild the house. Make each sentence fragment into a complete sentence. Write the sentence on a brick.

huffed and puffed
built a wall
called the police
one of my brothers
the big bad pig

① ② ③ ④ ⑤

12 Oink, Oink, Oink

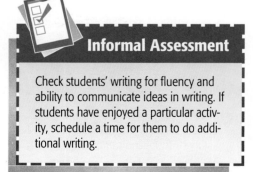

Informal Assessment

Check students' writing for fluency and ability to communicate ideas in writing. If students have enjoyed a particular activity, schedule a time for them to do additional writing.

INTERACTIVE LEARNING

Writing a Sentence

TESTED SKILL

LAB, p.12

Teach/Model Display Transparency 1–3. Have students read the three groups of words at the top of the transparency. Ask which group of words is a sentence. (the first) Remind students that a sentence is a group of words that tells a complete thought—it tells who or what the sentence is about and what happens. Ask students to explain why the second group of words is not a sentence. (It doesn't tell what happens—what the pig did.) Ask the same question about the third group. (It doesn't tell who or what built the house.)

Explain that it is important for writers to use complete sentences so their readers are not confused.

The wolves played croquet.	complete sentence
The big bad pig.	doesn't tell what happens
Built a house of bricks.	doesn't tell who built the house

Have students add to each fragment on the transparency to create a complete sentence. They might want to complete each sentence in several different ways. Ask volunteers to share their sentences by reading them aloud or by writing them on the transparency.

Practice/Apply Assign the activity Give Directions. Remind students to be sure that each of their sentences tells a complete thought.

SKILL FINDER

Grammar, pp. 60J–60K

Reading-Writing Workshop, p. 116–117F

Writing Activities

Shared Writing: A Reversed Tale

Work with students to write a story, reversing the roles in another traditional tale. Use one of the following ideas or brainstorm ideas together.

- The Three Trolls and the Billy Goat Gruff
- Baby Bear and the Goldilocks Family
- Rotten Red Riding Hood and the Little Wolf

(See the Writer's Craft Minilesson on page 59.)

Students can use The Learning Company's new elementary writing center for all their writing activities.

Write a Song
Cooperative Learning

Remind students that when the big bad pig smelled the flowers, he started to sing and dance the tarantella. Have students work in small groups to write a song that the pig might have sung. Have volunteers perform their songs for the class.

Give Directions

Remind students that the three little wolves enjoyed playing games, including croquet, battledore and shuttlecock, hopscotch, pig-pog, and piggy-in-the-middle. Have each student select a favorite game and write a set of directions for playing it.

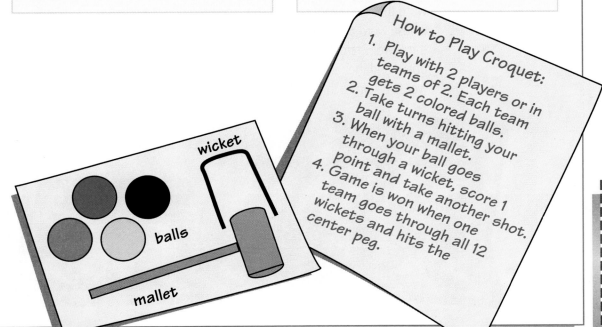

How to Play Croquet:
1. Play with 2 players or in teams of 2. Each team gets 2 colored balls.
2. Take turns hitting your ball with a mallet.
3. When your ball goes through a wicket, score 1 point and take another shot.
4. Game is won when one team goes through all 12 wickets and hits the center peg.

wicket

balls

mallet

Portfolio Opportunity

- Save *Literacy Activity Book* page 12 to record students' understanding of writing complete sentences.
- Save responses to activities on this page for writing samples.

Instruct *and* Integrate

Word Skills and Strategies

Literacy Activity Book, p. 13

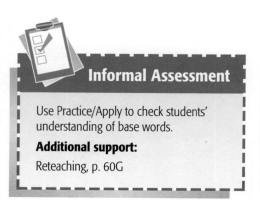

What a Gift

The three little wolves bought their new friend the pig a T-shirt. Solve the puzzle to find out what was printed on the shirt.

Each word has a base word. Write the base word. Then write each numbered letter on the T-shirt.

precooked	__ __ __ __ __ __ 8 14	agreement	__ __ __ __ __ 6 11
mislead	__ __ __ __ 4 9	unhappiness	__ __ __ __ __ 5
remover	__ __ __ __ 7	weekly	__ __ __ __ 15
unfolded	__ __ __ __ 2 13	lived	__ __ __ __ 12
enjoy	__ __ __ 1	selfish	__ __ __ __ 3 10

TESTED SKILL

Structural Analysis
Base Words
LAB, p. 13

Teach/Model

Write this sentence on the board.

> The little wolves were getting tired of rebuilding their house.

Ask students if they can find a word in the sentence that is made from the smaller word *build.* Repeat with *get, wolf,* and *tire.* As they find each word, write the base word above it. Tell students that many words are created by adding beginnings and endings to smaller words. Explain that the smaller words are called base words. Point out that the spelling of the base word sometimes changes when an ending is added, as in *wolf* and *wolves.*

Tell students that many words can be made from the same base word. Under *rebuilding* on the board, add *builds* and *builder.* Explain that *rebuilding, builds,* and *builder* are all part of the word family for *build.* Tell students that all of the words in a word family are related in meaning, for example, a builder is a person who builds. Point out that when students come across an unfamiliar word in their reading, finding the base word can be a clue to figuring out the meaning of the word.

Practice/Apply

Write each word below on an index card (not including the base words) and give one card to each student. Have students determine the base word that their word comes from and then find the other four students whose word comes from the same base word. Once students have found their "word-family members," have them write their base word on the board and their individual words beneath it. As a class, discuss how the words within each family are related in meaning.

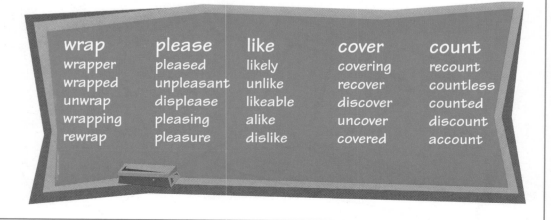

wrap	please	like	cover	count
wrapper	pleased	likely	covering	recount
wrapped	unpleasant	unlike	recover	countless
unwrap	displease	likeable	discover	counted
wrapping	pleasing	alike	uncover	discount
rewrap	pleasure	dislike	covered	account

Extra Support

Point out to students that the meaning of a base word is closely related to the meaning of the longer word. Make sure they understand that not every group of letters that happens to form a word within a longer word is a base word. For instance, *neigh* is not a base word in *neighbor.*

Informal Assessment

Use Practice/Apply to check students' understanding of base words.

Additional support:

Reteaching, p. 60G

Base Words

Draw three houses and mailboxes on the board. Label the mailboxes *lock, trust,* and *fair.* Remind students that many words come from a smaller base word, and that words that come from the same base words are all part of the same word family. Write each word below on the board in random order and ask students which word family it belongs to. Have a volunteer write the word in the appropriate house.

Word Skills Practice

Cumulative Skill Practice
Goldie Bear and the Three Locks
by Jed Mannheimer

WATCH **ME** READ

locked
locker
unlock
relock

lock

trustful
distrust
trusting
entrust

trust

MAIL

fairness
unfair
fairest
fairly

fair

MAIL

MAIL

M I N I L E S S O N

Reviewing Short Vowels

Teach/Model   Write this sentence on the board.

Nice pigs do not huff and puff to be let in!

Ask students which word or words in the sentence have the short *a* sound. *(and)* The short *e* sound? *(let)* The short *i* sound? *(pigs, in)* The short *o* sound? *(not)* The short *u* sound? *(huff, puff)*

Practice/Apply   *Cooperative Learning*   Divide the class into five groups and assign each group a short vowel sound. Have each group hunt for words in the story that contain their vowel sound. Write the headings *and, let, pigs, not,* and *puff* on the board. As students share their words with the class, write each word under the heading with the appropriate vowel sound.

Portfolio Opportunity

Use *Literacy Activity Book* page 13 to record students' understanding of base words.

3

Instruct *and* Integrate

Building Vocabulary

High-Frequency Vocabulary Practice

Cumulative Skill Practice
Goldie Bear and the Three Locks
by Jed Mannheimer

Literacy Activity Book, p. 14

A Bad Temper

The Big Good Pig is feeling like a Big Bad Pig again because he is having trouble with the sentences. Help him feel good by completing each sentence with the better of the two words in parentheses.

1. The three little wolves looked soft and
   _____ (cuddly, messy).

2. In order to sneak up on the wolves, the Big Bad Pig
   came _____ (running, prowling) through
   the trees.

3. The Big Bad Pig _____ (grunted, swayed)
   because he was big and bad.

4. When the wolves were scared, they began
   _____ (trembling, playing).

5. Each time one of their houses _____
   (crumbled, fetched), the wolves were
   _____ (frightened, determined) to build a
   better one.

14   Oink, Oink, Oink

Use this page to review Selection Vocabulary.

Workbench
saw
screwdriver
pliers
wren
pain

Garden Shed
shovel
spade
hoe
ake
wel

Sewing Box
needle
pins
thimble
scissors
measuring

Cleaning Closet
mop
broom
scrub brush
dustpan
sponge

Kitchen Drawer
knife
wooden spoon
strainer
egg beater
spatula

Vocabulary Activities

Synonyms for *big* and *bad*
Cooperative Learning

On the board, write the title *The Three Little Wolves and the Big Bad Pig.* Then cross out the words *Big* and *Bad* and above them write *Large* and *Wicked.* Ask students whether or not you've changed the meaning of the title. Point out that *large* and *big* are synonyms—words that have the same or nearly the same meaning. Explain that *wicked* and *bad* are also synonyms.

> The Three Little Wolves
> Large Wicked
> and the Big Bad Pig

Have students work in small groups to replace the words *big* and *bad* with more interesting synonyms.

Encourage groups to come up with several versions of the title and then to choose one or two favorites to share with the class.

Classifying/Categorizing

Remind students that the big bad pig couldn't destroy the little wolves' houses with his bare hoofs—he had to rely on tools such as a sledge-hammer and a pneumatic drill. Ask students to describe these tools. Point out that a tool is a hand-held object designed to do a certain kind of work.

Tell students that when the pig became good and moved in with the wolves, he needed tools for being helpful rather than harmful. Set up posters around the room with the labels *Workbench, Gardening Shed, Cleaning Closet, Sewing Box,* and *Kitchen Drawer.* Have students move independently from poster to poster, listing tools that the pig should keep in each area of his new home. Encourage students to read what their classmates have written and to think of new words.

Spelling

5-Day Planner

FIVE-DAY PLAN

DAY 1	DAY 2	DAY 3	DAY 4	DAY 5
Pretest; Minilesson; Challenge Words/ Additional Words (opt.); Take-Home Word Lists (LAB)	First LAB page; Challenge Words Practice (opt.)	Check first LAB page; Second LAB page (except writing application)	Check second LAB page; writing application (LAB)	Test

Teaching CHOICES

MINILESSON

TESTED SKILL

Short Vowels
LAB, pp. 15–16

- Say the word *ask*. Have students repeat the word. Ask them what vowel sound they hear in *ask*. (ă). Then write *ask* on the board. Have a volunteer tell how the vowel sound is spelled. (*a*) Underline the vowel.

- Introduce the /ĕ/,/ĭ/,/ŏ/, and /ŭ/, sounds, using *next, mix, lock,* and *shut.*

- Write the Spelling Words on the board. Tell students that each Spelling Word has a short vowel sound. Say the Spelling Words and have students repeat them.

- Encourage students to add to their Study List some words that they have misspelled in their own writing.

Spelling Words

*ask   *black
*next   *shut
*mix   *lock
*smell   *truck

Challenge Words

*knock   *plenty
*scent   *fetch

Additional Spelling Words

spill   crust
lunch   splash

*Starred words or forms of the words appear in *The Three Little Wolves and the Big Bad Pig.*

Literacy Activity Book, p. 15

Flower Power

Short Vowels Each Spelling Word has a short vowel sound. A short vowel sound is usually spelled *a, e, i, o,* or *u* and is followed by a consonant sound.

short a ask   short o lock
short e next   short u shut
short i mix

Write each Spelling Word next to the flower that has the matching vowel sound.

Spelling Words
1. ask   5. black
2. next   6. shut
3. mix   7. lock
4. smell   8. truck

My Study List What other words do you need to study for spelling? Add them to My Study List for *The Three Little Wolves and the Big Bad Pig* in the back of this book.

Literacy Activity Book, p. 16

Spelling Spree

Proofreading Find and circle four misspelled Spelling Words in this song. Then write each word correctly.

The Piggy Jig
Whenever the sky is rainy and blak,
I lock all my cares away.
Then I shut my eyes and smel the flowers,
And find the nixt mud hole for play!

Spelling Words
1. ask   5. black
2. next   6. shut
3. mix   7. lock
4. smell   8. truck

Riddles Write a Spelling Word to answer each riddle.

5. If you have a question, you do this. What is this?
6. Before you bake a cake, you do this. What is this?
7. This opens with a key. What is this?
8. This has four wheels. What is this?
9. Your nose can do this for you. What is this?
10. Your eyes do this when you fall asleep. What is this?

Build It Up Imagine that you are going to build something. On a separate paper, write step-by-step directions for how to do it. Use Spelling Words from the list.

16 Oink, Oink, Oink

Spelling Assessment

Pretest

Say each underlined word, read the sentence, and then repeat the word. Have students write only the underlined words.

1. Before you open the door, <u>ask</u> who it is.
2. What happens <u>next</u> in the story?
3. The first step is to <u>mix</u> the flour and the sugar.
4. Do you <u>smell</u> something burning?
5. Wolves can be <u>black</u>, white, or gray.
6. Remember to <u>shut</u> the windows.
7. It's a good idea to <u>lock</u> your door at night.
8. That <u>truck</u> is full of bricks.

Test

Spelling Words Use the Pretest sentences.

Challenge Words

9. Please <u>fetch</u> me some water.
10. Do you hear a <u>knock</u> at the door?
11. The <u>scent</u> of roses is in the air.
12. There is <u>plenty</u> of time to catch the bus.

SKILL FINDER

Daily Language Practice, p. 60K

Reading-Writing Workshop, p. 117E

Spelling Vocabulary Students can use the **Spelling Spree CD-ROM** for extra practice with the spelling principles taught in this selection.

MEETING INDIVIDUAL NEEDS

Challenge

Challenge Words Practice Have students use the Challenge Words to write tongue twisters.

3

Instruct *and* Integrate

Grammar

5-Day Planner

FIVE-DAY PLAN

DAY 1	DAY 2	DAY 3	DAY 4	DAY 5
Daily Language Practice 1; Teach/Model; First LAB page	Daily Language Practice 2; Check first LAB page; Cooperative Learning	Daily Language Practice 3; Writing Application	Daily Language Practice 4; Reteaching (opt.); Second LAB page	Daily Language Practice 5; Check second LAB page; Students' Writing

---

Transparency 1–4

Subjects and Predicates

SUBJECT	PREDICATE
The pig	came down the road.

He|was a big bad pig.

The three little wolves|escaped.

Their houses|were not as lucky.

Flowers|changed the pig.

SUBJECTS	PREDICATES

TRANSPARENCY 1-4
TEACHER'S BOOK PAGE 60J

Literacy Activity Book, p. 19

Picture Perfect

Literacy Activity Book, p. 17

Piece it Together

Subjects and Predicates
Color red each puzzle piece that has a subject. Color blue each puzzle piece that has a predicate. Then cut out and match the puzzle pieces to make sentences.

SUBJECT	PREDICATE
The wolf	laid the bricks.

this story

the four animals

many famous stories

is a very old one

scares some small children

it

live happily ever after

read the story to children

teachers

are about animals

On another piece of paper, write the sentences. Begin each sentence with a capital letter. End each sentence with a period.

Oink, Oink, Oink **17**

Informal Assessment

Responses to the activities should indicate a general understanding of subjects and predicates.

Additional Support:
Reteaching, p. 60K.

INTERACTIVE LEARNING

TESTED SKILL ✓ Subjects and Predicates

LAB, pp. 17, 19

> Every sentence has two parts.
> - The **subject** tells whom or what the sentence is about.
> - The **predicate** tells what the subject does or is.

Teach/Model

Write the following sentences on the chalkboard, and ask volunteers to role-play each one.

> The pig huffed and puffed.
> The wolves are scared.

Ask the class to tell who or what each sentence is about (pig, wolves) and then what the sentences say about the pig or the wolves (huffed and puffed; are scared). Introduce the terms *subject* and *predicate* and underline them in each sentence. Explain that every sentence has a subject and a predicate.

Show Transparency 1–4. Direct students to the example sentence. Have volunteers draw a line between the subject and the predicate in each of the other sentences. Point out that a subject and a predicate can be made up of one word or several words.

Divide the class into Subjects and Predicates. Have the Subjects take turns giving a subject to start a sentence, and have the Predicates take turns finishing it. Write their sentences on the transparency.

Note that a sentence begins with a capital letter and ends with an end mark.

Practice/Apply

***Cooperative Learning:* Build the Brick House** Have students work in small groups to build "brick houses" of subjects and predicates. Write the sentences below on the board. Have each group cut out sixteen "bricks" and write subjects and predicates from the eight sentences.

> **The wolves | lived with their mother.**
> **Tea | was their favorite drink.**
> **She | sent them into the world.**
> **Other animals | gave them supplies.**
> **Their first three houses | fell.**
> **The flowers | were a great idea.**
> **The big bad pig | became a big good pig.**
> **The last house | was a flower house.**

SKILL FINDER
Reading-Writing Workshop, p. 117E
Writing a Sentence, p. 60D

INTERACTIVE LEARNING *(continued)*

Practice/Apply *Cooperative Learning:* **Build the Brick House** *(continued)* Then ask students to match each subject with the correct predicate. Help students draw the outline of a house large enough to hold eight rows of bricks. Have students glue the bricks onto a sheet of paper, "stacking" them to create a "wall." When all groups are finished, students can check one another's subjects and predicates.

 Writing Application: Paragraph About a Character Invite students to write a paragraph about their favorite story character. Remind them to be sure that each sentence has a subject and a predicate.

 Students' Writing Have students look at a piece of writing they have done or are working on to make sure that all sentences have subjects and predicates.

Materials
- poster paper
- construction paper
- markers
- scissors

More Practice
Houghton Mifflin English Level 3
Workbook Plus, pp. 1–2, 7–10
Reteaching Workbook, pp. 1, 4, 5
Write on Track
Write on Track SourceBook, pp. 49–54

Daily Language Practice
Focus Skills

Grammar: Subjects and Predicates
Spelling: Short Vowel Sounds

Every day write one sentence fragment on the chalkboard. Tell students that each sentence is missing a subject or a predicate. Ask them to add the missing part. Remind them to begin each sentence with a capital letter and to end it with a period. Tell students also to check for misspelled words. Have each student write the sentence correctly on a sheet of paper. Have students correct their own papers as a volunteer corrects the sentence on the chalkboard.

Students Acquiring English: Have these students work with fluent English-speaking partners.

Sample responses:

1. Were gray and white and blak.
   The little wolves were gray and white and **black.**

2. Had only one loc and key.
   Their brick house had only one **lock** and key.

3. Their nixt house.
   Their **next** house **was stronger.**

4. A shutt door.
   A **shut** door **did not keep out the big bad pig.**

5. Loved the smel of flowers.
   The pig loved the **smell** of flowers.

 Reteaching

Subjects and Predicates

Have students work in pairs to draw picture sentences. First, ask them to draw a picture of the subject of a sentence, such as a dog. Next, ask them to draw a picture of the subject doing something, such as chasing a car. Then have them write the sentence shown in the pictures.

Ask each pair to share their pictures and sentences with the group and to identify who or what the sentence is about and what that person/animal/object is or is doing. Reinforce the terms *subject* and *predicate,* and have each pair identify them in their written sentences.

The pig danced a jig.
subject
predicate

Instruct
and
Integrate

Communication Activities

Audio Tape
for Oink, Oink, Oink: *The Three Little Wolves and the Big Bad Pig*

Listening and Speaking

Storytelling
Cooperative Learning

Suggest that students work in small groups to retell either *The Three Little Wolves and the Big Bad Pig* or some other once-upon-a-time tale. Provide the titles of several tales on chart paper and have students sign up for their retelling. Share and discuss the guidelines before they begin.

Students Acquiring English Students acquiring English can speak the refrain or other patterned parts of the story.

Tales to Retell:

- Cinderella
- Juan Bobo
- Jack and the Beanstalk
- The Princess and the Pea

Guidelines for Storytelling

Read the story several times. Try telling it aloud without looking at the book. Practice out loud to yourself or a friend.

Divide the story into big sections, such as beginning, middle, and end.

Do not memorize the story. Use your own words. Memorize only key phrases or rhymes, such as "huff and puff."

Speak loudly and clearly. Use your hands and body to show expression.

Consider using a prop, such as a hat or a scarf.

Interviewing the Big Bad Pig
Cooperative Learning

Invite students to plan a TV or radio talk show interview with the Big Bad Pig. They can work together to develop a list of possible questions. For example,

- Why did you behave so violently toward the wolves?

- What made you change?

- What advice do you have for other pigs?

Students can take turns playing either host or guest. The audience can also ask questions.

Informal Assessment

Use the Guidelines for Storytelling to evaluate students' storytelling presentations.

Additional Support:

- Review the guidelines.
- Have students work in pairs to practice the story before sharing it with the group.

Viewing

Watching a Video

There are several videotape versions of the original story of "The Three Little Pigs." If students have the opportunity to watch one, have them discuss the difference between reading a story and watching one on television.

Resources
The Three Little Pigs by James Marshall. Weston Woods.
The Three Little Pigs by Erik Blegvad. Weston Woods.

Using Facial Expressions and Body Language

Students Acquiring English You can learn a lot about how a person feels by examining his or her body language and facial expressions. Encourage students to look at the following illustrations from *The Three Little Wolves and the Big Bad Pig:* pages 40, 42, and 51. What emotions are being expressed? Invite volunteers to pantomime emotions, such as the ones listed in the box, as other students guess what feeling is being expressed.

anger	hate
fear	joy
surprise	confusion
sadness	love

Note: Body language and expressions vary in meaning from culture to culture.

Examining Real Wolves and Pigs
Cooperative Learning

What do real wolves and pigs look like? Provide several nonfiction books on wolves and pigs. Students can also refer to the articles "What's Up, Pup?" (page 61) and "This Little Piggy" (page 64). They can work in small groups to compare pictures of real wolves and pigs with the story illustrations.

Portfolio Opportunity

Film or tape-record students' storytelling sessions.

Cross-Curricular Activities

Book List

Science

Unbuilding
by David Macaulay

*Hammers, Nails, Planks and Paint:
How a House Is Built*
by Thomas Campbell Jackson

spade

bricks

trowel

level

Choices for Science

Careers in Construction

Brainstorm with students the different professions on a construction site. (carpenters, electricians, insulation workers, plasterers, plumbers, etc.) What kind of expertise is required for each job? Encourage students to interview family or friends in these professions and report back to the class.

Students Acquiring English Encourage students to work with a partner to prepare interview questions beforehand.

Tools of the Trade

Students Acquiring English If possible, visit a hardware store or lumberyard with students. Perhaps an employee can explain the construction tools and materials to students. Alternatively, show students the photos of tools on this page, and discuss each tool's name and function.

Looking at Blueprints

Challenge Give students the opportunity to study the blueprint on pages 30 and 31 and to draw blueprints for a room of their own at home.

Students Acquiring English Students can draw or explain types of houses found in their birthplaces. Discuss how the houses are similar and different.

Building Your School

Lead students on a discovery tour of your school, examining the walls, floors, and ceilings to determine what materials were used. Then invite a knowledgeable person (town engineer, school maintenance employee, architect, or construction worker) to describe the less visible features of the building. Perhaps students can recommend repairs or improvements to the building.

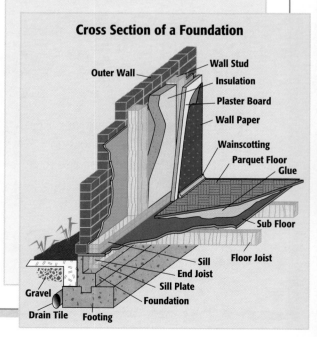

Cross Section of a Foundation

Outer Wall

Wall Stud

Insulation

Plaster Board

Wall Paper

Wainscotting

Parquet Floor

Glue

Sub Floor

Floor Joist

Sill

End Joist

Sill Plate

Foundation

Gravel

Drain Tile

Footing

Math

Playing a Huff-and-Puff Game
Cooperative Learning

Ask students to collect objects they think will not be able to withstand a strong gust of air. Students can then use their measurement skills to play Huff-and-Puff in teams.

Rules:

1. Take turns using a straw to blow the objects across a desk top.
2. Measure the distances traveled.
3. After several rounds, add up team totals to determine a winner.

Materials
- drinking straws
- objects such as paper clips and bottle caps
- measuring tape or ruler

Dance

Dancing the Tarantella

Did you know that the tarantella was originally danced as a cure for the bite of a tarantula spider? Teach students this dance using a famous tarantella by Liszt, Chopin, or Weber.

Resources

Jorge Bolet Plays Liszt, London/ Decca Chamber Music series

Arthur Rubinstein—The Chopin Collection, RCA Victor Gold Seal

1 Do a simple hop or double hop while waving a scarf. Move in a wide circle.

2 Continue to dance in smaller and smaller circles as your audience closes in.

3 As the music slows and the dance ends, fall into the arms of your audience.

Materials
- colorful scarf
- tape or CD player

Students Acquiring English Students may enjoy teaching a dance from their culture.

What's Up, Pup?

Building Background

Previewing/Predicting

Ask students to examine the photographs and use them as the basis for making predictions about how wolves are alike and different from dogs. You might use a Venn diagram like this.

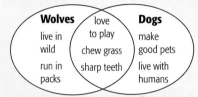

Wolves	love to play	**Dogs**
live in wild	chew grass	make good pets
run in packs	sharp teeth	live with humans

Selection Vocabulary

You may wish to review the following vocabulary before students begin to read. Invite students to make up sentences using each word.

romp: to play in a lively way

mischief: naughty or bad behavior

autumn: the season that follows summer

 ## Students Acquiring English

Students may not be familiar with the female name *Gretta*. Tell them it is a short form of the name *Margaret*. It is derived from *margaron*, a word meaning "pearl."

Eight-week-old gray wolf pups are usually busy little creatures. Luckily, this one is sitting still long enough for us to get a good look. Gretta is her name, and she's taking a break after a morning romp. She won't rest for long, though. What's next? Turn the page to see what kind of mischief she might stir up.

What's UP, Pup?

by Lyle Prescott
photos by Art Wolfe

✎ Writer's Craft

Narrative Nonfiction Ask students whether or not they think Gretta is a good name for a wolf pup. Discuss how naming the pup makes the article immediately more appealing. Why is nonfiction that reads like a story often easier to read?

Media Literacy

Magazines Ask students if they have ever read *Ranger Rick* before. If they haven't, ask them to examine the cover and speculate what subjects a magazine like *Ranger Rick* might cover.

61

Extra Support

Parentheses Point out the directional words in parentheses throughout the article. Discuss with students how helpful it is for an author to include this information in an article with many photos.

 Challenge

Observations Ask students to make two lists—one of Gretta's behaviors that a scientist could observe, and the other of thoughts and actions the writer assigns to Gretta.

Science Link

Canines Explain that *canine* is the name of an animal family that includes foxes and dogs. Ask students to identify dogs that look like wolves. If possible, bring in pictures of different dog breeds for students to look through.

Chomp! "OK, grass — you haven't got a chance against a tough wolf like me," Gretta might be thinking (**right**). Like other young wolf pups, she likes to play with and explore almost everything around her. (She may even eat the grass after she finishes "attacking" it.)

Gretta is also practicing using her teeth. See those pointy ones at the sides of her mouth? They're called *canines* (KAY-nines), and they'll help her hunt when she gets older.

Every day, wolf pups tumble and wrestle together (**left**). Playing like this helps the pups figure out which ones will later be bosses and which ones will get bossed around. Plus, the fast-growing pups need to exercise their muscles. By the time autumn comes, they'll have to be strong enough to join the adults at hunting time.

62

Social Studies Link

Wolf Survival Discuss how wolves were once plentiful in the United States, but now many of them live in protected areas. If possible, bring in maps and information about the range of wolves. Have volunteers point to areas where wolves remain in significant numbers.

The other frisky wolf pups have dashed off without Gretta. They couldn't have gone far — but where are they? She throws back her head and lets out a long, sad howl (**right**). "Hey, guys, you left me here all alone — *please* come back," the little pup seems to be calling.

A wolf may howl alone, or a pack may howl together in a chorus. Either way, the sounds can carry for a long distance. Sometimes wolves may howl messages to each other from a mile or two apart.

The wolf pups like to hang out all over Mom (**above**). That's Gretta in front, giving Mom a lick. Luckily for the little pups, the adult wolves are never too old to play.

63

Interact with Literature

Students Acquiring English

Punctuation/Expressions Be sure students understand that the dialogue is set off by quotation marks. Also point out the punctuation. Explain that to *hang out* is slang meaning "to keep company."

Instruct *and* Integrate   **MINILESSON**

Study Skill
Taking Notes

Teach/Model

Explain that the article describes not only what wolf pups do, but why they do it. Discuss how taking notes is a good strategy when you have a lot of information. Then model with this Think Aloud.

Think Aloud

If I don't write down the reasons why Gretta does different things, I know I'll forget them. I don't need to write everything down, just the most important facts. I think making a chart will be easier than writing sentences.

What She Does	Why She Does It
eats grass	to strengthen teeth
wrestles	to exercise muscles; to determine who is boss

Begin filling in a chart like this.

Practice/Apply

Have students continue taking notes on why Gretta howls (to tell where she is) and why she plays with her mom (to show affection).

SKILL FINDER   Full lesson, p. H2

Building Background

Have students recite the rhyme "This Little Piggy." Discuss how this rhyme is usually recited. (by pinching a person's toes) Have students preview the article. Ask if, given the title and format of the article, they think this selection will be fun facts or serious information.

Discuss the questions listed at the beginning of the article. Ask students to suggest possible answers. List the questions and students' responses on chart paper, and save for future use.

Reading Strategies

Predict/Infer

Ask students what they expect to find out as they read the selection. Then have them preview the selection, paying special attention to the key words (in larger type) in the headlines. Students should be able to predict that the selection will give answers to the questions at the beginning. Have them read to find out the answers.

It oinks! It wallows! It hangs out with the litter! Here's all the dirt on . . .

This Little Piggy!

by Linda Granfield

Can pigs swim?

What good are pigs' snouts?

Are pigs smart?

Are all pigs born with curly tails?

Do pigs prefer to be dirty?

Do pigs really make pigs of themselves?

Go hog wild. Take a look at these questions and see how many you can answer. If you think pigs are hard to peg down, you're right!

64

Students Acquiring English

Expressions Ask students what it means to *go hog wild*. Explain that *to make a pig of yourself* is to eat too much and *hard to peg down* means "difficult to understand." Point out that these expressions are like the ones listed in the box on page 65.

Pigs swim
on hot, sunny days.

You might be surprised to know that pigs are great dog paddlers! Sometimes, they'll escape the burning sun by taking a swim at a water hole. The large amount of fat in their bodies helps keep even heavy pigs floating in the water. Pigs are such good swimmers they can cross rivers many kilometers (miles) wide.

A pig's snout
is a pig's best friend.

Sure, a pig's snout is used for breathing — but it's also great for sweating, digging, and reaching out to other pigs! Like a dog, a pig sweats through its nose instead of its skin. A pig counts on its snout's flat front and bony upper rim as it digs in the dirt and unearths tasty roots. But all that digging doesn't harden a pig's nose. It remains moist and tender — perfect for greeting another pig snout-to-snout when they meet!

When Pigs Fly

Pigs have trotted their way into many of our expressions. See if you can match each of these with its meaning. Then check your answers on page 66.

1.	pigpen	a.	stubborn
2.	pig-headed	b.	braid
3.	go whole hog	c.	living well
4.	pigtail	d.	never
5.	high off the hog	e.	messy place
6.	when pigs fly	f.	take to the limit

65

MINILESSON

Study Skill
K–W–L

Teach/Model

Explain to students that K-W-L is a strategy that will enable them to understand, organize, and remember information in nonfiction selections. The *K* stands for what students already know, the *W* stands for what they want to know, and the *L* stands for what they learn. Model with this Think Aloud.

Think Aloud

I know some obvious things about pigs—that they're big and they like mud—but I still have a lot of questions. I'll put these questions in a chart like this and when I find the answers, I'll write them in the column titled "What I Learned About Pigs."

What I Know About Pigs	What I Want to Know About Pigs	What I Learned About Pigs
Pigs are big.	Do they eat a lot?	
Pigs like mud.	Why do they like it?	

Practice/Apply

Have students work in small groups to list other things they know about pigs and questions they have about pigs. Afterward have them list what they have learned and share their findings.

SKILL FINDER

Full lesson, p. H3

Extra Support

Expressions You may want to have students work with partners to match the expressions with their meanings. Afterward ask students which expressions they've heard before. In each case, what or who was being described?

Visual Literacy

Advertisements Ask students to compare the way the advertisement on page 66 presents information with the way the article "This Little Piggy!" does. Discuss how large type and exclamation marks are an effective way of attracting a reader's attention.

 Students Acquiring English

Word Meaning Discuss the meaning of *stuff themselves silly*. (eat much too much) Point out these other meanings of *stuff*:

• to pack something (a bag) tightly

• to fill with a soft material, or stuffing

• to stop up, as in a nose being stuffed

Ask students to recall an occasion on which they ate too much. How did it make them feel? Did they also feel like napping afterward?

Point out that *curly* and *kinky* are synonyms. Ask a volunteer to demonstrate the meaning of *clockwise*. (You might also use the face of a clock for this purpose.)

Also, explain that a *maze* is a complicated network of passages and paths.

Straight or curly pig tails tell tales.

Many, but not all breeds of pigs are born with curly tails. But when a kinky-tailed pig is scared or not feeling well, its tail may straighten out. Do all curly pig tails curl in the same direction? One old American saying claims that pigs' tails in the south twist clockwise, while pigs' tails in the north twist the opposite way.

66

Pigs are smarter than you think!

Pigs were one of the first animals to be trained by people. In 1785, a famous hog, called the Learned Pig, was taught to spell words, tell time, and solve math problems with the help of rewards. Today, some scientists believe that pigs are very intelligent and easier to train than dogs. They report that pigs can easily find their way through mazes that prove too difficult for many other animals.

Pigs won't stuff themselves silly.

Pigs will eat almost anything — even snow! But that doesn't mean pigs go hog wild over food. Unlike cows and horses, which will eat until they are ill, pigs stop when they feel full. After they have eaten, they usually nap until the next meal. Even without snacking between breakfast and dinner, pigs grow very quickly!

Answers to "When Pigs Fly": 1. e 2. a 3. f 4. b 5. c 6. d

🏠 Home Connection

Animal Stories What are students' experiences with animals? Have they ever owned one, or visited a zoo? Invite them to share their experiences, and to compare their animals with pigs.

Picks of the Litter

Whether you're in Africa or Asia or somewhere in South America, you'll find a wild pig cousin or two! The **bush pig (a)** lives in the grasslands of Africa and Madagascar. Like a wart hog (another African wild pig), male bush pigs have warts on their faces. These warts help protect their faces from the tusks of other bush pigs when they fight. The **babirusa (b)** makes its home in southeast Asia. Its teeth, which can be longer than your foot, grow through the roof of its mouth and out the top of its snout. The **collared peccary (c)**, from South and Central America, is a more distant pig relation. A peccary will "woof" like a dog when its enemy the jaguar is nearby.

Pigs look dirty but really they're cool.

If you visit a farm, you'll probably find pigs covered with dried, caked mud. But it's not because pigs want to be dirty. They need the moisture found in mud. Pigs are very sensitive to heat but have no sweat glands to help them cool off. A coating of mud lowers their body temperature and stops sunburn. If there's clean water nearby, pigs will use that, too.

Instruct and Integrate

Science Link

Animal Myths Have students create bulletin board displays that highlight myths about animals and present the true facts. Students might write the myth on the face of file cards and put factual information on the back.

Health Link

Staying Cool Discuss the ways human beings can stay cool in hot weather. (Encourage students acquiring English to share ways to stay cool associated with their cultural groups.) How can someone avoid sunburn? What foods are good to eat on a hot day?

Social Studies Link

Habitats Using a map or globe, help students locate the habitats of the bush pig (Africa and Madagascar) and the collared peccary (South and Central America). Invite students acquiring English to share stories and descriptions of wild pigs or pig-like animals from their native countries.

✎ Journal

Have students list more animal expressions in their journals. Allow students time to share these expressions and to explain when they might be used.

Interact with Literature

MEETING INDIVIDUAL NEEDS

Students Acquiring English

Word Meaning Discuss the meaning of the phrase *sensitive to heat*. Ask students how they feel when playing outside on very hot days. What do they do to cool off? Also, explain that wart hogs have many warts—hard, rough lumps that grow on the skin.

SELECTION:
The Three Little Javelinas

by Susan Lowell
Illustrated by Jim Harris

- Arizona Young Readers' Award
- Reading Rainbow Book

AWARD WINNER

by Susan Lowell

Other Books by the Author

The Tortoise and the Jackrabbit

Selection Summary

Three little javelinas (pronounced ha-ve-LEE-nas)—"wild, hairy, southwestern cousins of pigs"—set out to seek their fortunes in the desert. As in the traditional tale, each little javelina builds a house. But the materials they use are true to the desert. The first house is of tumbleweed, the second, saguaro (sa–WA–ro) ribs (sticks from the inside of a dried-up cactus), and the third, adobe (a–DOE–be) bricks.

Of course, only the adobe house can withstand the huffing and puffing of their tireless foe, Coyote. As he tries to enter the house through the stove pipe, the third little javelina lights a fire in the stove, and Coyote takes off in a puff of smoke.

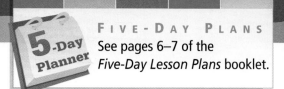
Lesson Planning Guide

	Skill/Strategy Instruction	Meeting Individual Needs	Lesson Resources
1 Introduce *the* Literature *Pacing: 1 day*	**Preparing to Read and Write** Prior Knowledge/Building Background, 67C **Selection Vocabulary**, 67D • desert • dust storm • whirlwind • tumbleweeds • cactus • adobe **Spelling Pretest**, 88I • nose • these • shade • use • mice • smoke • snake • ripe	**Support in Advance**, 67C **Students Acquiring English**, 67C **Other Choices for Building Background**, 67C **Spelling Challenge Words:** • escape • amaze • arrive • fortune	*Literacy Activity Book:* Vocabulary, p. 20 **Transparency:** Vocabulary, 1–5 **Great Start** CD-ROM software, "Oink, Oink, Oink" CD
2 Interact *with* Literature *Pacing: 1–3 days*	**Reading Strategies:** Predict/Infer, 70, 72 Monitor, 70, 78 Think About Words, 76 Summarize, 80 Evaluate, 84 **Minilessons:** ✓ Compare and Contrast, 75 Predicting Outcomes, 79 Summarizing: Story Structure, 83 Writer's Craft: Setting, 85	**Choices for Reading**, 70 **Guided Reading**, 70 Comprehension/Critical Thinking, 74, 78, 86 **Students Acquiring English**, 69, 70, 72, 75, 77, 80, 82, 83, 85, 86, 88 **Extra Support**, 73, 74, 78, 87 **Challenge**, 76, 81	**Reading-Writing Workshop** A Story, 116–117F *Literacy Activity Book,* pp. 40–42 The Learning Company's Ultimate Writing & Creativity Center software
3 Instruct *and* Integrate *Pacing: 1–3 days*	✓ **Comprehension:** Compare and Contrast, 88B ✓ **Writing:** Writing a Book Report, 88D **Word Skills and Strategies:** ✓ Structural Analysis: Inflected Endings *-ed* and *-ing*, 88F Phonics Review: Long Vowel Pairs and Vowel-Consonant-*e*, 88G **Building Vocabulary:** Vocabulary Activities, 88H ✓ **Spelling:** Vowel-Consonant-*e*, 88I ✓ **Grammar:** Correcting Run-on Sentences, 88J–88K **Communication Activities:** Listening and Speaking, 88L–88M; Viewing, 88M **Cross-Curricular Activities:** Science, 88N; Art, 88O; Math, 88O	**Reteaching:** Compare and Contrast, 88C **Activity Choices:** Write a Book Report, Shared Writing: Same Plot, Different Setting, Create a Cartoon, 88E **Reteaching:** Inflected Endings *-ed* and *-ing*, 88G **Activity Choices:** Selection Vocabulary Extension, Words from Spanish, Rhyming Words, 88H **Challenge Words Practice**, 88I **Reteaching:** Correcting Run-on Sentences, 88K **Activity Choices:** Listening and Speaking, 88L–88M; Viewing, 88M **Activity Choices:** Science, 88N; Art, 88O; Math, 88O	**Watch Me Read:** *Ham and Eggs for Jack* **Reading-Writing Workshop** A Story, 116–117F **Transparencies:** Comprehension, 1–6, Writing, 1–7, Grammar, 1–8 *Literacy Activity Book:* Comprehension, p. 22; Writing, p. 23; Word Skills, p. 24; Building Vocabulary, p. 25; Spelling, pp. 26–27; Grammar, pp. 28–29 The Learning Company's Ultimate Writing & Creativity Center software **Spelling Spree** CD-ROM **Video:** *Along Sandy Trails* **Audio Tape** for Oink, Oink, Oink: *The Three Little Javelinas*

✓ *Indicates Tested Skills. See page 34F for assessment options.*

Introduce *the* **Literature**

Preparing to Read and Write

Support in Advance

Use this activity with students who need extra support before participating in the whole-class activity.

Desert Talk Ask students what they know about the desert. Use the story illustrations, especially on pages 73 and 78, as a guide. You might have students draw pictures of a desert environment and share them with the class.

Management Tip
During this time, have other students describe in their journals one story or TV show that was set in the desert.

Students Acquiring English

This story contains words describing motion, such as *trotted away* and *wandered lazily,* that students may not know. Start a word wall with these words. Have students pantomime them. Students can then add other motion words as they read the story.

Prior Knowledge/Building Background

**Key Concept
Life in the Desert**

Cooperative Learning Have groups of students work together to make lists of the sights, sounds, and feelings a person walking through the desert might experience.

**Key Concept
Coyote and
Javelinas**

Have students preview the illustrations. Note that in this story the pigs have been replaced by javelinas (ha-ve-LEE-nas) and the wolf by a coyote. Have students compare these animals and discuss how they are often depicted in stories.

Why Pigs/Javelinas Are Seen As Good	Why Wolf/Coyote Is Seen As Bad
They have round bodies and are cute-looking.	He is lean and his teeth are sharp and scary.
They help each other out.	He is alone.
They want to live in peace.	He wants to eat them.

Students Acquiring English If possible, show pictures of a desert or a video such as *Let's Explore the Desert* (National Geographic) to build background.

Other Choices for Building Background

Drawing Settings

Students Acquiring English Have students draw two houses: one in a city setting and one in a desert setting. Ask them to compare and contrast the settings. What special needs would someone who lives in a desert environment have?

Being Prepared

Cooperative Learning

Have students work in small groups to make lists of clothing and other supplies that would help a person survive in the desert. Afterward students can share their lists and combine them into a master list.

Great Start
For students needing extra support with key concepts and vocabulary, use the Oink, Oink, Oink CD.

INTERACTIVE LEARNING

Spelling
You may want to give the Spelling Pretest on p. 88I before students read the selection.

Daily Language Practice
Use the sentences on page 88K as daily practice of the spelling and grammar skills taught with this selection.

Selection Vocabulary

Key Words

desert

dust storm

whirlwind

tumbleweeds

cactus

adobe

Display Transparency 1–5. After volunteers have read aloud the Key Words, use these questions to discuss the captions.

- What would you need to protect yourself in a dust storm?

- What would it feel like to brush against some tumbleweeds?

- How can a cactus survive in a dry place like the desert? (It absorbs huge amounts of water during occasional desert rains.)

- How is an adobe brick different from a regular brick? (It is baked in the sun, not an oven; adobe is a light color, not red.)

Two Key Words are compounds. Challenge students to define them using the parts of the compound. (Example: *Tumbleweeds* are *weeds* that *tumble.*)

Students Acquiring English You might wish to introduce these additional words: *hooves, hairy, sneaky, shade, heat, magic,* and *suspicious.*

Vocabulary Practice Have students work independently or together to complete the activity on *Literacy Activity Book* page 20.

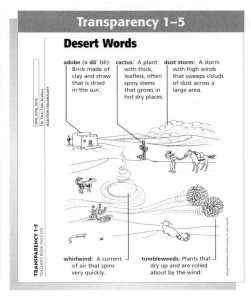

Transparency 1–5

Desert Words

adobe (a dō′ bē): Brick made of clay and straw that is dried in the sun.

cactus: A plant with thick, leafless, often spiny stems that grows in hot dry places.

dust storm: A storm with high winds that sweeps clouds of dust across a large area.

whirlwind: A current of air that spins very quickly.

tumbleweeds: Plants that dry up and are rolled about by the wind.

TRANSPARENCY 1-5
TEACHER'S BOOK PAGE 67D

Science

Teacher FactFile
Desert Food Chain

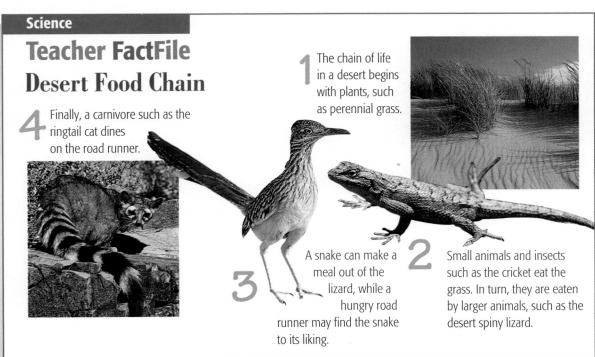

4 Finally, a carnivore such as the ringtail cat dines on the road runner.

1 The chain of life in a desert begins with plants, such as perennial grass.

3 A snake can make a meal out of the lizard, while a hungry road runner may find the snake to its liking.

2 Small animals and insects such as the cricket eat the grass. In turn, they are eaten by larger animals, such as the desert spiny lizard.

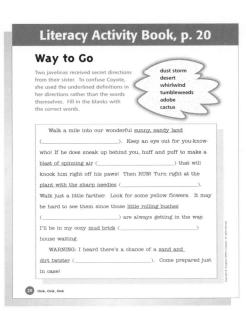

Literacy Activity Book, p. 20

Way to Go

Two javelinas received secret directions from their sister. To confuse Coyote, she used the underlined definitions in her directions rather than the words themselves. Fill in the blanks with the correct words.

> dust storm
> desert
> whirlwind
> tumbleweeds
> adobe
> cactus

Walk a mile into our wonderful <u>sunny, sandy land</u>

(_____). Keep an eye out for you-know-who! If he does sneak up behind you, huff and puff to make a <u>blast of spinning air</u> (_____) that will knock him right off his paws! Then RUN! Turn right at the <u>plant with the sharp needles</u> (_____).

Walk just a little farther. Look for some yellow flowers. It may be hard to see them since those <u>little rolling bushes</u>

(_____) are always getting in the way.

I'll be in my cozy <u>mud brick</u> (_____) house waiting.

WARNING: I heard there's a chance of a <u>sand and dirt twister</u> (_____). Come prepared just in case!

20 Oink, Oink, Oink

2

Interact
with
Literature

More About the Author

Susan Lowell

Susan Lowell describes javelinas as being "extremely bristly—very hairy on the chinny-chin-chin. Oddly enough, they are also related to the hippopotamus." The name comes from the Spanish word for the collared peccary, a member of the swine family that ranges from the southwestern United States down to the tip of South America. In the American Southwest, another common local name for peccaries, besides javelinas, is "wild pigs."

Lowell's sources for this story include the many Coyote legends told by Native Americans of the Southwest, especially the Tohono O'Odham (toe-HO-no O-OH-tam) or Desert People, formerly known as the Papago tribe, of southern Arizona and northern Mexico.

More About the Illustrator

Jim Harris

The coyote in *The Three Little Javelinas* is no stranger to Jim Harris. The illustrator lives at the end of a dirt road on the slope of a mesa in Colorado. Every night he hears the coyotes howl. Sometimes an elk walks across the deck of his art studio. Harris has been drawing and painting since he was four years old.

MEET THE AUTHOR

SUSAN LOWELL has some wild neighbors who often come over for a cactus dinner. That's because she lives in the Arizona desert, and her neighbors are pig-like animals called *javelinas* (ha-ve-LEE-nas). The javelinas like to eat the thorny stems of the cactuses that grow near her ranch. Lowell enjoys watching the javelinas so much that she made up a story about them.

MEET THE ILLUSTRATOR

JIM HARRIS lives in Colorado on the side of a flat-topped mountain called a *mesa*. Every night, he can hear coyotes howling outside. Sometimes he even sees an elk walk across the deck outside his art studio. Harris has been drawing and painting since he was four years old.

68

THE THREE LITTLE JAVELINAS

by Susan Lowell
Illustrated by Jim Harris

69

Science Link

Javelinas Although javelinas look like pigs, they are not. They are classified as peccaries, which are members of the swine family. Have students turn to "My Hairy Neighbors" on page 89 to study photos of real javelinas.

 MEETING INDIVIDUAL NEEDS

Students Acquiring English

This story makes use of descriptive words, dialogue, and action that can be acted out or pantomimed by students as they read it.

Visual Literacy

Discuss the javelinas' clothing. Ask why chaps and bandannas are worn. (Chaps protect your legs and bandannas cover your mouth in dust and sand storms.) If you have students from arid countries, ask them to share how people dress.

Interact
with
Literature

Reading Strategies

▶ **Monitor**
  Predict/Infer

Discussion Discuss with students how good readers adjust the way they read depending on the kind of material they are reading.

Ask students what reading strategies might help them with this story. Discuss how the story might be surprising, so they may need to make predictions and monitor their reading.

Predicting/Purpose Setting

Have students summarize the simple structure of the traditional tale "The Three Little Pigs" and predict how *The Three Little Javelinas* will be similar to it.

Choices for Reading

Independent Reading	**Cooperative Reading**
Guided Reading	**Teacher Read Aloud**

Guided Reading

Students using the Guided Reading option should read to page 75, keeping their predictions in mind as they read. Use the questions on page 74 to check comprehension.

ONCE UPON A TIME, way out in the desert, there were three little javelinas. Javelinas (ha-ve-LEE-nas) are wild, hairy, southwestern cousins of pigs.

Their heads were hairy, their backs were hairy, and their bony legs — all the way down to their hard little hooves — were very hairy. But their snouts were soft and pink.

One day, the three little javelinas trotted away to seek their fortunes. In this hot, dry land, the sky was almost always blue. Steep purple mountains looked down on the desert, where the cactus forests grew.

Soon the little javelinas came to a spot where the path divided, and each one went a different way.

70

QuickREFERENCE

 Journal

Encourage students to record their predictions and inferences in their journals. You might also point out the phrase *Once upon a time* and ask students to add it to their journals as a story starter.

Students Acquiring English

Idiom/Multiple-Meaning Word
The phrase *to seek their fortunes* means the javelinas left home to work and look for success. You may want to ask students what success means to them. Also, explain that a *spot* is a place or location.

71

Math Link

Numbers vs. Numerals Discuss the difference between a number and a numeral. A number is something said out loud. A numeral is a symbol. When we write a number, we can write the numeral (*3*) or the word for that number (*three*).

Music Link

Cowboy Songs Do students know any cowboy songs, such as "Home on the Range" or "Red River Valley"? During long cattle drives, these songs helped alleviate a cowboy's loneliness. They were also an effective way to quiet the cattle!

Interact
with
Literature

Reading Strategies

▶ **Predict/Infer**

Remind students that in the original tale the wolf blew the pigs' houses down. Tell them they can use this knowledge to make a prediction about how Coyote will approach the first javelina. Do they think the javelina will escape? Why or why not?

The first little javelina wandered lazily along. He didn't see a dust storm whirling across the desert — until it caught him.

The whirlwind blew away and left the first little javelina sitting in a heap of tumbleweeds. Brushing himself off, he said, "I'll build a house with them!" And in no time at all, he did.

72

QuickREFERENCE

MEETING INDIVIDUAL NEEDS

Students Acquiring English

Motion Words Have a student pantomime the action of *wandered lazily,* and discuss how its meaning differs from the word *walked.* Explain what it means to be *caught* by something and the meaning of the word *heap.*

Then along came a coyote. He ran through the desert so quickly and so quietly that he was almost invisible. In fact, this was only one of Coyote's many magical tricks. He laughed when he saw the tumbleweed house and smelled the javelina inside.

"Mmm! A tender juicy piggy!" he thought. Coyote was tired of eating mice and rabbits.

73

Interact *with* Literature

 Guided Reading

Comprehension/Critical Thinking

1. Why is Coyote called sneaky? (He used magic to make himself almost invisible. He tried to fool the first javelina by calling out sweetly. He tiptoed when he moved.)

2. Why did Coyote laugh when he saw the tumbleweed house and smelled the javelina inside? (He knew that the house would not be strong enough to protect the javelina.)

3. Why didn't the first javelina choose something better than tumbleweeds to build with? (He was lazy and chose the first material that he stumbled onto.)

Predicting/Purpose Setting

Ask students to compare the first part of the story with other versions they know. Discuss whether their purpose-setting predictions were correct. Tell students to revise their predictions, if necessary, and to read to the end of page 79 to find out what happens to the second javelina.

He called out sweetly, "Little pig, little pig, let me come in."

"Not by the hair of my chinny-chin-chin!" shouted the first javelina (who had a lot of hair on his chinny-chin-chin!).

"Then I'll huff, and I'll puff, and I'll blow your house in!" said Coyote.

74

Informal Assessment

If students' responses indicate that they are understanding the story, have them finish reading independently or in a cooperative group.

QuickREFERENCE

 ★★★ **Multicultural Link**

Tricksters The word *coyote* comes from the Aztec *coyotl.* In many Native American tales Coyote is a trickster who is often outsmarted. Students might enjoy reading *Coyote Steals a Blanket: A Ute Tale* by Janet Stevens.

Extra Support

Rereading Aloud Students may better appreciate the end rhyme and rhythm in the exchange between Coyote and the javelina if they reread the dialogue aloud. Also, discuss the humor in the parenthetical remark.

And he huffed, and he puffed, and he blew the little tumbleweed house away.

But in all the hullabaloo, the first little javelina escaped — and went looking for his brother and sister.

Coyote, who was very sneaky, tiptoed along behind.

75

Students Acquiring English

Word Meaning Explain that *hullabaloo* is a nonsense word that describes a state of confusion.

Motion Words Demonstrate *tiptoed* by tiptoeing in a sneaky way. Then have students add the word to their journals or to the wall chart.

MINILESSON

Compare and Contrast

Teach/Model

Discuss with students how reading different versions of the same tale can be fun. Point out that part of the fun is comparing the new story with the original.

Think Aloud

One big way this story is different from "The Three Little Pigs" is the desert setting. The characters have changed too—there are javelinas instead of pigs, and a coyote has replaced the wolf. The first part is like "The Three Little Pigs" because the coyote asks to be let in and the javelina refuses him in the same way as in the original story.

Practice/Apply

Ask students to point out other ways the traditional tale and *The Three Little Javelinas* are alike and different. Map responses in a Venn diagram.

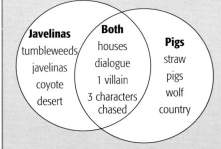

Javelinas
tumbleweeds
javelinas
coyote
desert

Both
houses
dialogue
1 villain
3 characters
chased

Pigs
straw
pigs
wolf
country

SKILL FINDER
Full lesson/Reteaching, pp. 88B–88C

Minilessons, p. 103; Theme 4, p. 47

Interact
with
Literature

Reading Strategies

▶ **Think About Words**

Discuss with students how they can use context clues to figure out the following about saguaros:

• They're tall. (clue: *Giant cactus plants called saguaros*)

• They grow fruit. (clue: *They held their ripe red fruit high in the sky.*)

• Not much grows outward from them. (clue: *But they made almost no shade.*)

The second little javelina walked for miles among giant cactus plants called saguaros (sa-WA-ros). They held their ripe red fruit high in the sky. But they made almost no shade, and the little javelina grew hot.

Then he came upon a Native American woman who was gathering sticks from inside a dried-up cactus. She planned to use these long sticks, called saguaro ribs, to knock down the sweet cactus fruit.

The second little javelina said, "Please, may I have some sticks to build a house?"

"*Ha'u,*" (how) she said, which means "yes" in the language of the Desert People.

76

Quick REFERENCE

★★★ **Multicultural Link**

The Tohono O'Odham (toe-HO-no O-OH-tam), or Desert People, conduct a harvest in the early summer, when cactus flowers begin to bear fruit. This harvest was so important that it marked the beginning of the new year.

MEETING INDIVIDUAL NEEDS

Challenge

Saguaros Have students research
• how long saguaros live
• what animals live in them
• the kinds of food they provide
Explain that cactus fruit looks like watermelon when it is broken open.

★★★ **Multicultural Link**

Word Origins Note that the word *saguaros* came from Mexican Spanish. Invite students to research other English words that have been borrowed from other languages and to report back to the class.

When he was finished building his house, he lay down in the shade. Then his brother arrived, panting from the heat, and the second little javelina moved over and made a place for him.

Visual Literacy

Have students find the mouse on page 77 and then on pages 72 and 75. Discuss how the mouse's facial expressions are a commentary on the story action. Students will enjoy looking for the mouse as they continue to read.

MEETING INDIVIDUAL NEEDS

Students Acquiring English

Word Meaning Have a volunteer demonstrate *panting.* Ask students why animals pant. (to cool off or to catch their breath after running) Also, discuss the phrase *made a place for him.* ("provided a space or area for him to rest")

Interact
with
Literature

Reading Strategies

▶ **Monitor**

Discuss the humor in Coyote's response about not wanting to eat the javelinas' hair. Recall that the author poked fun at the "chinny-chin-chin" response in a parenthetical remark on page 74.

 Guided Reading

Comprehension/Critical Thinking

1. Why are saguaro ribs stronger to build with than tumbleweeds? (They are long sticks that are hard enough to knock fruit off a cactus.)

2. Do you think that Coyote is big and bad like the big bad pig? Why or why not? (He is not as big physically, but he's threatening because he is so clever.)

Predicting/Purpose Setting

Have students summarize the story so far. Then ask them to make predictions about the ending. Comprehension questions can be found on page 86.

Pretty soon, Coyote found the saguaro rib house. He used his magic to make his voice sound just like another javelina's.

"Little pig, little pig, let me come in!" he called.

But the little javelinas were suspicious. The second one cried, "No! Not by the hair of my chinny-chin-chin!"

"Bah!" thought Coyote. "I am not going to eat your *hair.*"

78

Self-Assessment

Reflecting Invite students to ask:

• How am I enjoying the story?
• Do I understand everything that has happened so far?
• What was the hardest part so far?

QuickREFERENCE

Vocabulary

Word Meaning If students have difficulty with *suspicious,* point out context clues: Coyote calls out in a javelina-like voice, but the ones inside don't open the door; they don't completely trust what they're hearing.

 **Extra Support**

Reading Dialogue Point out that Coyote changes his voice to mimic a javelina. Ask students to try reading the dialogue the way either a coyote and a javelina might talk or the way some other animal they know might.

Then Coyote smiled, showing all his sharp teeth: "I'll huff, and I'll puff, and I'll blow your house in!"

So he huffed, and he puffed, and all the saguaro ribs came tumbling down.

But the two little javelinas escaped into the desert.

Still not discouraged, Coyote followed. Sometimes his magic did fail, but then he usually came up with another trick.

79

Journal

Advice If students can think of a better way to trick the javelinas, have them write their words of advice to Coyote in their journals.

MINILESSON

Predicting Outcomes

REVIEW & MAINTAIN

Teach/Model

Discuss how most stories have a sequence of events that result in an outcome. Explain that one way readers can anticipate this outcome is by making predictions. Use this chart to illustrate the process.

What I Learn from the Story	+	What I Know	=	Prediction: What Might Happen

Practice/Apply

Help students predict the outcome of *The Three Little Javelinas* by expanding the chart like this.

What I Learn from the Story	+	What I Know	=	Predicted Outcome
This story is like "The Three Little Pigs."		In the original, the wolf tried to come down the chimney.		Coyote will try the chimney, but, like the wolf, he will fall into boiling water.

Encourage students to develop a similar chart for other stories they read in the future. (You may wish to have them copy the format of the chart above in their journals for reference.)

SKILL FINDER

Full lesson/Reteaching, Theme 4, pp. 58B–58C

Minilessons, Theme 4, pp. 53, 67

Interact
with
Literature

Reading Strategies

▶ **Summarize**

Ask students to summarize how the javelinas have tried to protect themselves against Coyote thus far. Remind them that in the original story, the houses are built of pro- gressively stronger materials. Have them consider whether Coyote will be able to blow down an adobe house or whether this is the house he will have to enter some other way.

The third little javelina trotted through beautiful palo verde trees, with green trunks and yellow flowers. She saw a snake sliding by, smooth as oil. A hawk floated round and round above her. Then she came to a place where a man was making <u>adobe</u> (a-DOE-be) bricks from mud and straw. The bricks lay on the ground, baking in the hot sun.

80

QuickREFERENCE

Science Link

Palo Verde Trees There are ten species of palo verdes, but all of them bear fruit shaped like a pea-pod. This tree also has spines that jut out like thorns. *Palo verde* is a Spanish phrase that perfectly describes the trees: "green sticks."

MEETING INDIVIDUAL NEEDS
Students Acquiring English

Motion Words Discuss with students the mental pictures these images create: *snake sliding by, smooth as oil* and a *hawk floated round and round.* Discuss substitutions for *smooth as oil* and *floated.* What pictures do they make in your mind?

You might wish to bring in pictures and illustrations to reinforce the images, or have a student panto-mime the actions.

The third little javelina thought for a moment, and said, "May I please have a few adobes to build a house?"

"*Sí,*" answered the man, which means "yes" in Spanish, the brick-maker's language.

So the third javelina built herself a solid little adobe house, cool in summer and warm in winter. When her brothers found her, she welcomed them in and locked the door behind them.

Coyote followed their trail.

81

"Little pig, little pig, let me come in!" he called. The three little javelinas looked out the window. This time Coyote pretended to be very old and weak, with no teeth and a sore paw. But they were not fooled.

"No! Not by the hair of my chinny-chin-chin," called back the third little javelina.

"Then I'll huff, and I'll puff, and I'll blow your house in!" said Coyote. He grinned, thinking of the wild pig dinner to come.

"Just try it!" shouted the third little javelina. So Coyote huffed and puffed, but the adobe bricks did not budge.

Again, Coyote tried. "I'll HUFF ... AND I'LL PUFF ... AND I'LL BLOW YOUR HOUSE IN!"

82

Informal Assessment

Oral Reading Have individual students read aloud pages 82–83 as a check of oral reading fluency. Use the Oral Reading Checklist in the *Teacher's Assessment Handbook* as a guide for assessment.

Quick**REFERENCE**

Students Acquiring English

Word Meaning Explain that *did not budge* means "did not move slightly." Discuss how this is a humorous word choice by the author because it emphasizes how solid the adobe house is.

The three little javelinas covered their hairy ears. But nothing happened. The javelinas peeked out the window.

Summarizing: Story Structure

Teach/Model

REVIEW & MAINTAIN

Review the elements of a story: setting, characters, problem, events, and solution. Discuss how a good story summary includes most of these elements. Then map out *The Three Little Javelinas* like this.

Setting: southwestern U.S.

Characters: Coyote, 3 javelinas

Problem: Three javelinas must escape a clever coyote.

Events: 1. Javelinas leave to seek fortunes. 2. Coyote blows down tumbleweed house. 3. Coyote blows down rib house. 4. Coyote slips through stove pipe in the adobe house.

Solution: Javelinas light fire in stove that chases Coyote away.

Practice/Apply

Have students use the chart to summarize. Here is an example.

This version of "The Three Little Pigs" takes place in the Southwest. This time it's a coyote chasing three javelinas. Their houses made of tumbleweed and saguaro ribs are no match for Coyote. But the third house, made of adobe, does the trick. When Coyote tries to enter this house, his tail is scorched and he runs away in pain.

SKILL FINDER

Full lesson/Reteaching, pp. 60B–60C

Minilessons, p. 45; Theme 2, p. 207

Extra Support

Dialogue Coyote's second warning to the javelinas (page 82) is in all capital letters. Ask students why the words were printed this way. Then have groups of students form a chorus to read the line the way Coyote would say it.

Students Acquiring English

Word Meaning Explain that to *peek* means "to look quickly or secretly." Ask volunteers to pantomime peeking out a window or door.

Interact
with
Literature

Reading Strategies

▶ **Evaluate**

Encourage students to evaluate what makes the climactic scene in the story work well. Discuss how the author uses sound words such as *whoosh* and *sizzle.* Point out how she put extra letters in front of the word *sizzle* to emphasize the initial sound. Ask students to reread the line with this word slowly to emphasize the sound.

84

The tip of Coyote's raggedy tail whisked right past their noses. He was climbing upon the tin roof. Next, Coyote used his magic to make himself very skinny.

"The stove pipe!" gasped the third little javelina. Quickly she lighted a fire inside her wood stove.

"What a feast it will be!" Coyote said to himself. He squeezed into the stove pipe. "I think I'll eat them with red hot chile sauce!"

Whoosh. S-s-sizzle!

85

QuickREFERENCE

Writer's Craft
Setting

Teach/Model

Ask students to describe where *The Three Little Javelinas* takes place. Spark discussion by asking:

- Where do the javelinas live?
- What is the weather like there?
- What grows there?
- What sounds are there?
- What does the place look like?

Remind students that the setting is where a story takes place. Explain that a rich setting can make a story vivid and interesting.

Practice/Apply

Work together with students to make a chart that compares the setting of *The Three Little Javelinas* with another story. Here is an example.

The Three Little Javelinas	The Three Little Wolves and the Big Bad Pig
Sights: javelinas; purple mountains; blue sky; cactus and palo verde trees; flowers; adobe	**Sights:** forest; houses of brick and concrete; gardens; trucks; various animals
Sounds: wind blowing dust; panting; howls; different languages	**Sounds:** animals talking and playing; construction work
Weather: hot; dry	**Weather:** pleasant

SKILL FINDER

Writing Activities: Same Plot, Different Setting, p. 88E

Reading–Writing Workshop, p. 117A

Interact *with* Literature

 Guided Reading

Comprehension/Critical Thinking

1. Why was the noise Coyote made so amazing? (The javelinas had never heard it before. It was a combination of different sounds.)

2. How did the author write down the noise Coyote made? (She broke it into little sounds, and then one long howl.)

3. Coyote was clever but in the end his tricks weren't good enough. How would you describe the third little javelina? (Accept reasonable responses.)

4. Do you think the desert made a good setting? Why or why not? (Students should cite details of the setting in their answers.)

Then the three little javelinas heard an amazing noise. It was not a bark. It was not a cackle. It was not a howl. It was not a scream. It was all of those sounds together.

"Yip

    yap

     yeep

        YEE-OWW-OOOOOOOOOOOOOO!"

Away ran a puff of smoke shaped like a coyote.

86

Self-Assessment

Encourage students to assess their own reading by asking

- Did my predictions help me understand the story?
- Were any parts of the story confusing? What did I do to understand them?
- How did knowing the original story help me understand this one?

Quick**REFERENCE**

Visual Literacy

The *Mona Lisa* Point out that the painting on the wall is called the *Mona Lisa,* by Leonardo da Vinci. Ask students how it adds to the story's humor. (It's a serious work in the middle of a comical and often silly story.)

 Students Acquiring English

Vocabulary Discuss the words *bark, howl, cackle,* and *scream,* and have volunteers demonstrate how each sound differs. You may wish to make a list of these and other related sound words for students to add to their journals.

The three little javelinas lived happily ever after in the adobe house.

And if you ever hear a Coyote's voice, way out in the desert at night . . . well, you know what he's remembering!

87

Science Link

Coyotes The coyote is famous for its evening serenade of howls and yelps. In fact, its scientific name, *Canis latrans*, means "barking dog."

Interact
with
Literature

Responding Activities

Personal Response

- What did students like or dislike about this story? Would they recommend it to a friend? Encourage them to write their thoughts in their journals.

- Allow students to choose their own ways of responding to the selection.

Anthology Activities

Choose, or have students choose, a response activity from page 88.

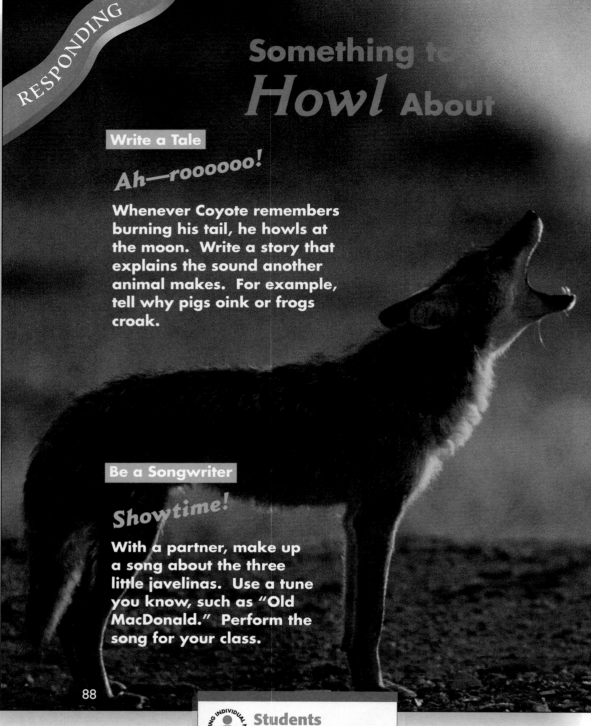

RESPONDING

Something to *Howl* About

Write a Tale

Ah—roooooo!

Whenever Coyote remembers burning his tail, he howls at the moon. Write a story that explains the sound another animal makes. For example, tell why pigs oink or frogs croak.

Be a Songwriter

Showtime!

With a partner, make up a song about the three little javelinas. Use a tune you know, such as "Old MacDonald." Perform the song for your class.

88

Informal Assessment

Check responses for a general understanding of the selection.

Additional Support:

- Use the Guided Reading questions to review and, if necessary, reread.

- Have students summarize the story or parts of it.

- Reread aloud the original tale on pages 35A–35B and have students compare the selection to it.

QuickREFERENCE

MEETING INDIVIDUAL NEEDS
Students Acquiring English

For the "Create a Refrain" activity on page 88A, encourage students who are acquiring English to create rhymes in their primary language. They can then teach the refrain to the class in their primary language and explain its meaning.

Home Connection

Encourage students to retell the story to their families. Suggest that they think of other stories that involve threes (*Goldilocks and the Three Bears, Three Little Kittens,* and so on).

More Choices for Responding

Conduct an Interview
Cooperative Learning

Have students take the roles of the javelinas, Coyote, and interviewers. Students should probe into the characters' backgrounds, finding out as much as they can about each and taking notes.

Draw the Coyote in Action

What other kinds of tricks might Coyote have played? Have students draw new possibilities for catching the javelinas.

The Tumbleweed Surprise Trick

Create a Refrain

Students may like to think of a new response to Coyote's "*Little pig, little pig, let me come in?*" refrain.

Encourage them to create a refrain that rhymes, as in the original.

Selection Connections
LAB, p. 8

Have students complete the portion of the chart relating to *The Three Little Javelinas.*

Literature Discussion

- Which retelling of "The Three Little Pigs" did you prefer, this one or *The Three Little Wolves and the Big Bad Pig?* Why?

- Would trying to get Coyote to change his mind have worked, or were the javelinas wise to just keep running?

- How was Coyote like the big bad pig? How was he different?

Comprehension Check

Use the following questions and/or *Literacy Activity Book* page 21 to check understanding of the story.

1. What are two ways in which Coyote tried to use his magical powers to catch the javelinas? (He made his voice sound like a javelina's to try to get in the rib house and he made himself skinny enough to fit down the stove pipe.)

2. According to this story, what is a coyote remembering when you hear him howling at night? (He's remembering how he was scorched by the javelinas.)

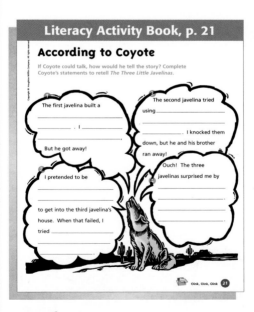

Literacy Activity Book, p. 21

According to Coyote

If Coyote could talk, how would he tell the story? Complete Coyote's statements to retell *The Three Little Javelinas.*

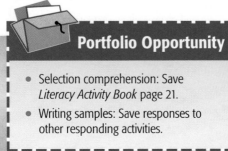

Portfolio Opportunity

- Selection comprehension: Save *Literacy Activity Book* page 21.
- Writing samples: Save responses to other responding activities.

3

Instruct
and
Integrate

Comprehension

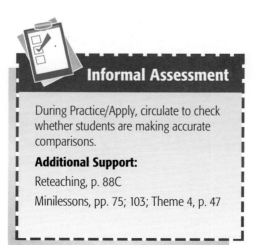

Literacy Activity Book, p. 22

Like It or Not

How does the desert setting of *The Three Little Javelinas* compare and contrast with where you live? Think about the weather, the land, the plants, and the animals.

Write your responses in the Venn diagram. Remember that similar things in both settings go in the middle.

Desert

Both Settings

My Home Region

22   Oink, Oink, Oink

Compare and Contrast

LAB, p. 22

Teach/Model

Discuss with students how appreciating a good story often involves comparing it to other stories. Tell students that good readers often compare and contrast story details. They stop and ask themselves questions like:

- Does this character remind me of a character from another story I've read? Are the story events similar?

- How is this story different from other stories I've read? What do I think of these differences?

Read aloud the original version of "The Three Little Pigs" on pages 35A–35B. Then have students compare and contrast it with *The Three Little Javelinas.* Use these prompts. Chart students' responses.

- Which stories have animal characters? human characters?

- What building materials are used in each story?

- What happens to the villain in each story?

- In which stories does the wolf huff and puff and the pigs say *"not by the hair of my chinny-chin-chin"?*

3 Little Pigs
straw, sticks, bricks
villain boiled

chinny-chin-chin
animal characters
3 pigs
predator
huff and puff

3 Little Javelinas
tumbleweeds, adobe, saguaro ribs
villain scorched

Practice/Apply

- Have students use *Literacy Activity Book* page 22 to compare and contrast the desert setting of *The Three Little Javelinas* with the setting (region) in which they live.

- Have small groups use a Venn diagram to compare and contrast the illustrations in *The Three Little Wolves and the Big Bad Pig* and *The Three Little Javelinas.* Students might analyze the colors used and what makes each style of illustration funny.

SKILL FINDER
Minilessons, pp. 75; 103;
Theme 4, p. 47

Informal Assessment

During Practice/Apply, circulate to check whether students are making accurate comparisons.

Additional Support:

Reaching, p. 88C

Minilessons, pp. 75; 103; Theme 4, p. 47

Reteaching

Compare and Contrast

Cooperative Learning Divide students into small groups. Assign one of the following animals to each group: pigs, javelinas, coyotes, and wolves. Have students work together to describe different features of the animals. Students should use illustrations and photos from the stories and articles such as "This Little Piggy!" as guidance.

Encourage them to ask themselves questions like the following:

- hair: is it furry? rough? short? long?

- eyes: are they large? narrow?

- body size: is the animal large or small? fast or slow?

- ears: are they pointy or flat? how big are they?

Afterward display Transparency 1–6. Have the groups make comparisons and then fill in the chart. For example:

	Javelinas	Pigs	Wolves	Coyotes
pointy ears			+	+
curly tails	+	+		
big snouts	+	+		

Additionally, you might invite students to make animal riddle cards. Tell them to take one feature of the animal they chose, and think of another animal that has the same feature. They should then write the riddle on the face of the card and answer it inside.

Transparency 1–6

Compare and Contrast

	Javelinas	Pigs	Wolves	Coyotes
pointy ears				
curly tails				
big snouts				

How is an elephant like a pig on vacation?

How is an elephant like a pig on vacation?

They both have trunks.

Portfolio Opportunity

Save *Literacy Activity Book* page 22 to record students' understanding of comparison and contrast.

3

Instruct *and* Integrate

Writing Skills and Activities

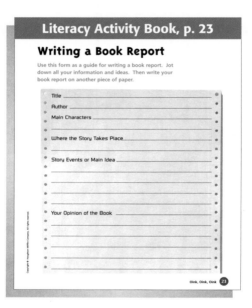

Literacy Activity Book, p. 23

Writing a Book Report

Use this form as a guide for writing a book report. Jot down all your information and ideas. Then write your book report on another piece of paper.

- Title _____
- Author _____
- Main Characters _____
- Where the Story Takes Place _____
- Story Events or Main Idea _____
- Your Opinion of the Book _____

Oink, Oink, Oink 23

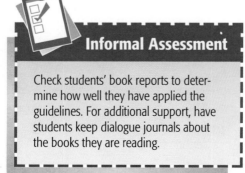

Informal Assessment

Check students' book reports to determine how well they have applied the guidelines. For additional support, have students keep dialogue journals about the books they are reading.

INTERACTIVE LEARNING

Writing a Book Report

LAB, p. 23

Teach/Model

Hold up a storybook that is a favorite of yours and identify it as such. Tell students that one way to share your thoughts about a book is to write a book report. Explain that a book report tells what the book is about and also gives your opinion of the book.

Display Transparency 1–7 and read the model book report aloud as students follow along. Then ask the following questions:

- What does this student tell about the story?
- What is this student's opinion of *The Three Little Javelinas?*

Discuss with students these guidelines for writing a good book report.

Guidelines for Writing a Book Report

- Tell the title of the book and the author's name.
- Tell a little about the main characters and where the story takes place.
- Tell about important events or the story's main idea. Don't give away the ending.
- Give your opinion of the book.

Practice/Apply

Assign the activity Write a Book Report. Encourage students to use *Literacy Activity Book* page 23 to plan their book reports.

Writing Activities

Students can use The Learning Company's new elementary writing center for all their writing activities.

Create a Cartoon

Suggest that students write and draw cartoons telling the story of *The Three Little Javelinas.* Students might tell the whole story individually or work in small groups to divide up scenes and cartoon frames.

Coyote climbed onto the roof, used his magic to become very skinny, and climbed into the stovepipe.

The javelinas saw him and quickly lit a fire in the wood stove.

Snap, crackle, pop! Coyote shot out of the stovepipe like a cannonball!

Write a Book Report

Have students write a book report about a book they have read recently. Collect their book reports in a loose-leaf notebook and keep it in an accessible place in the classroom. Encourage students to look in the notebook for ideas for books to read and to add book reports whenever they want to share their opinions about books they have read.

Shared Writing: Same Plot, Different Setting

Work with students to write the three little pigs story in another story setting. Remind them that the story characters, building materials, and other story elements might have to change to fit the new setting. A polar cap setting might involve three little penguins and a big bad bear, for example. You might want to try several ideas and brainstorm for each before choosing one and beginning to write. (*See the Writer's Craft Minilesson on page 85.*)

Portfolio Opportunity

Save responses to activities on this page for writing samples.

Instruct *and* Integrate

Word Skills and Strategies

Literacy Activity Book, p. 24

Which Ending?

Coyote is clever, but he can't read the words on the chalkboard. Fill in the chart to help him to see that each word is made from a base word plus the ending *-ed* or *-ing*.

	Base Word	-ed or -ing
scaring	scare	ing
flipped	flip	ed
1. sneaking		
2. thanked		
3. chased		
4. topping		
5. piling		
6. jogged		
7. giggling		
8. mixed		
9. winning		
10. dared		

24 Oink, Oink, Oink

Copyright © Houghton Mifflin Company. All rights reserved.

MEETING INDIVIDUAL NEEDS

Extra Support

Be sure students understand that not every word that ends with the letters *ed* or *ing* is made up of a base word and ending. Use the words *red, tumbleweed,* and *nothing* as examples.

Informal Assessment

Use Practice/Apply to check students' understanding of the endings *-ed* and *-ing*.

Additional Support:

Reteaching, p. 88G

INTERACTIVE LEARNING

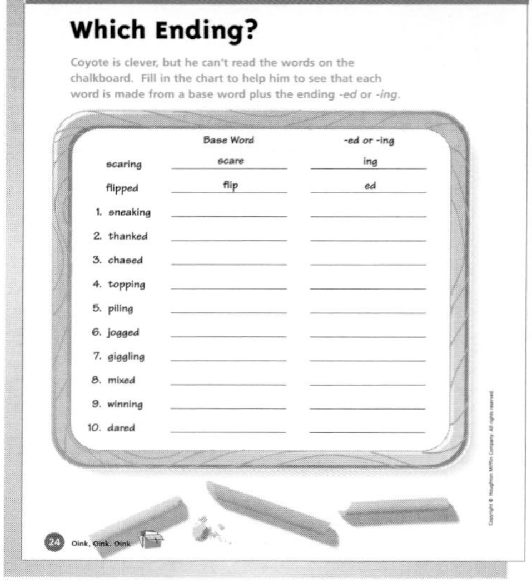

TESTED SKILL

Structural Analysis

Inflected Endings *-ed* and *-ing*

LAB, p. 24

Teach/Model

Write these sentences on the board.

> One javelina finished his house of sticks.
> Another is building an adobe house.

Ask students to find the words in the sentences that are made up of a base word, or smaller word, plus the ending *-ed* or *-ing*. As students find each word, underline its *-ed* or *-ing* ending and write its base word above it. Tell students that *-ed* and *-ing* usually appear at the end of verbs, or action words. Explain that *-ed* at the end of a word usually means that the action happened in the past. An *-ing* ending usually means that the action is happening in the present.

Point out to students that learning to recognize word endings can sometimes help them read unfamiliar words. Once they recognize the ending, they may discover that they know the base word as well.

Practice/Apply

Cooperative Learning Divide the class into small groups. For each group, divide a sheet of paper into two columns. Label one column *-ed* and the other *-ing*. Have the students in each group search through the story to find words with *-ed* or *-ing* endings and list them in the columns. When they have listed all the words they can, have them identify each base word.

-ed	-ing
trotted	whirling
looked	brushing
divided	eating
wandered	looking
laughed	gathering
smelled	building
tired	panting
called	showing
shouted	tumbling

SKILL FINDER

Spelling, Theme 5

Inflected Endings *-ed* and *-ing*

Write the words *walked, dropped, running,* and *taking* on the board. Remind students that many words are made up of a smaller word and the ending *-ed* or *-ing.* Have volunteers break apart the words on the board by writing each base word and ending.

Then have students look in a favorite storybook for more examples.

Word Skills Practice

Cumulative Skill Practice
Ham and Eggs for Jack
by Andrew Clements

WATCH **ME** READ

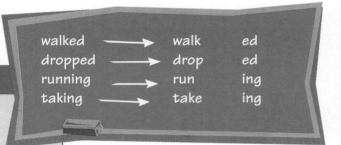

walked ⟶	walk	ed
dropped ⟶	drop	ed
running ⟶	run	ing
taking ⟶	take	ing

M I N I L E S S O N

Phonics Review
Long Vowel Pairs and Vowel–Consonant-*e*

Teach/Model Write these nonsense words on the board. Tell students that the words don't mean anything but to try pronouncing them anyway.

tweel   jeam   chay   blail   prew   bife

Remind students that they can often make good guesses about the pronunciation of a new word by looking for familiar groups of letters. Discuss the letters students based their guesses on. *(ee* and *ea* often have the long *e* sound; *ay* and *ai* often have the long *a* sound; *ew* often has the long *u* sound; any vowel followed by a single consonant and *e* usually has the long vowel sound.) Circle each pair of vowels and *ife* in *bife.* Point out that by knowing vowel patterns, they can pronounce unfamiliar words or even nonsense words!

Practice/Apply ***Cooperative Learning*** Divide the class into small groups. Have each group try to be the first to find three words in *The Three Little Javelinas* that follow each vowel pattern on the board.

Possible responses:

ee	*ea*	*ay*	*ai*	**vowel-consonant-*e***		
three	each	way	fail	came	divided	fire
seek	heap	day	trail	escaped	inside	like
steep	eating	lay	tail	shade	tired	coyote
tumbleweeds	sneaky			make/made	mice	adobe
sweetly	heat			snake	miles	stove
teeth	please			place	ripe	noses
trees	weak			bake	arrived	smoke
green	feast			shaped	smiled	used
peeked	scream			these	sometimes	
squeezed				time	pipe	

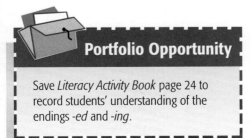

3

Instruct *and* Integrate

Building Vocabulary

High-Frequency Vocabulary Practice

Cumulative Skill Practice
Ham and Eggs for Jack
by Andrew Clements

WATCH **ME** READ

Literacy Activity Book, p. 25

Word Families

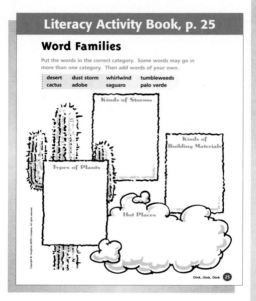

Use this page to review Selection Vocabulary.

tornado
plaza
siesta
fiesta
burro
hammock
chocolate
alligator
tomato
patio
cargo
poncho
cocoa
vanilla
pueblo

iguana
saguaro
mesa
stampede
chile
lariat
bronco
barbecue
jaguar
mosquito
avocado
coyote
cafeteria
pimento
adobe

Vocabulary Activities

Rhyming Words
Cooperative Learning

Ask students what rhyming words the coyote used each time he came to the house of a little javelina. (*huff and puff*) Point out to students that words rhyme when they begin with different sounds but end with the same sound. Have the class brainstorm for other words that rhyme with huff and puff, and write the words on the board. (*stuff, muff, cuff, fluff, gruff, bluff, scuff, rough, enough, tough*)

Divide students into small teams. Tell them that when you say "Go," they will have one minute to list words that rhyme with *trick*. When the time is up, have the team with the most words read their list. Write the words on the board, and ask the other teams to mention words on their own list that the winning team did not include. Repeat the game two more times, having students rhyme with *snake* and then *heat*.

Words from Spanish

Tell students that many Spanish words have become part of the English language. Then tell them that they will each create one page of a Words from Spanish pictionary.

Write each word on the list to the left on a slip of paper and put the slips in a bag. Have students pick a word, write it on a sheet of paper, and draw a picture to show what it means. Help students use a dictionary or encyclopedia if they are not sure what the word means or how to illustrate it. Have them show and explain their drawings to the class. Then bind the drawings into a book to display in the classroom.

Selection Vocabulary Extension

Display again Transparency 1–5 and review the Selection Vocabulary Words, *desert, dust storm, whirlwind, tumbleweeds, cactus,* and *adobe.*

Encourage students to add other desert-related words to the list. To think of words have them look at the transparency, revisit *The Three Little Javelinas,* and use their own knowledge of deserts.

partial word list:

saguaro, coyote, javelina, hawk, lizard, scorpion, sand, oasis, mesa, butte, dunes, mirage

Spelling

5-Day Planner **FIVE-DAY PLAN**

DAY 1	DAY 2	DAY 3	DAY 4	DAY 5
Pretest; Minilesson; Challenge Words/ Additional Words (opt.); Take-Home Word Lists (LAB)	First LAB page; Challenge Words Practice (opt.)	Check first LAB page; Second LAB page (except writing application)	Check second LAB page; writing application (LAB)	Test

Teaching CHOICES

MINILESSON

Spelling Words

*nose	*mice
*these	*smoke
*shade	*snake
*use	*ripe

Challenge Words

*escape	*arrive
*amaze	*fortune

Additional Spelling Words

stove	life
smile	tune

*Starred words or forms of the words appear in *The Three Little Javelinas.*

✓ TESTED SKILL Vowel-Consonant-*e*

LAB, pp. 26–27

- Write the words *rip* and *ripe* on the board. Say the words, and have students repeat them. Have a volunteer name the vowel sound in *rip*. (/ĭ/)

- Ask students if the vowel sounds in *rip* and *ripe* are the same or different. (different) Explain that the word *ripe* has the /ī/ sound because it ends in the vowel-consonant-*e* pattern. Underline the letters *ipe*.

- Introduce the /ā/, /ē/, /ō/, and /yōō/ sounds, using the words *shade, these, nose,* and *use.* Point out that the vowel sound in the *u*-consonant-*e* pattern can be pronounced /ōō/, or /yōō/, as in *use.*

- Write the Spelling Words on the board. Tell students that each Spelling Word has the vowel-consonant-*e* pattern. Say the Spelling Words and have students repeat them.

Spelling Assessment

Pretest

Say each underlined word, read the sentence, and then repeat the word. Have students write only the underlined words.

1. A pig's nose is called a snout.
2. Where do these animals live?
3. It's hard to find shade in the desert.
4. They will use bricks to build a house.
5. The wolf was tired of eating mice.
6. The fire sent smoke up the chimney.
7. The snake slid along the sand.
8. Those berries look ripe to me.

Test

Spelling Words Use the Pretest sentences.

Challenge Words

9. This story will really amaze you!
10. We must find a way to escape from the wolf.
11. The sailor went to seek his fortune.
12. Plan to arrive at my house by six.

SKILL FINDER

Daily Language Practice, p. 88K	
Reading-Writing Workshop, p. 117E	

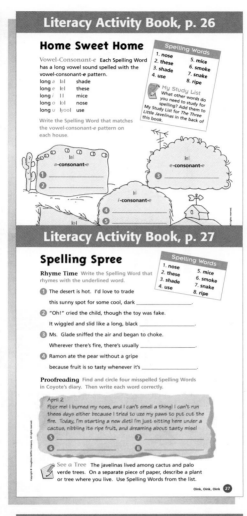

Literacy Activity Book, p. 26

Home Sweet Home

Spelling Words
1. nose
2. these
3. shade
4. use
5. mice
6. smoke
7. snake
8. ripe

Vowel-Consonant-*e* Each Spelling Word has a long vowel sound spelled with the vowel-consonant-*e* pattern.

long a		a		shade
long e		e		these
long i		ī		mice
long o		o		nose
long u		yoo		use

Write the Spelling Word that matches the vowel-consonant-*e* pattern on each house.

My Study List What other words do you need to study for spelling? Add them to My Study List for *The Three Little Javelinas* in the back of this book.

Literacy Activity Book, p. 27

Spelling Spree

Spelling Words
1. nose
2. these
3. shade
4. use
5. mice
6. smoke
7. snake
8. ripe

Rhyme Time Write the Spelling Word that rhymes with the underlined word.

1. The desert is hot. I'd love to trade
   this sunny spot for some cool, dark _____.
2. "Oh!" cried the child, though the toy was fake.
   It wiggled and slid like a long, black _____.
3. Ms. Glade sniffed the air and began to choke.
   Wherever there's fire, there's usually _____.
4. Ramon ate the pear without a gripe
   because fruit is so tasty whenever it's _____.

Proofreading Find and circle four misspelled Spelling Words in Coyote's diary. Then write each word correctly.

April 2
Poor me! I burned my nose, and I can't smell a thing! I can't run thees days either because I tried to uze my paws to put out the fire. Today, I'm starting a new diet! I'm just sitting here under a cactus, nibbling ite ripe fruits, and dreaming about tasty mise!

5. _____
6. _____
7. _____
8. _____

 See a Tree The javelinas lived among cactus and palo verde trees. On a separate piece of paper, describe a plant or tree where you live. Use Spelling Words from the list.

Oink, Oink, Oink 27

Literacy Activity Book

Take-Home Word Lists: pp. 161–162

Spelling Vocabulary Students can use the **Spelling Spree CD-ROM** for extra practice with the spelling principles taught in this selection.

 MEETING INDIVIDUAL NEEDS **Challenge**

Challenge Words Practice Have students use the Challenge Words to write newspaper headlines.

Grammar

5-Day Planner

FIVE-DAY PLAN

DAY 1	DAY 2	DAY 3	DAY 4	DAY 5
Daily Language Practice 1; Teach/Model; First LAB page	Daily Language Practice 2; Check first LAB page; Cooperative Learning	Daily Language Practice 3; Writing Application	Daily Language Practice 4; Reteaching (opt.); Second LAB page	Daily Language Practice 5; Check second LAB page; Students' Writing

Transparency 1–8

TRANSPARENCY 1–8
TEACHER'S BOOK PAGE 88J

Correcting Run-On Sentences

RUN-ON	The javelinas lived in the desert it was very hot and dry.
CORRECT	The javelinas lived in the desert. It was very hot and dry.

Cactus forests grew in the sand the mountains looked purple.

Each javelina took a different path a dust storm came along.

The first javelina got an idea he built his house very fast.

Coyote huffed and puffed it was an easy job.

Literacy Activity Book, p. 29

It's a Secret!

Literacy Activity Book, p. 28

Run-on Riddles

Run-on This is the largest desert plant its fruit is red.

This is the largest desert plant. Its fruit is red.

Correcting Run-on Sentences Read each run-on sentence. Then write the two sentences correctly. Last, answer the riddles!

1. She built a strong house it had a tin roof. **ANSWERS?**

2. He could make himself small he knew many tricks.

3. He fell down his house fell down, too.

4. Its fire did the trick Coyote was gone for good.
   Its fire did the trick. Coyote was gone for good. (1)

5. They are made of mud people build with them.

28 Oink, Oink, Oink

Informal Assessment

Responses to the activities should indicate students' ability to recognize and correct run-on sentences.

Additional Support:
Use Reteaching, p. 88K.

INTERACTIVE LEARNING

TESTED SKILL

Correcting Run-on Sentences
LAB, pp. 28–29

> Two or more sentences that run together form a **run-on sentence.** Correct run-on sentences by adding end marks and capital letters.

Teach/Model

Invite volunteers to make up two or three sentences about the story. Write students' sentences on the chalkboard as a run-on sentence. Read the run-on sentence rapidly without any pauses or vocal inflections to indicate the end of any sentence other than the run-on one.

Elicit from students that run-on sentences are confusing because they lack the signals that tell where one sentence ends and another begins—end marks and capital letters.

Ask volunteers to draw lines separating the run-on sentence into individual sentences. Ask other volunteers to add periods and capital letters.

Display Transparency 1–8. Point out that two or more sentences that run together make a *run-on sentence.* Ask the class to help you rewrite these run-on sentences. Have students read each run-on sentence aloud with you. Then call on volunteers to draw a line between the complete thoughts. If the class agrees, invite other volunteers to add capital letters and end marks. Point out that this is what they should do when they proofread their work.

Practice/Apply

Cooperative Learning: **Correcting a Letter** Duplicate the following letter, and distribute copies to small groups of students. Explain that the javelina did not understand about run-on sentences. Have each group work together to correct the letter. Then have each student create a decorated sheet of stationery and write the corrected letter on it.

SKILL FINDER Reading-Writing Workshop, p. 117E

Dear Friend,

I now live with my brother and sister in an adobe brick house the coyote tried to trick us and eat us he was burned by the fire in the stove we played in the desert every day I hope you come to visit me soon you will be safe because the coyote is gone.

Sincerely,
A. Javelina

INTERACTIVE LEARNING (continued)

Practice/Apply

 Writing Application: A Place Ask students to imagine that the javelinas could change their voices or appearance the way Coyote did. What trick would they play to scare him away? Suggest that students write a plan describing what the javelinas could do. Remind them to avoid run-on sentences.

Students' Writing Encourage students to check their works in progress for run-on sentences. Point out that one way to proofread for this kind of error is to read their sentences aloud, listening for the beginning and the end of each complete thought.

More Practice
Houghton Mifflin English Level 3
Workbook Plus, pp. 11–12
Reteaching Workbook, p. 6
Write on Track
Write on Track SourceBook, pp. 61–62, 116

Daily Language Practice
Focus skills

Grammar: Correcting Run-on Sentences
Spelling: Vowel-Consonant-*e*

Every day write one run-on sentence on the chalkboard. Have each student write the sentence correctly on a sheet of paper. Tell students to separate the sentences in the run-on sentence by adding an end mark and a capital letter. Tell students also to correct any misspelled words. Have students correct their own papers as a volunteer corrects the sentence on the chalkboard.

1. The sand is hot there is almost no shaade.
The sand is hot. **T**here is almost no **shade.**

2. A snake crossed our path mise also live here.
A snake crossed our path. **M**ice also live here.

3. People build cool houses they uze mud bricks.
People build cool houses. **T**hey **use** mud bricks.

4. The cactus has rype fruit people get it down with sticks.
The cactus has **ripe** fruit. **P**eople get it down with sticks.

5. The dust storm looks like smok you must cover your nose.
The dust storm looks like **smoke. Y**ou must cover your nose.

Reteaching

Correcting Run-on Sentences

MEETING INDIVIDUAL NEEDS

Write the run-on sentences below on sentence strips. Display the first sentence strip, and have students read it aloud with you. Discuss with students what is wrong with it, and review the term *run-on sentence*. Then have students tell where the sentence should be cut apart and where the end mark and capital letter are needed. Invite different volunteers to cut apart the sentence strip and to write the correct end mark and capital letter. Repeat for the other run-on sentences. Post the cut-apart sentences.

cut apart here   capital letter here

People helped the javelinas ┊ they gave sticks and bricks.

end mark needed here

The sticks came from a cactus the bricks baked in the sun.

The stick house fell quickly it was not strong enough.

Coyote found the brick house he huffed and puffed as usual.

Adobe bricks are strong the little javelinas were safe.

3

Instruct
and
Integrate

Communication Activities

Listening and Speaking

Audio Tape
for Oink, Oink, Oink: *The Three Little Javelinas*

Listening to a Poetic Picture

Read aloud "August" for students' listening pleasure. Invite them to share their reactions. Then tell students the first listening guideline, and read the poem again. Ask students to focus on that point. Encourage them to discuss the word picture drawn by the poet. Use this same method with the other guidelines.

Invite each student to bring a poem to class to share. They can then pair up with a listening partner or in small groups, read the poem aloud, practice their listening skills, and discuss how the guidelines apply to their poem.

Guidelines for Listening to Poetry

Listen for feelings that the poet expresses. What words does he or she use to describe them?

Think about how the poet's experiences are like yours. Have you ever felt the same way?

Listen for something ordinary that the poet describes in a new and fresh way.

Listen for when the poet uses the word *like* or *as* to make a comparison. What is being compared?

August

The desert sun of August
Is shimmering my street
And turning houses into dunes
That glitter in the heat.
One tree is my oasis.
I need the ice cream man!
His truck comes just as slowly
As a camel caravan.

by Sandra Liatsos

Building a Language Tree

★★★ **Multicultural Link** Students tap into their own diverse backgrounds by creating a language tree. First, have them recall the people in the desert who said *yes* to the javelinas. Then volunteers draw a tree on poster board and label two branches "Spanish" and "Desert People." They write *sí* and *ha'u* on leaves off these branches. Invite them to share how to say *yes* in other languages and to add these words and languages to the tree.

Ja · Da · Hai
Oui · French · German · Russian · Japanese · Hai
Sí · Spanish · Hebrew · Kein
Desert People · Ha'u

YES

Informal Assessment

Circulate among the listening groups, and encourage students to use the "Guidelines for Listening to Poetry" as the basis of their discussions.

Listening and Speaking continued

Hearing a Range of Sounds

Resources
Listen to the Desert
by Pat Mora

Challenge students to focus on desert sounds. First, they can rehearse and present a choral reading of Pat Mora's book *Listen to the Desert.* Then they can work in small groups to recreate a desert sound, such as an animal sound, desert rain, thunder, or wind. Each group presents its sound alone and then together with other groups as you orchestrate.

Viewing

Watching a Video of Desert Life

VIDEO *Along Sandy Trails*
by Ann Nolan Clark

There are many fine videos about the desert. Ask your school librarian or media specialist for a suggestion, or consider showing *Along Sandy Trails,* by Ann Nolan Clark, which depicts desert life as it is experienced by a young Tohono O'Odham (Papago) girl on a walk with her grandmother. Before watching the video, use a K-W-L chart to brainstorm questions.

DESERTS		
What do you KNOW?	What do you WANT to find out?	What did you LEARN?

Taking a Walking Tour

Lead students on a walking tour of the buildings in your community. Have students use a chart to group the buildings into general types, such as wood houses, brick apartment buildings, etc.

Portfolio Opportunity

Save the language tree from Building a Language Tree in a class portfolio.

Instruct *and* Integrate

Cross-Curricular Activities

Book List

Science

Cactus Hotel
by Brenda Z.
Guiberson

Materials

- glass or plastic container
- pebbles
- watering can
- water
- sponge or paper towels
- cactus soil—available in garden centers or hardware stores
- sand
- cacti
- rocks or other props
- mesh cover—available at pet shops

Choices for Science

Making a Desert Terrarium

Students may enjoy building their own desert terrarium.

 Line a tank with small pebbles for drainage. Carefully add a layer of commercial cactus soil—a handful at a time.

 Moisten the soil. Clean the sides of the tank.

 Plant a variety of small cacti, allowing plenty of space for growth. Add $1/4$ inch layer of sand.

Add props or rocks. Protect the plants with a mesh cover that allows air in. Set in a sunny spot.

Exploring the Saguaro Cactus

Challenge The saguaro is a commanding presence in the Sonoran Desert because of its size and longevity. Invite students to research the saguaro cactus and report on questions such as

- Where do saguaros grow?
- What are the average height and weight of mature saguaros? How old do they get?
- What animals live in or near saguaros?

Students can then collaborate on a saguaro poster for classroom display. They can draw one life-size saguaro or several at different stages of growth. Some students can draw birds in nest holes and Sonoran Desert animals.

Resource
Saguaro National Monument
3693 South Old Spanish Trail
Tucson, AZ 85730-5699

Materials

- encyclopedias or other reference books
- poster board or butcher paper
- markers

Art

Designing Outfits
Cooperative Learning

Students can work in small groups. Each group draws a pig and creates outfits for desert, Arctic, country, and city settings. (The illustrations in *The Three Little Javelinas* can serve as a starting point.)

Materials
- construction paper
- markers or crayons
- glue
- yarn
- clothing scraps
- cotton balls

Math

Graphing Desert Weather
Cooperative Learning

Resource
The Arizona-Sonora Desert Museum
2021 North Kinney Road
Tucson, AZ 85743

The Sonoran Desert is spread across southern Arizona and the Mexican state of Sonora. Have students work in teams to collect temperature and rainfall data for Tucson and four other major U.S. cities of their choice. Have students develop graphs and post them on a bulletin board.

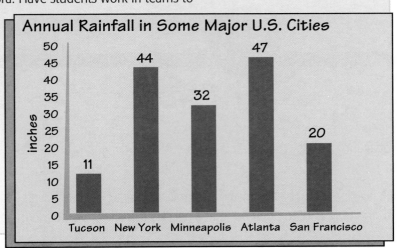

Annual Rainfall in Some Major U.S. Cities

City	inches
Tucson	11
New York	44
Minneapolis	32
Atlanta	47
San Francisco	20

My Hairy Neighbors

Building Background/Prior Knowledge

Remind students of the story *The Three Little Javelinas*. Ask:

- What kind of animal is a javelina? (a wild, hairy, piglike animal)

- Where do javelinas live? (southwestern United States)

Point out that this is factual information they learned while reading a story. Use this information to begin modeling a K-W-L chart.

Javelinas

What I Know	What I Want to Find Out	What I Learned
wild and hairy piglike live in Southwest		

Cooperative Learning Tell students the article they are about to read will contain many more facts about javelinas. Have small groups of students work together to fill out their own K-W-L charts. Tell them to list in the second column other things they would like to know about javelinas. Then have students read the selection, and meet again to fill out the third column of their charts.

Background: FYI

Feeding Time During the summer, the collared peccary eats only in the early morning or evening, when it's cool. During the day the collared peccary rests under shady bushes for over ten hours.

Bristles Explain that a javelina's long hair is bristly, or coarse and stiff. Compare it with the bristles on a hairbrush. You may want to point out that a peccary's bristles may be as long as seven inches!

My Hairy Neighbors

by Susan Lowell
photos by
Thomas A. Wiewandt

Meet some pig-like animals that "talk" with stinky smells!

Welcome to my ranch. I live deep in a rocky canyon way out in the Arizona desert. I have many wild neighbors. At the end of a summer day, three of my favorites often come for dinner. Just watch!

There — a hairy animal is peeking through the bushes. And another. And another. It's Juan, José, and Josefina!

The animals are each about 20 inches (50 cm) high, with rounded backs. And they look and act a bit like pigs. But they're *peccaries* (PECK-a-rees). Some people around here also call them *javelinas* (ha-ve-LEE-nas).

 Check out the rings of light hair around the necks of these peccaries. They look like collars, don't they? That's why the animals are called *collared peccaries*.

89

Discussion

- Why are javelinas called collared peccaries? (because of the ring of light hair around their necks)

- Why does a javelina need sharp teeth? (because it has to gnaw through hard surfaces, such as prickly pear cactuses)

- Why do you think javelinas snuggle together when they sleep? (to keep each other warm and also to make sure they're all safe)

- Can you name any other animals that travel in herds? (elephants, horses, cattle, etc.)

- How do javelinas communicate? (by rubbing musk on one another)

◄ A peccary can use its long, sharp teeth to bite a prickly pear cactus. Those teeth may look nasty, but this animal is probably just yawning.

▲

Peccaries live in groups called *herds*, which helps them protect each other from their enemies. And when it's snooze time, the herd snuggles close together.

◄ Peccaries often kneel to dig for food. See this one's knees? It has thick pads of skin there from kneeling so much!

90

 Students Acquiring English

Word Meaning Students may enjoy saying the word *snooze* several times, drawing it out so that the relationship of the sound of the word to its meaning is clearer. Explain that *snooze time* is merely a more colorful way of saying "time to sleep."

A drippy hole on the javelina's back oozes a smelly liquid called *musk*. Family members rub the musk on each other. That helps them keep track of each other.

Peccaries don't live just in deserts. In Mexico and much of South America, they also can be found in mountains and rain forests. They live only in wild areas. But some of those wild areas are very close to the homes of people.

As I go into my house, I suddenly hear some loud noise. *Clang! Bang! Clatter!*

What's that? Uh-oh! Outside my ranch house, Josefina just knocked over one of the trash cans. Her babies poke their snouts inside it and sniff for something good to eat.

"Shoo!" I say. "No junk food! Go find some nice cactus fruit." Josefina grunts. Together the herd starts moving. "Good night!" I call to them. Then I watch the herd gallop off into the desert darkness.

Peccary herds stick close together. This young one found a safe place in its herd — right in the thick of things.

91

Instruct and Integrate

Math Link

A Javelina's Height Ask students to read aloud the sentence that tells how high a peccary is. Ask them to identify objects in the classroom that are about 20 inches (50 cm) high. Have students compare their own heights with the height of a typical peccary. Is the peccary as tall? Almost as tall? Half as tall?

Science Link

Omnivorous Animals A javelina's snout enables it to uproot logs and dig in the ground for roots and underground stems. Javelinas are omnivorous—they eat anything that is available. Ask students to brainstorm what plants and animals a javelina might find in a desert or forest. (snakes, eggs, fruit, cactus, acorns)

 Home Connection

Wild Areas What is the "wild area" nearest your school? The front section of your phone book is a good place to find a listing of parks and preserves in your area. Ask students if they have ever visited these places. What wild animals are there?

Interact with Literature

MEETING INDIVIDUAL NEEDS

 ## Students Acquiring English

Expressions Explain the meaning of the phrase *keep track of*. Ask students what things they try to keep track of. Point out that this caption explains the comment made at the top of page 89 about how javelinas "talk."

Explain that *in the thick of things* means "right in the middle of what is going on." Point out that *thick* also refers to the peccaries' thick, hairy coats.

SELECTION:

The Three Little Hawaiian Pigs and the Magic Shark

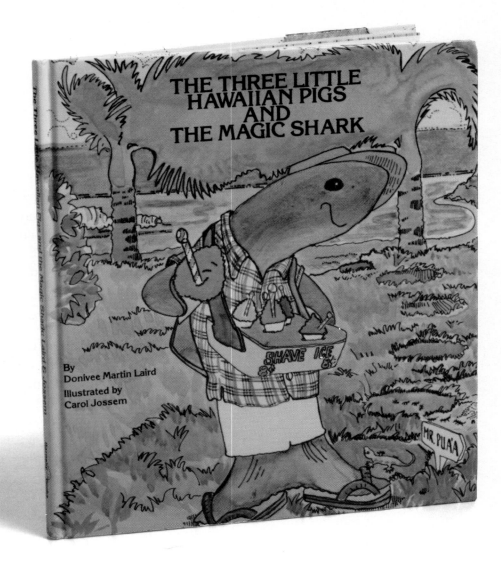

by Donivee Martin Laird

Other Books by the Author

Keaka and the Liliko'i Vine

Wili Wai Kula and the Three Mongooses

Selection Summary

The story of "The Three Little Pigs" moves to Hawaii, where the first two little pigs quickly build their houses out of pili grass and driftwood, respectively. The third pig takes the time to build a sturdy house of lava rock before joining his brothers on the beach.

A magic shark sees them surfing and craves a pig dinner. Disguised first as a shave ice man and then as a beachboy, he cannot con his way into the first and second little pigs' houses; so he blows their houses down as the pigs escape. Frustrated and hungry, the shark goes as a lei seller to the third pig's house but still cannot fool the pigs. This time, the magic shark futilely huffs and puffs until he is out of air and the pigs can dispose of him like a rug.

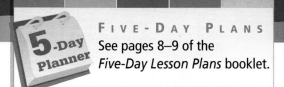

FIVE-DAY PLANS
See pages 8–9 of the
Five-Day Lesson Plans booklet.

Lesson Planning Guide

	Skill/Strategy Instruction	Meeting Individual Needs	Lesson Resources
1 Introduce *the* Literature *Pacing: 1 day*	**Preparing to Read and Write** Prior Knowledge/Building Background, 91C **Selection Vocabulary,** 91D • craving • anxiously • plot • scheme • pangs • furious **Spelling Pretest,** 114I • three • tail • beach • play • deep • away • please • chain	**Support in Advance,** 91C **Students Acquiring English,** 91C **Other Choices for Building Background,** 91C **Spelling Challenge Words:** • easy • really • reef • creature	*Literacy Activity Book:* Vocabulary, p. 30 **Transparencies:** Building Background, 1–9, Vocabulary, 1–10 **Great Start** CD-ROM software, "Oink, Oink, Oink" CD
2 Interact *with* Literature *Pacing: 1–3 days*	**Reading Strategies:** Monitor, 94, 98, 100 Think About Words, 94, 108 **Minilessons:** ✓ Fantasy/Realism, 95 Writer's Craft: Anthropomorphism, 97 Compare and Contrast, 103 Sequence, 107	**Choices for Reading,** 94 **Guided Reading,** 94 Comprehension/Critical Thinking, 96, 102, 106, 112 **Students Acquiring English,** 94, 95, 96, 97, 98, 99, 102, 105, 106, 109, 110, 112, 114 **Extra Support,** 100, 111, 113 **Challenge,** 103	**Reading-Writing Workshop** A Story, 116–117F *Literacy Activity Book,* pp. 40–42 The Learning Company's Ultimate Writing & Creativity Center software
3 Instruct *and* Integrate *Pacing: 1–3 days*	✓ **Comprehension:** Fantasy/Realism, 114B ✓ **Writing:** Combining Sentences: Compound Sentences, 114D **Word Skills and Strategies:** ✓ Using Context, 114F Dictionary: Alphabetical Order, 114G **Building Vocabulary:** Vocabulary Activities, 114H ✓ **Spelling:** Long *a* and Long *e*, 114I ✓ **Grammar:** Kinds of Sentences, 114J–114K **Communication Activities:** Listening and Speaking, 114L; Viewing, 114M **Cross-Curricular Activities:** Social Studies, 114N; Science, 114O	**Reteaching:** Fantasy/Realism, 114C **Activity Choices:** Creative Writing: Animal Characters, 114E; Plan a House, 114E; Write a Poem, 114E **Reteaching:** Using Context, 114G **Activity Choices:** Selection Vocabulary Extension, Synonym Search, Vocabulary Notebook, 114H **Challenge Words Practice,** 114I **Reteaching:** Kinds of Sentences, 114K **Activity Choices:** Listening and Speaking, 114L; Viewing, 114M **Activity Choices:** Social Studies, 114N; Science, 114O	**Watch Me Read:** *Red Riding Hood and Gray Wolf* **Reading-Writing Workshop** A Story, 116–117F **Transparencies:** Comprehension, 1–11; Writing, 1–12; Grammar, 1–13 *Literacy Activity Book:* Comprehension, p. 32; Writing, p. 33; Word Skills, p. 34; Building Vocabulary, p. 35; Spelling, pp. 36–37; Grammar, pp. 38–39 **Spelling Spree** CD-ROM **Audio Tape** for "Oink, Oink, Oink": *The Three Hawaiian Pigs and the Magic Shark* **Channel R.E.A.D.** videodisc: "The Ordinary Princess" The Learning Company's Ultimate Writing & Creativity Center software

✓ **Indicates Tested Skills.** *See page 34F for assessment options.*

Introduce *the* **Literature**

Preparing to Read and Write

Support in Advance

Use this activity for students who need extra support before participating in the whole-class activity.

Picture Walk Preview the illustrations with students and make a web using words such as *ocean, reef, ukulele, surfboard,* and *lei.*

 Management Tip
Suggest that other students spend a few minutes writing a description of a tropical place in their journals.

Students Acquiring English
This story has boxes that help define many Hawaiian words. Preview them with students to build background.

Prior Knowledge/Building Background

Key Concept
Hawaii

Ask students to share what they know about Hawaii. Tell them that the next version of "The Three Little Pigs" takes place in Hawaii. Ask:

- If you were building a house out of things you could find in Hawaii, what would you use?

- What kind of animal in Hawaii would make a good villain for this story?

Then work with the class to plan a "trip" to Hawaii. Organize the trip by completing the planner on Transparency 1–9 with students.

Class Trip to Hawaii	
What we might find there: ocean, palm trees, mountains	**Clothes we need to pack:** T-shirts, shorts, sandals

Transparency 1–9

Aloha, Hawaii!

CLASS TRIP TO HAWAII

What we might find there:

Clothes we need to pack:

Activities we might do:

Foods we might eat:

TRANSPARENCY 1-9
TEACHER'S BOOK PAGE 91C

Other Choices for Building Background

Rehearsing the Lines

Students Acquiring English Reread the traditional tale (pages 35A–35B). Invite students to chime in on (or recite from memory) the dialogue between the wolf and the pigs.

Map Study

Challenge Have students find Hawaii on a map. Then ask: Where is Hawaii? What is it near? What other places are about the same size as Hawaii? Which states are closest to Hawaii?

 ### Quick Writing
Cooperative Learning

Have students work in small groups to brainstorm a list of ways the story of "The Three Little Pigs" might change when it is set in Hawaii.

Great Start
For students needing extra support with key concepts and vocabulary, use the "Oink, Oink, Oink" CD.

Spelling
You may want to give the Spelling Pretest on page 114I before students read the selection.

Daily Language Practice
Use the sentences on page 114K as a daily practice of the spelling and grammar skills taught with this selection.

Selection Vocabulary

Key Words

craving

anxiously

plot

scheme

pangs

furious

Display Transparency 1–10. Point out that all the words are used in the story to tell about the villain, or evil character. Read each of these sentences aloud and ask students to place the under-lined words on the map based on how they are used in the sentence.

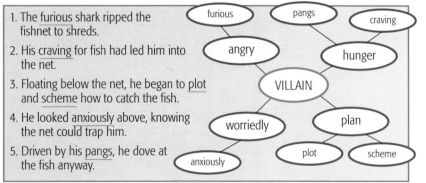

1. The furious shark ripped the fishnet to shreds.
2. His craving for fish had led him into the net.
3. Floating below the net, he began to plot and scheme how to catch the fish.
4. He looked anxiously above, knowing the net could trap him.
5. Driven by his pangs, he dove at the fish anyway.

Vocabulary Practice Students can work independently or in pairs to complete the activity on *Literacy Activity Book* page 30.

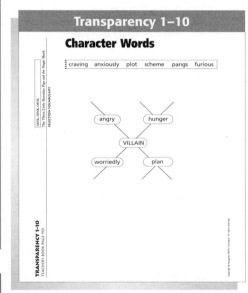

Transparency 1–10

Character Words

craving anxiously plot scheme pangs furious

angry   hunger

VILLAIN

worriedly   plan

Multicultural

Teacher FactFile
Hawaiian Islands

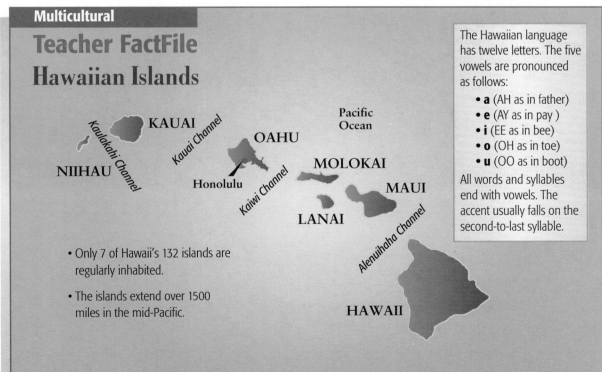

KAUAI

Kaulakahi Channel

Kauai Channel

OAHU

Pacific Ocean

NIIHAU

Honolulu

Kaiwi Channel

MOLOKAI

MAUI

LANAI

Alenuihaha Channel

HAWAII

- Only 7 of Hawaii's 132 islands are regularly inhabited.

- The islands extend over 1500 miles in the mid-Pacific.

The Hawaiian language has twelve letters. The five vowels are pronounced as follows:
- **a** (AH as in father)
- **e** (AY as in pay)
- **i** (EE as in bee)
- **o** (OH as in toe)
- **u** (OO as in boot)

All words and syllables end with vowels. The accent usually falls on the second-to-last syllable.

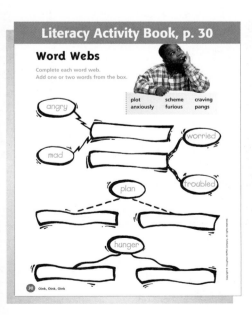

Literacy Activity Book, p. 30

Word Webs

Complete each word web.
Add one or two words from the box.

plot   scheme   craving
anxiously furious pangs

angry

worried

mad

troubled

plan

hunger

30 Oink, Oink, Oink

Interact
with
Literature

More About the Author

Donivee Martin Laird

Donivee Martin Laird grew up in Hawaii, which she describes as "one of the most beautiful places in the world." After living in Puerto Rico for several years, and then attending school at Pennsylvania State University, she returned to Hawaii in 1973, where she still lives today with her family.

A teacher in Honolulu since 1977, Laird began writing children's stories to fill a void in contemporary Hawaiian literature for the early grades. She began experimenting with Hawaiian adaptations of well-known folktales, using her own classroom as her "laboratory." Her books, including *Wili Wai Kula and the Three Mongooses* (Hawaii's own "Goldilocks and the Three Bears") and *'Ula Li'i and the Magic Shark* (a Hawaiian "Little Red Riding Hood"), have been well-received by teachers and schoolchildren.

About the Author

Donivee Martin Laird

The beautiful state of Hawaii is home to Donivee Martin Laird. She was born there and lives there today with her family and a mongoose named Custard. Laird has written several Hawaiian versions of popular tales, such as *Wili Wai Kula and the Three Mongooses*, a Hawaiian "Goldilocks and the Three Bears."

About the Illustrator

Don Stuart

Don Stuart didn't have any brothers or sisters growing up, so he used to entertain himself by drawing. Making his own comic books was a favorite thing to do. Among the illustrators Stuart admires today is Lane Smith, the illustrator of *The True Story of the 3 Little Pigs*.

92

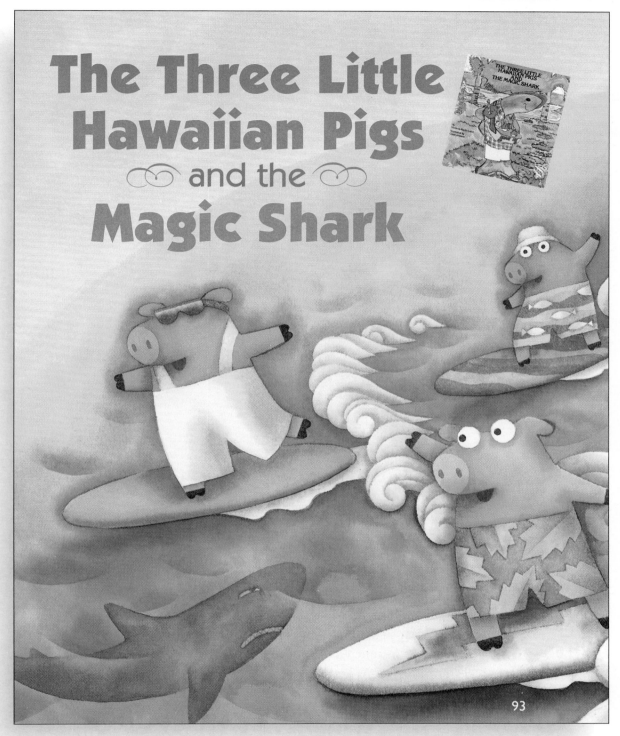

The Three Little Hawaiian Pigs ∽ and the ∽ Magic Shark

More About the Illustrator

Don Stuart

Growing up as an only child, Don Stuart entertained himself by writing and drawing his own comic books. Although he says he frequently got into trouble for drawing during class, he credits a high school art teacher with putting the idea into his head that he could one day make a living at something he enjoyed so much.

Today, Stuart lives in Ohio with his wife and three sons, all of whom spend a lot of time drawing. "I think there's at least one artist among them," he says. For the illustrations for *The Three Little Hawaiian Pigs and the Magic Shark*, Stuart used bright liquid watercolors called luma dyes.

Interact *with* Literature

One morning in Hawaii a mother and father pig called their children together.

"Our dear pua'a keikis," they said with sorrow in their voices. "As much as we love you, it is time for you to become grown-ups and seek your own way in the

94

Reading Strategies

▶ **Think About Words Monitor**

Student Application

Ask students to preview the selection and talk about what strategies they think will be useful in understanding it. If necessary, lead students to note that since the story is set on an island, there may be details that will confuse them at first, so they should monitor their reading. Also, discuss how thinking about the Hawaiian words that are in boxes may be necessary.

Predicting/Purpose Setting

Have students make predictions on how the shark will try to catch the pigs. Have them read to find out.

Choices for Reading

| Independent Reading | Cooperative Reading |
| Guided Reading | Teacher Read Aloud |

 **Guided Reading**

Because of the Hawaiian words in this story, you may wish to read aloud parts of the story. Pronunciations are found in boxes. Have students read to the end of page 97, keeping their purpose in mind. Then use the questions on page 96 to check comprehension.

QuickREFERENCE

★★★ Multicultural Link

Most Hawaiians speak English but some incorporate words from the Hawaiian language into their everyday speech. The language sounds very melodic to English speakers, perhaps because words are made up mostly of vowels.

 Students Acquiring English

Expressions Note that the phrase *seek your own way in the world* has the same meaning as *seek your fortune*: to leave home and earn money on one's own.

 Journal

Encourage students to explore their thinking by writing in their journals. In their entries they could discuss
- questions they had while reading
- evaluations they made
- how they figured out word meanings

pua'a (poo AH ah) a Hawaiian word meaning pig

keiki (kay EE kee) what Hawaiians call a child

aloha (ah LOH ha) a Hawaiian word with meanings such as hello, goodbye, and love

world. Here is a sack of money for each of you. Spend it wisely and always be careful of strangers."

After saying aloha to their parents, the three little pigs set off down the road looking forward to a life full of happiness, adventure, and riches.

95

MINILESSON

Fantasy/ Realism

TESTED SKILL

Teach/Model

Remind students that fantasies contain both real and make-believe elements. Begin mapping them out for this story using the illustration on pages 94–95.

Real	Fantasy
palm trees	pigs dressed like people

Then reread the text on these two pages with students. Ask:

- Can pigs really talk?
- Can pigs collect riches?

Add these details to the Fantasy column. To add to the Real column, students can pull out elements such as the buckets and fishing rods from the illustration.

Practice/Apply

Have students review the story and add other real and make-believe details to the chart.

SKILL FINDER

Full lesson/Reteaching, p. 114B–114C

Minilessons, p. 57; Theme 5, p. 211

Interact *with* Literature

Guided Reading

Comprehension/Critical Thinking

1. What has happened in the story so far? (The little pigs left their parents and built their own homes. The first pig built a house out of pili grass, while the second built his out of driftwood.)

2. Why were the first two pigs able to build their houses so quickly? (The materials they used were light.)

3. Do you think they spent their money wisely? What other material could they have chosen? (Have students cite alternate materials that could be found on an island.)

4. What kind of house do you think the third Hawaiian pig will build? (one that is stronger than a pili grass house or a driftwood house)

Predicting/Purpose Setting

Ask students to predict whether the first two pigs' houses will be strong enough to stop the villain. Then have them read to the end of page 102 to find out what the third pig does.

> **pili** (PEE lee) **grass** a grass used to thatch grass houses in old Hawaii
>
> **opihi** (oh PEE hee) a shallow, cone-shaped limpet shell whose animal is prized eating

They had gone only a short distance when they met a man with a load of pili grass. "Ah ha," said the first little pig. "This is for me. I will build myself a grass house and live beside the sea."

So, he bought the pili grass and happily headed towards the beach where he built his house. It was finished quickly and he took his pole, his net, his small bucket for opihi, and he went fishing.

96

Informal Assessment

If students' responses indicate that they are understanding the effect the setting has on the story, have them finish reading the story independently or with partners.

Quick REFERENCE

Vocabulary

Pronunciations Model for students the pronunciations on page 96 and then have them try. Ask them what a reader could infer about the sound of the vowel *i* in Hawaiian from the pronunciations of *pili* and *opihi*.

Students Acquiring English

Word Meaning Point out that to *live beside the sea* means "to live near the water." Have students demonstrate standing *beside* their desks. Ask students why the pigs want to live by the sea.

Social Studies Link

Physical Features Ask students if they know these words, used to describe mountainous areas:
- *plateau:* an area of flat land that is higher than the land around it
- *valley:* a long, narrow area of low land between mountains

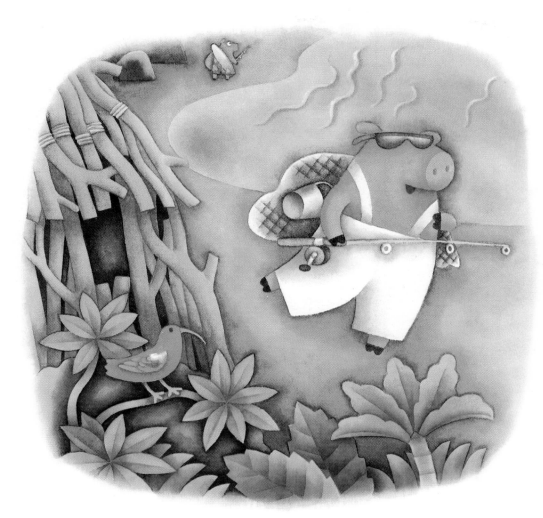

The other two little pigs went on until they met a man selling driftwood. "Ah ha," said the second little pig. "This is for me. I will build myself a house of driftwood and live beside the sea."

Feeling pleased with himself, he quickly built his house and went to join the first little pig fishing and scraping opihi off the slippery rocks.

97

Writer's Craft

Anthropomorphism

Teach/Model

Tell students that the pigs in this story do many things that real-life pigs could never do. Spark discussion by asking:

- What is funny about the idea of a pig fishing?

- What would the story be like if the pigs acted like real pigs do?

- What is your favorite story with talking animals? Why do you like it?

Point out that in fantasies, animals often do things that only people can do in real life, and this is called *anthropomorphism*. This adds to the humor of the story.

Practice/Apply

Have students make a list of all the things the pigs do in this story that are make-believe. Suggest that they draw a smiling face next to those actions (such as pigs surfing) that they think help make the story a funny one.

SKILL FINDER

Writing Activities: Animal Characters, p. 114E

Reading–Writing Workshop, pp. 116–117F

Students Acquiring English

MEETING INDIVIDUAL NEEDS

Word Meaning Explain that opihi cling to rocks. Have a student demonstrate *scraping*. Discuss objects that serve as good scrapers. Ask students what it would sound like if they were scraping a rock with a knife.

Science Link

Opihi Opihi are mollusks— animals that usually live in water and have a hard outer shell. Ask students if they know the names of any other sea animals that live inside shells, such as clams, oysters, or limpets.

Interact *with* Literature

Reading Strategies

▶ **Monitor**

Ask students why, even though they may know little about pili grass, driftwood, and lava rock, they can still conclude that the third pig's house is probably the strongest. Volunteers might cite these clues:

- the original story of "The Three Little Pigs" (The first two houses were built out of weaker materials than the third.)

- the materials the first two Hawaiian pigs used (Pili grass and driftwood can fall apart easily.)

- how quickly the pigs finished building their houses (The first two pigs finished quickly, while the third pig worked longer on his house.)

Discuss how these clues come to the surface when a reader stops and rereads. Ask students what other steps a reader can take when a story becomes confusing. (read further to see if the story becomes clearer; study the illustrations)

lava rock formed by a volcano

pau (POW) finished, all done

The third little pig went on until he met a man selling lava rock. "Ah ha." said the third little pig. "This is for me. I will build myself a house of lava rock and live beside the sea and go fishing with my brothers."

It took many days to build the house and before it was done, one brother came to visit the third little pig.

"Why are you wasting your time on such a hard house to build?" he asked. "We are pau with our houses and have time to fish and take it easy surfing and playing. Forget this house, come with us."

The third little pig just shook his head and said he would rather take his time and build a strong house.

98

QuickREFERENCE

Students Acquiring English

MEETING INDIVIDUAL NEEDS

Word Meaning Use the illustration on page 98 to discuss why the house is *hard* (difficult) to build. Point out that since it is *hard* (solid), it will also be difficult to destroy. Use the illustration on page 102 to explain what *surfing* is.

After many days of hard work, the lava rock house was finished. It was sturdy and strong and the third little pig was pleased with his work. He checked his doors and windows carefully to be sure his house was snug and safe.

Then off he went to join his brothers beside the sea.

Science Link

Volcanoes The Hawaiian islands were formed from volcanoes. At least two volcanoes, Mauna Loa and Kilauea, are still active.

MEETING INDIVIDUAL NEEDS
Students Acquiring English

Pantomime Have a student pantomime the action of checking doors and windows. Discuss the meaning of *snug and safe*.

★★★ Multicultural Link

Ancestry The first Hawaiians were Polynesian, but now many people of European and Japanese descent live there. Have students study a map and name different Pacific islands where the first Hawaiians came from.

Interact
with
Literature

Reading Strategies

▶ **Monitor**

Ask students if they have had diffi-culty understanding any part of the story thus far. For example, has the setting made the story harder to understand? If so, encourage stu-dents to discuss how they have dealt with these difficulties. Have they tried rereading certain parts? Have they used the illustrations? Have they asked a reading partner for help?

yellow tang a small bright yellow reef fish

humuhumu (hoo moo HOO moo) a member of the trigger fish family; one of whom is the humuhumu-nukunuku-a-pua'a or fish with a snout like a pig, made famous in a popular Hawaiian song

he'e (HAY ay) the Hawaiian word for octopus

puhi paka (POOK hee PAH kah) a ferocious eel with sharp teeth

The three little pigs threw their nets and pulled in reef creatures like the brilliant yellow tang, the horned humuhumu, or the slimy octopus, he'e. They climbed over the wet rocks scraping off the delicious opihi and once in a while they caught puhi paka, the fierce fanged eel.

100

QuickREFERENCE

Visual Literacy

Ask students to identify fish in the illustration using
- the definitions in the box
- context clues such as *brilliant, horned, slimy, delicious,* and *fierce fanged*
- their prior knowledge of fish

MEETING INDIVIDUAL NEEDS **Extra Support**

Word Meaning If necessary, explain that a *reef* is a strip of rock, sand, or coral that rises close to the surface of the sea. *Tide pools* are puddles of water that the sea leaves behind when the tide goes out.

Science Link

Tropical Fish The yellow tang and the opihi live in reefs because reefs provide a food source (they eat growths on the coral reef) and offer them protection. Can students name other animals that hide in caves or holes to avoid enemies?

ulua (oo LOO ah) a kind of crevalle or jack fish

opakapaka (oh pah kah PAH kah) a blue snapper fish

ahi (AH hee) a yellow fin tuna fish

trade winds breezes which keep Hawaii cool

Sometimes they took their poles, and standing far out on the rocks, fished the deeper waters for the larger ulua, opakapaka, and ahi. They played tag, splashed in the tide pools, and chased tiny sand crabs. Their days were clear and sunny, and cooled by gentle trade winds.

101

Vocabulary

Ask students what sound the vowel *u* makes in Hawaiian, based on the pronunciations of *humuhumu, puhi paka,* and *ulua*. (It makes the sound *oo*.) Some students acquiring English will enjoy helping others pronounce these words.

2

Interact
with
Literature

Guided Reading

Comprehension/Critical Thinking

1. How would you summarize this part of the story? (The third pig built a strong house of lava rock; then he went to fish and surf with his brothers. An evil shark saw the pigs and wanted to eat them.)

2. Why couldn't the shark catch the pigs on the lava rocks? (They were too quick; the lava was sharp.)

3. How does the author describe the shark? Do you think he is scary? (Students should cite details such as the shark's teeth and his drooling.)

Predicting/Purpose Setting

Ask students to make predictions about what the shark may do. Then have them read to the end of page 107 to find out what scheme the shark chooses.

When the waves broke just right beside the reef, they took their surfboards and caught long breathtaking rides to the beach.

Meanwhile, an evil magic shark watched them from deep down where the water is green. Back and forth swam the magic shark, his long teeth shining in the gloomy water. He especially wanted to eat the three little pigs since they looked so sweet and tender.

102

Self-Assessment

Reflecting Ask students if they are thinking about how late the villain appears in this version of "The Three Little Pigs." How might this make his first appearance more suspenseful?

QuickREFERENCE

Students Acquiring English

Word Meaning Discuss the meaning of *the waves broke just right*. Point out that surfers look for waves they can ride for long distances. Ask why such a ride might be exciting. If necessary, demonstrate *breathtaking*.

He knew he couldn't catch them on the rocks, for the lava was sharp and the pigs too quick. He wished they would fall off their surfboards, but the pigs were too good and went too fast through the rough water.

So, watching and planning, the magic shark drooled and thought of the yummy little pigs.

103

Challenge

Waves Invite students to research how ocean waves are created (by wind) and what *tsunamis* are (tidal waves caused by earthquakes). If possible, let students tie a jump rope to a stationary object and demonstrate how waves move.

Compare and Contrast

REVIEW & MAINTAIN

Teach/Model

Work with students to complete a chart that compares and contrasts the building materials used by the pigs in the following stories.

House

Tale	#1	#2	#3
3 Hawaiian Pigs	pili grass	driftwood	lava rock
3 little javelinas	tumble-weeds	saguaro ribs	adobe
traditional 3 little pigs	straw	sticks	brick

Discuss how comparing and contrasting these details helps readers better understand the relative strength of these materials. Point out that it also helps a reader remember what he or she has read.

Practice/Apply

Have students prepare a chart like the following that compares the villains' strategies in the different versions of "The Three Little Pigs."

Villain	Prey	Strategy
wolf	pigs	huff and puff
coyote	javelinas	magic
shark	pigs	disguise

SKILL FINDER

Full lesson/Reteaching, pp. 88B–88C

Minilessons, p. 75; Theme 4, p. 47

2

Interact
with
Literature

---

shave ice powdery ice shavings put in a paper cone and covered with sweet, flavored syrup

One morning, unable to stand his craving any longer, the magic shark disguised himself as a shave ice man and knocked on the door of the first little pig's house. "Little Pig, Little Pig, let me come in," he called. "I have plenty shave ice!"

The little pig peeked out of the window. He was hot and thirsty and the cool, colorful shave ice looked so tasty. He grabbed his money and started to open the door.

But, just in time, he saw a fin on the shave ice man's back and he knew it was really the magic shark. He quickly shut and locked the door.

The shark knocked harder and called, "Little Pig, Little Pig, let me come in."

"Oh no," cried the little pig. "Not by the hair on my chinny, chin, chin."

104

Informal Assessment

Oral Reading Have individual students read aloud pages 104–105 as a check of oral reading fluency. Use the Oral Reading Checklist in the *Teacher's Assessment Handbook* as a guide for assessment.

QuickREFERENCE

Vocabulary

Word Meaning Ask students if they have ever eaten *shave ice* or a similar treat such as snowcones. What kinds of tropical fruits might be used as the syrup in shave ice? What are the colors of the fruits?

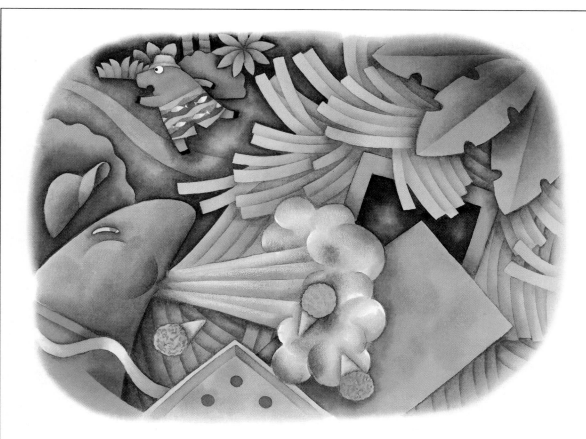

The magic shark was hot and hungry and the little pig's answer made him very mad. He yelled, "Little Pig, Little Pig, let me come in or I will huff and I will puff and I will blow your house down."

The little pig did not open his door. (After all he wasn't crazy, he knew what the magic shark wanted.)

So, the very mad magic shark huffed and the very mad magic shark puffed and the very mad magic shark blew down the first little pig's house.

The first little pig ran out of the back door and down the path to the house of the second little pig. The very mad magic shark went back to the ocean to cool off and make a new plan.

105

Students Acquiring English

MEETING INDIVIDUAL NEEDS

Idioms Explain that *to stand* in this context means "to put up with" or "to endure." The expression *to cool off* can mean to calm down or to do something—such as swimming—that will make one feel less hot.

Interact *with* Literature

Guided Reading

Comprehension/Critical Thinking

1. What happened to the first two little pigs? (The shark blew down the first pig's pili grass house and the second pig's driftwood house. The pigs ran to the lava house of the third little pig.)

2. What tricks did the shark try and how well did they work? (He disguised himself as a shave ice man and a beachboy. Neither disguise fooled the pigs.)

3. What do you think of the two pigs so far? (Answers will vary.)

4. Why must the magic shark plan so much more than the big bad pig or Coyote did? (He is not as strong as the big bad pig or as clever as Coyote. Also, he is a sea animal rather than a land animal, and, given his great hunger, his attack must be quick and effective.)

Predicting/Purpose Setting

Ask if students' predictions were accurate. Have them read to the end of the story to find out what the shark does and how the story ends.

---

lei (LAY) a garland (usually of flowers)

ukulele (oo koo LAY lay) a four stringed instrument played by strumming, 'uke' is short for ukulele

nose flute a flute like instrument played by blowing air with the nose

---

In a few days, the magic shark was hungry for little pigs again. This time he dressed up as a beachboy, wearing white pants, a coconut leaf hat, and a lei around his neck. He knocked on the door of the second little pig's house and called, "Little Pig, Little Pig, let's talk story and play ukes."

The little pigs grabbed their ukulele and nose flute and opened the door. The beachboy smiled and the little pigs saw rows and rows of long, sharp white teeth and just in time, they slammed the door.

106

QuickREFERENCE

★★★ Multicultural Link

Folktales Tell students that to *talk story* means to tell stories. Explain that many folktales were originally passed down from generation to generation by word of mouth. They were often polished and embellished with each retelling.

Students Acquiring English

Word Meaning As necessary, explain the following:
- A *beachboy* is someone who spends a lot of time at the beach, surfing and swimming and relaxing in the sun.
- *Ukes* is short for *ukuleles*.

"Little Pig, Little Pig, let me come in," called the hot and hungry magic shark anxiously.

"Oh no," cried the little pigs. (They knew that was no friendly beachboy out on the steps.) "Not by the hairs on our chinny, chin, chins."

This made the magic shark upset so he roared, "Then I will huff and I will puff and I will blow your house down." Just as he said he would, the very upset magic shark huffed and the very upset magic shark puffed and the very upset magic shark blew down the house of the second little pig.

The little pig and his brother jumped out of the window and ran down the path to the house of the third little pig.

107

Sequence

REVIEW & MAINTAIN

Teach/Model

Tell students that noting the sequence of events in a story makes it easier to understand.

Write these sentences on the board and ask students what's wrong with the sequence of events. Then have students rearrange the events in the proper order.

1. The first two little pigs ran to their brother's lava rock house.
2. The shark blew down the house of the second little pig.
3. Disguised as a beachboy, the shark knocked on the second pig's door.

Discuss how remembering the sequence in a story helps a reader summarize. Ask students what they could do if they failed to remember the sequence of events in a story. (reread; review with someone who's also read it)

Practice/Apply

After students have read pages 108–111, ask them to list the events in the order in which they occur. You may want to leave the list from this lesson on the board for reference.

SKILL FINDER

Full lesson/Reteaching, Theme 4, pp. 84B–84C
Minilessons, Theme 4, pp. 33, 77

Music Link

Ukulele The word *ukulele* means "leaping flea" in Hawaiian because the instrument is played as if a person's fingers are jumping off the strings. If possible, share some ukulele music with the class, such as *Hawaiian Mood* by Ohta-San.

Interact *with* Literature

Reading Strategies

▶ **Think About Words**

Have a volunteer model the kinds of questions a reader might ask in order to figure out the meaning of the word *pangs*. For example:

- What word or words are around *pangs* that might provide a clue to its meaning? (*Hunger* modifies it. Hunger is a feeling, so perhaps *pangs* has something to do with feeling.)

- What happens when I try to substitute *feeling* for *pangs*? Does it make sense? (Yes. The sentence would read: *After a few days his hunger* feeling *was so bad that the magic shark decided to try again.*)

---

mu'u mu'u (MOO oo MOO oo) a long, loose fitting woman's dress

lauhala (loo HAH lah) leaf of the hala or Pandanus tree; used in weaving hats, rugs, and baskets

---

Once more the magic shark, hot and still hungry, swam angrily down to his watery home to plot and scheme. After a few days his hunger pangs were so bad that the magic shark decided to try again.

This time he went pretending to be a lei seller. He knocked on the third little pig's door and called sweetly, "Little Pig, Little Pig, let me come in. I have leis to sell."

The three little pigs loved to wear leis and were happy to hear a sweet voice calling.

They looked out and saw the lei seller in her mu'u mu'u and lauhala hat, with flower leis on her arms. But then, they also saw a shark's tail sticking out from under the mu'u mu'u. They knew who that was so they rushed around locking the doors and windows.

108

Journal

Saying "Welcome" Visitors to Hawaii are often greeted with leis made from orchids, carnations, and/or jasmines. Have students acquiring English share customs and greetings in their primary languages. Then invite students to write in their journals about other ways of saying "welcome" to someone. Have they ever greeted a person by giving him or her a gift?

"Little Pig, Little Pig, let me come in," called the magic shark, growing upset.

"Oh no," answered the little pigs. "Not by the hairs on our chinny, chin, chins."

"You will be sorry!" screamed the furious magic shark in his loudest voice. "I will huff and I will puff and I will blow your house down." No one answered and no one opened the door, so the furious magic shark huffed and the furious magic shark puffed and he huffed and he puffed and he blew . . . and nothing happened!

Again he huffed and he puffed and he huffed and he puffed and he blew and he blew and still nothing happened.

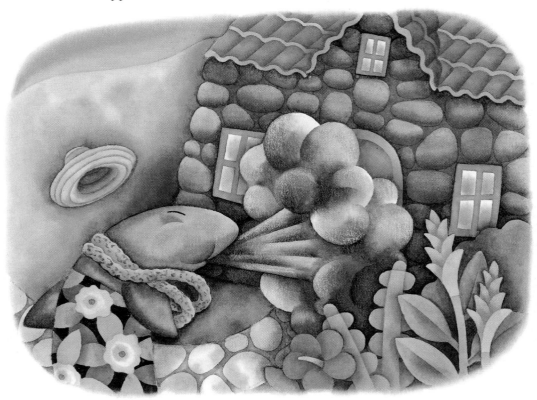

109

Interact
with
Literature

Once more the furious magic shark huffed and the furious magic shark puffed and the furious magic shark huffed and the furious magic shark puffed and the furious magic shark blew and blew and still . . . the lava rock house stood firm.

Now this made the magic shark extremely furious. So, gathering up all of his air, the extremely furious magic shark huffed and puffed and huffed and puffed and huffed and puffed

and blew
and blew
and blew
and blew
and blew
and blew
and blew

until . . . whoosh; ker-splat, he fell on the ground all out of air looking like a flat balloon!

110

QuickREFERENCE

 Journal

Have students describe in their journals how the author builds suspense by

- repeating *huffed* and *puffed*
- unusual line breaks
- sound words such as *ker-splat*

MEETING INDIVIDUAL NEEDS

Students Acquiring English

Explain that *stood firm* means that the lava house remained standing. Have students demonstrate the sound words *whoosh* and *ker-splat*. Invite them to give examples of other sound words in several languages and in English.

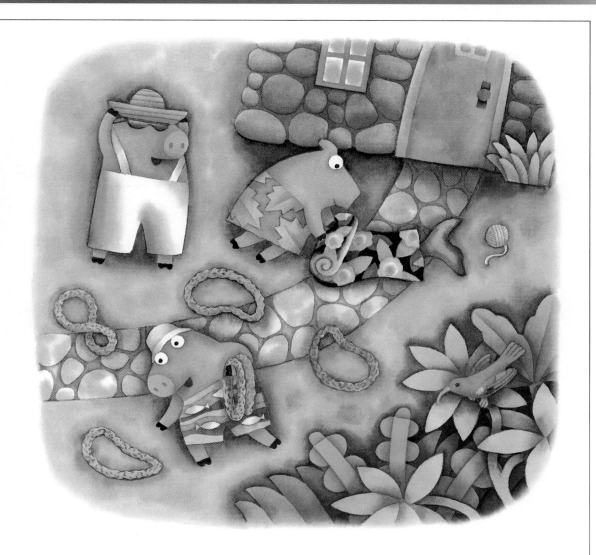

It was quiet and still and the three little pigs
cautiously peeked out of the house. Seeing the very flat
magic shark, they quickly ran outside, rolled him up
like a straw mat, and tied a string around him.

Then . . . taking him off to the dump they threw
him away.

111

Interact *with* Literature

Guided Reading

Comprehension/Critical Thinking

1. What happened to the magic shark at the end of this story? (He blew so hard trying to knock down the lava house that he blew himself all out of air; he ended up looking like a flat balloon; the pigs rolled him up and took him to the dump.)

2. Why is an island a fun place for a party? (Answers will vary, but students might cite a variety of outdoor activities.)

3. What would the pigs' parents think of where their children are living? (They would be happy because the little pigs are safe and living close to one another.)

When they returned to the seashore, the third little pig helped his brothers build sturdy rock houses and once they were finished, the three little pigs gave a large party. They invited all their friends and relatives as well as a shave ice man (without a fin) to serve

112

Self-Assessment

Ask students to assess their reading with questions such as the following:

• Were there any places where I had trouble understanding the story? What did I do?
• How did I handle the hard words in the story?
• Do I think this is a good story?

QuickREFERENCE

Students Acquiring English

Expressions Explain that *gave a large party* means "had a big party." Explain that the party was *given* as a gift by the hosts (the pigs) to their guests.

refreshments, a beachboy (without rows of sharp white teeth) to join the musicians, and a lei seller (without a shark's tail) to give out leis.

From then on the three little pigs lived safely and peacefully beside the sea.

113

Home Connection

Stick Puppets Students may enjoy drawing their own pictures of the characters in this story. They might make stick puppets of the characters, which they can then use to retell the story to family members.

MEETING INDIVIDUAL NEEDS

Extra Support

Reader's Theater This selection lends itself to Reader's Theater. To aid comprehension, consider assigning parts to students and having them perform important scenes.

Interact *with* Literature

Responding Activities

 Personal Response

- Suggest that students choose a favorite part of the story to describe in their journals.

- Allow students to choose their own way of responding to the selection.

Anthology Activities

Choose one of the activities on page 114 for students to do or have them choose one independently.

 Informal Assessment

Responses should indicate a general understanding of the story and its structure.

Additional Support:

- Use the Guided Reading questions to review and if necessary reread.

- Have students summarize the story.

- Reread confusing sections aloud.

RESPONDING

Aloha, Little Pigs

Write a Paragraph

Dear Magic Shark

The shark didn't have much luck fooling the pigs. Can you think of a better disguise he could have used? Write a paragraph to give the shark advice on what to wear and how to act.

Act Out a Scene

Let Me Come In!

With a group of friends, act out your favorite scene from the story. You'll need one person to play each part and another to be the narrator. It might be fun to make props to help you tell the story.

114

QuickREFERENCE

 Students Acquiring English

Students who are gaining proficiency with written English may respond by role-playing or by drawing. For example, for the activity "Dear Magic Shark," students can draw a picture of a shark in disguise and work with a classmate to label it.

Home Connection

News from Hawaii Encourage students to work with family members to find magazine and/or newspaper articles about Hawaii.

More Responding Activities

Materials
- paper plates
- scissors
- string or yarn
- markers or crayons

Make Masks
Cooperative Learning

Students may enjoy working together to make masks of the story characters. These can be used to re-enact the story.

1 Draw a pig or a shark face on a paper plate.

2 Cut out the face and eyes. Make holes on the side for string.

3 Run the string through the side holes and secure with knots or staples.

Literature Discussion

Note: Guidelines for conducting a literature discussion can be found on page 114L.

- Were you satisfied with the ending of this story, or can you think of a different ending?
- Who is the trickiest villain—the big bad pig, Coyote, or the shark? Why?

Selection Connections

LAB, p. 8

Have students complete the portion of the chart relating to the story.

Compose a Song

Invite students to write a song that the three Hawaiian pigs might sing at the party. For example: "Ding, Dong, the Shark Is Dead"; "He'll Be Comin' Round the Coral Reef When He Comes"; "He's Huffing, He's Puffing" (melody: "It's Raining, It's Pouring").

Comprehension Check

To check selection comprehension use these questions and/or *Literacy Activity Book* page 31.

1. What did the Hawaiian pigs do for fun? (They played tag and went fishing and surfing.)

2. Why couldn't the shark catch the pigs when they were on their surfboards? (He knew they were too good at surfing and they traveled very fast.)

3. Why didn't the shark's disguises work? (Parts of the shark showed through, or he smiled and the pigs could tell he was a shark by his teeth.)

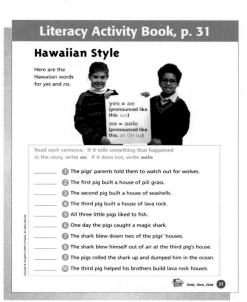

Literacy Activity Book, p. 31

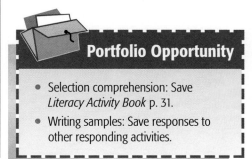

Portfolio Opportunity

- Selection comprehension: Save *Literacy Activity Book* p. 31.
- Writing samples: Save responses to other responding activities.

Instruct and Integrate

Comprehension

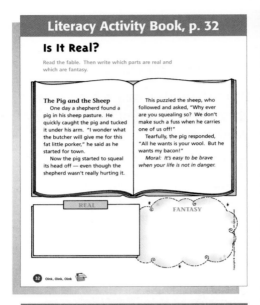
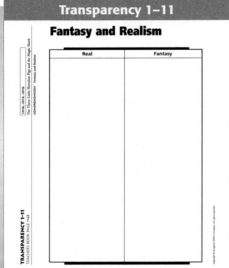

Transparency 1–11

Fantasy and Realism

Real	Fantasy

Informal Assessment

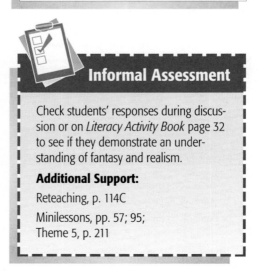

Check students' responses during discussion or on *Literacy Activity Book* page 32 to see if they demonstrate an understanding of fantasy and realism.

Additional Support:

Reteaching, p. 114C

Minilessons, pp. 57; 95;
Theme 5, p. 211

INTERACTIVE LEARNING

Fantasy/Realism

TESTED SKILL

LAB, p. 32

Teach/Model

Invite students to role-play the difference between realism and fantasy. For example, have a volunteer role-play a dog drinking water out of a dog dish. Then ask another volunteer to turn this realistic scene into a fantasy one, perhaps by having the dog drink water out of a glass with a straw. Encourage other such demonstrations.

Ask students what makes it obvious that *The Three Little Hawaiian Pigs and the Magic Shark* is a fantasy. (animals talking) Then discuss what makes the story funny. (the animals do many things humans do)

Display Transparency 1–11. Then ask students to tell which of these details about Hawaii from the story are real and which are fantasy.

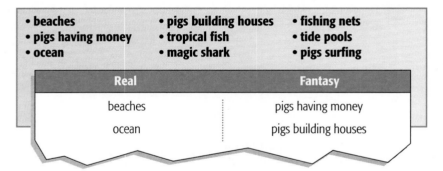

- beaches
- pigs having money
- ocean
- pigs building houses
- tropical fish
- magic shark
- fishing nets
- tide pools
- pigs surfing

Real	Fantasy
beaches	pigs having money
ocean	pigs building houses

Explain that the real details were not made up–they actually exist. Add that although the fantasy details use some part of reality–there are pigs–they contain other parts that were made up by the author.

Practice/Apply

- Have students use *Literacy Activity Book* page 32 to identify the fable as a fantasy.

- Have students classify several fiction books from the classroom library as fantasy or realism.

SKILL FINDER

Minilessons, pp. 57; 95;
Theme 5, p. 211

Reteaching

Fantasy/Realism

Fantasy and reality are an integral part of comic strips, and the following activity capitalizes on this fact.

Cut out two kinds of comic strips from your daily newspaper: ones that are set in the "real world" and ones that employ fantasy elements, such as talking animals and robots. Then put the strips in a box.

Invite students to select a strip from the box and identify the strip as an example of realism or fantasy. Ask them to name elements that are real and fantastical in each strip. You might use the questions in the box below to prompt students' responses.

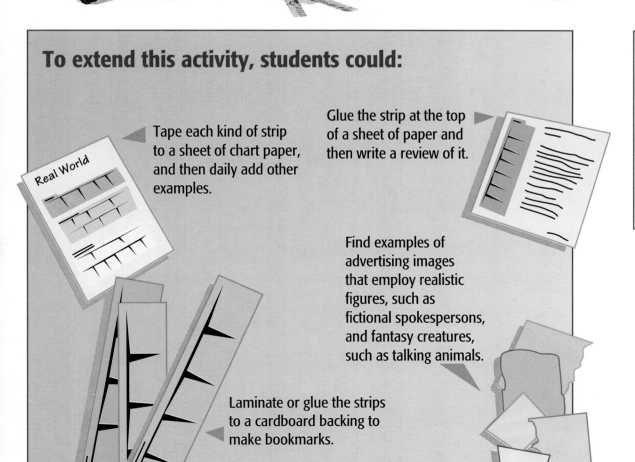

To extend this activity, students could:

▶ Tape each kind of strip to a sheet of chart paper, and then daily add other examples.

Real World

▶ Glue the strip at the top of a sheet of paper and then write a review of it.

Find examples of advertising images that employ realistic figures, such as fictional spokespersons, and fantasy creatures, such as talking animals.

▶ Laminate or glue the strips to a cardboard backing to make bookmarks.

Questions About Comics

• What is real in the comic strip? What's make-believe?

• Why do you think this comic strip is popular?

• How could you change the comic strip to make it more real (or fantastical)?

Portfolio Opportunity

Save *Literacy Activity Book* p. 32 to record students' understanding of fantasy and realism.

3

Instruct *and* Integrate

Writing Skills and Activities

Transparency 1–12

Combining Sentences: Compound Sentences

Simple Sentences	Compound Sentences
The pigs surfed. The shark watched them from below.	The pigs surfed, and the shark watched them from below.

❶ One little pig built his house. The others went fishing.

❷ The gentle trade winds blew. The sun shined.

❸ The shark knocked on the door. The pig peeked out of the window.

❹ The beachboy played music. The shave ice man served refreshments.

TRANSPARENCY 1–12
TEACHER'S BOOK PAGE 114D

Two to One

This story is about the three little pigs and the magic shark. Look for five sentences that could be combined. Write them as compound sentences.

Three Little Heroes

This week, three little pigs have become heroes! They took care of a pesky shark. The shark came into their yard. The pigs ran inside to hide. One pig began closing windows. Another locked the front door. The shark started knocking with his big fin. He was very hungry. The pigs were very scared. The angry shark began to huff and puff. The house shook. Finally, the shark ran out of air. He fell in a heap. The pigs took him off to the dump. The shark won't be bothering them anymore!

① ② ③ ④ ⑤

Oink, Oink, Oink **33**

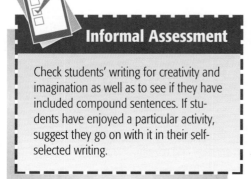

Informal Assessment

Check students' writing for creativity and imagination as well as to see if they have included compound sentences. If students have enjoyed a particular activity, suggest they go on with it in their self-selected writing.

TESTED SKILL

Combining Sentences: Compound Sentences
LAB, p. 33

Teach/Model

Write these sentences on the board.

The pigs surfed.

The shark watched them from below.

Point out that sometimes the idea in one sentence can go with the idea in another sentence. Tell students that they can combine the two sentences to make a longer sentence called a compound sentence. Combine the sentences on the board as shown.

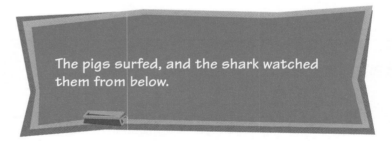

The pigs surfed, and the shark watched them from below.

Explain that the two sentences are joined by using a comma and the word *and*.

Display Transparency 1–12. Have volunteers combine the pairs of simple sentences. Tell students that using sentences of different lengths will make their writing more interesting.

Practice/Apply

Assign the activity Creative Writing: Animal Characters. Encourage students to vary the length of their sentences by using some compound sentences.

SKILL FINDER

Reading-Writing Workshop, p. 116–117F

Writing Activities

Plan a House

Remind students that the three Hawaiian pigs built their houses from pili grass, drift-wood, and lava rock. Have students write a paragraph of at least five sentences about the kind of house they would want to build.

- What would it be made of?
- What would it look like?
- Where would it be?

MY HOUSE

I would like to build a log cabin. I'd build it in the woods. I'd have a room full of video games. My dog would have his very own bedroom. There would be a big porch out front. We'd sleep on it on hot summer nights.

Students can use The Learning Company's new elementary writing center for all their writing activities.

Creative Writing: Animal Characters

Suggest that students write their own stories using animal characters. Encourage them to have their characters do some things that only humans could really do. Suggest that in planning their stories, they make a list of human behaviors that might work well with their story idea. (*See the Writer's Craft Minilesson on page 97.*)

Write a Poem

Have students write poems using the Hawaiian words in *The Three Little Hawaiian Pigs and the Magic Shark.* Suggest that they might want to rhyme the Hawaiian words with English ones, but explain that their poems do not nave to rhyme at all.

Portfolio Opportunity

- Save *Literacy Activity Book* page 33 to record students' understanding of combining sentences to form compound sentences.
- Save responses to activities on this page for writing samples.

Instruct
and
Integrate

Word Skills and Strategies

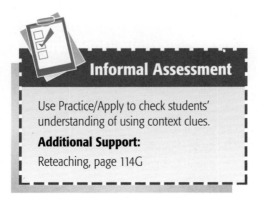

Literacy Activity Book, p. 34

Figure It Out

Use context clues to figure out the meaning of each underlined word. Circle the clues in the sentence. Then write the meaning.

1. The mother and father warned the little pigs not to squander their money but to spend it wisely.

2. The shark wore a costume to deceive the little pigs.

3. The sharp teeth of the shark filled the little pigs with trepidation.

4. The shark blew so hard that he collapsed like a deflated balloon.

5. When the shark was gone, the jubilant pigs laughed with joy.

6. At the party, the pigs wore leis of yellow, pink, and magenta flowers.

INTERACTIVE LEARNING

Using Context
TESTED SKILL
LAB, p. 34

Teach/Model

Write this sentence on the board.

Tell students that if they don't know the meaning of *yellow tang*, they could make a good guess by using clues from the other words in the sentence. Ask them what clues they would use. (Yellow tang are listed with tuna and snapper fish, so they are probably a kind of fish.)

> The pigs brought home tuna, snapper fish, and yellow tang.

Tell students that context clues are other words in a sentence that can be used to figure out the meaning of an unfamiliar word. Point out that lists of words are useful context clues but that there are other types of clues as well.

Practice/Apply

Cooperative Learning Write the following sentences on three sheets of paper, one sentence per sheet. On the opposite side of each sheet, write the definition of the underlined word. Fold the sheet and paperclip it so that the sentence is visible but the definition is not. Divide the class into groups and give each group one of the sentences. Have students guess the meaning of the underlined word and identify the clues they used. When the group thinks they have figured out the meaning, have them remove the paperclip to find out if they are right. Then have them reclip the paper and pass the sentence on to another group.

Sentence	Meaning	Clues
The villain was hated by everyone for his <u>nefarious</u> deeds.	evil, wicked	villain, hated
The salad contained leaves of spinach, lettuce, and <u>escarole</u>.	a leafy vegetable	leaves, spinach, lettuce
The winners wore cheerful grins, but the losers looked <u>morose</u>.	gloomy, unhappy	losers opposite of winners suggests morose is opposite of cheerful

Informal Assessment

Use Practice/Apply to check students' understanding of using context clues.

Additional Support:
Reteaching, page 114G

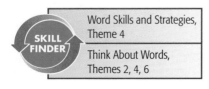

SKILL FINDER

Word Skills and Strategies, Theme 4

Think About Words, Themes 2, 4, 6

Using Context

Write the first sentence at right on the board and read it aloud.

Ask students what *puhi paka* means. (a fierce fanged eel)

Point out that the meaning of the word is given in the sentence. Write the second sentence at right on the board and read it aloud.

Ask students what they think *ravenous* means. (hungry) Point out that although the sentence doesn't tell the meaning of *ravenous,* some of the words are clues to the meaning. Ask students what clues they used. (couldn't wait, eat)

Tell students that when they come to an unfamiliar word in their reading, other words in the sentence will often help them figure it out.

Word Skills Practice

Cumulative Skill Practice
Red Riding Hood and Gray Wolf
by Rob Hale

> Once in a while the pigs caught <u>puhi paka</u>, the fierce fanged eel.

> The shark was <u>ravenous</u> and couldn't wait to eat all three pigs.

MINILESSON

Dictionary
Alphabetical Order

Teach/Model

Write these words in a random cluster on the board.

reason   listen   butter   rent   elephant   load

Ask students to help you list the words in alphabetical order. Model the process by starting with the first letter of each word, and where the letters are the same, going on to the second letter, and so on.

Practice/Apply

Write each of these words on a large index card and group the cards as shown. Divide the class into teams of five, and give each team one set of words. Tell students that when you say "Go," they should each take a word, hold it up for the group to see, and then arrange themselves in alphabetical order. The first group to arrange themselves correctly scores a point. After the first round, have groups exchange words and play again.

early	great	nine	clean	order
ever	itch	parent	clover	organ
nothing	quiz	repeat	history	queen
perfect	quote	roam	honey	silly
storm	thank	weather	interest	uncle
stump	toward	went	keep	upset

early

ever

nothing

perfect

storm

stump

Portfolio Opportunity

Save *Literacy Activity Book* page 34 to record students' understanding of using context clues.

3

Instruct *and* Integrate

Building Vocabulary

High-Frequency Vocabulary Practice

Cumulative Skill Practice
Red Riding Hood and Gray Wolf
by Rob Hale

Literacy Activity Book, p. 35

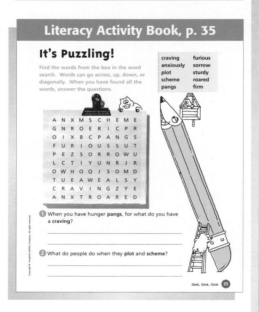

It's Puzzling!

Find the words from the box in the word search. Words can go across, up, down, or diagonally. When you have found all the words, answer the questions.

craving	furious
anxiously	sorrow
plot	sturdy
scheme	roared
pangs	firm

```
A N X M S C H E M E
G N R O E R I C P R
O I X B C P A N G S
F U R I O U S S U T
P E Z S O R R O W U
L C T I Y U N R J R
O W H O Q J S O M D
T U E A W E A L S Y
C R A V I N G Z Y E
A N X T R O A R E D
```

❶ When you have hunger **pangs**, for what do you have a **craving**?

❷ What do people do when they **plot** and **scheme**?

Oink, Oink, Oink **35**

Use this page to review Selection Vocabulary.

Vocabulary Activities

Synonym Search

Remind students that when the little pigs escaped from the shark, the shark was very mad. Write *mad* on the board, and ask students what other words they can think of that have the same or nearly the same meaning. (*annoyed, angry, furious*) Write their responses on the board and draw a circle around all of the words. Tell students that words with the same or nearly the same meaning are called synonyms.

Write each of the words shown (with its corresponding number) on a separate slip of paper, and give one slip to each student. Have students find the other student or students whose words are synonyms for their own word. The number on each slip will tell them how many other students they must find. Once students have formed their synonym pairs or groups, have them write their synonyms on the board and draw a circle around them.

sorrow 1	plan 2	quickly 2
sadness 1	plot 2	speedily 2
	scheme 2	rapidly 2
sack 1		
bag 1	finished 2	extremely 1
	completed 2	very 1
frightened 2	done 2	
scared 2		happily 2
afraid 2	hurt 3	cheerfully 2
	harmed 3	joyfully 2
delicious 1	damaged 3	
tasty 1	injured 3	carefully 1
		cautiously 1
creatures 1	strong 1	
animals 1	sturdy 1	certainly 2
		surely 2
shining 2		absolutely 2
gleaming 2	certainly 2	
glowing 2	surely 2	
	absolutely 2	

Vocabulary Notebook

Ask students what they would do to remember a friend's telephone number. (write it down) Point out that the same idea can be applied to learning the meaning of a new word.

Tell students that they will be making special notebooks for recording new words that they want to learn or remember. Have each student staple or three-hole punch 26 sheets of lined paper and write a letter of the alphabet at the top of each sheet. Students can use construction paper to make a cover for their notebook.

Suggest that when students record a word, they write it in a sentence and also write down its meaning. They might even want to draw a picture.

Spelling

5-Day Planner

FIVE-DAY PLAN

DAY 1	DAY 2	DAY 3	DAY 4	DAY 5
Pretest; Minilesson; Challenge Words/ Additional Words (opt.); Take-Home Word Lists (LAB)	First LAB page; Challenge Words Practice (opt.)	Check first LAB page; Second LAB page (except writing application)	Check second LAB page; writing application (LAB)	Test

Teaching CHOICES

MINILESSON

Spelling Words

*three	*deep
*tail	*away
*beach	*please
*play	*chain

Challenge Words

*easy	*reef
*really	*creature

Additional Spelling Words

*sea	main
*sweet	*leaf

*Starred words or forms of the words appear in *The Three Little Hawaiian Pigs and the Magic Shark.*

Spelling Long *a* and Long *e*

LAB, pp. 36–37

- Write *chain* and *play* on the board. Say the words and have students repeat them. Ask students to name the vowel sound in each word. (/ā/) Have students tell how the /ā/ sound is spelled in these words. (*ai, ay*) Point out that the *ai* pattern appears in the middle of a word, and the *ay* pattern appears at the end of a word.

- Write *beach* and *deep* on the board. Say the words and have students repeat them. Ask students to name the vowel sound in each word. (/ē/) Elicit the two spelling patterns for the /ē/ sound. (*ea, ee*)

- Write the Spelling Words on the board. Tell students that each Spelling Word has the /ā/ sound or the /ē/ sound. Say the Spelling Words and have students repeat them.

Spelling Assessment

Pretest

Say each underlined word, read the sentence, and then repeat the word. Have students write only the underlined words.

1. The three pigs live by the sea.
2. That pig has a curly tail.
3. Bring your fishing rod to the beach.
4. It's fun to play in the waves!
5. Do sharks stay in deep water?
6. Stay away from the rocks when you surf.
7. Can you please pass me my towel?
8. I lost my gold chain in the sand.

Test

Spelling Words Use the Pretest sentences.

Challenge Words

9. Let's go diving near the coral reef.
10. It's not easy to catch a big fish.
11. What sea creature has eight long arms?
12. Those sand crabs are really fast.

SKILL FINDER
| Daily Language Practice, p. 114K |
| Reading-Writing Workshop, p. 117E |

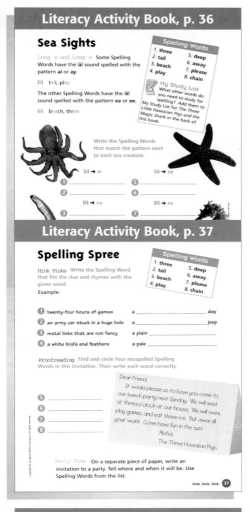

Literacy Activity Book, p. 36

Sea Sights

Long *a* and Long *e* Some Spelling Words have the [ā] sound spelled with the pattern *ai* or *ay*.

[ā]   tail, play

The other Spelling Words have the [ē] sound spelled with the pattern *ea* or *ee*.

[ē]   beach, three

Spelling Words
1. three   5. deep
2. tail   6. away
3. beach   7. please
4. play   8. chain

My Study List What other words do you need to study for spelling? Add them to My Study List for *The Three Little Hawaiian Pigs and the Magic Shark* in the back of this book.

Write the Spelling Words that match the pattern next to each sea creature.

[ā] → ai   [ā] → ay
1 ____   5 ____
2 ____   6 ____

[ē] → ea   [ē] → ee
3 ____   7 ____
4 ____

Literacy Activity Book, p. 37

Spelling Spree

Hink Pinks Write the Spelling Word that fits the clue and rhymes with the given word.
Example:

1 twenty-four hours of games   a _____ day
2 an army car stuck in a huge hole   a _____ jeep
3 metal links that are not fancy   a plain _____
4 a white bird's end feathers   a pale _____

Spelling Words
1. three   5. deep
2. tail   6. away
3. beach   7. please
4. play   8. chain

Proofreading Find and circle four misspelled Spelling Words in this invitation. Then write each word correctly.

Dear Friend,
   It would please us to have you come to our beach party next Sunday. We will meet at three o'clock at our house. We will swim, play games, and eat shave ice. Put away all your work. Come have fun in the sun!
      Aloha,
      The Three Hawaiian Pigs

5 ____
6 ____
7 ____
8 ____

Party Time On a separate piece of paper, write an invitation to a party. Tell where and when it will be. Use Spelling Words from the list.

Oink, Oink, Oink 37

Literacy Activity Book

Take-Home Word Lists: pp. 161–162

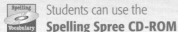

Students can use the **Spelling Spree CD-ROM** for extra practice with the spelling principles taught in this selection.

Challenge

Challenge Words Practice Have students use the Challenge Words to write safety tips for beachgoers.

3

Instruct *and* Integrate

Grammar

FIVE-DAY PLAN

DAY 1	DAY 2	DAY 3	DAY 4	DAY 5
Daily Language Practice 1; Teach/Model; First LAB page	Daily Language Practice 2; Check first LAB page; Cooperative Learning	Daily Language Practice 3; Writing Application	Daily Language Practice 4; Reteaching (opt.); Second LAB page	Daily Language Practice 5; Check second LAB page; Students' Writing

---

Transparency 1–13

Kinds of Sentences

STATEMENT: The little pigs are almost grown.

QUESTION: Should they leave home?

COMMAND: Let them go.

EXCLAMATION: How happy they are!

Look at the first little pig.
Is that a grass house?
How quickly he builds it!
Is his house strong enough?
Now he is going fishing.
Will he see the shark?

Literacy Activity Book, p. 39

What Kind?

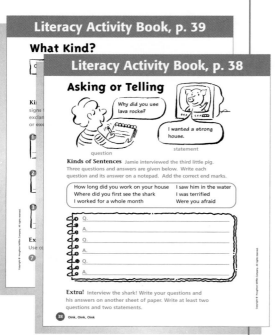

Literacy Activity Book, p. 38

Asking or Telling

Why did you use lava rocks?

I wanted a strong house.

question   statement

Kinds of Sentences Jamie interviewed the third little pig. Three questions and answers are given below. Write each question and its answer on a notepad. Add the correct end marks.

How long did you work on your house	I saw him in the water
Where did you first see the shark	I was terrified
I worked for a whole month	Were you afraid

Q. ____
A. ____
Q. ____
A. ____
Q. ____
A. ____

Extra! Interview the shark! Write your questions and his answers on another sheet of paper. Write at least two questions and two statements.

38 Oink, Oink, Oink

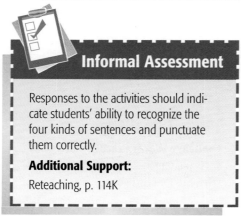

Informal Assessment

Responses to the activities should indicate students' ability to recognize the four kinds of sentences and punctuate them correctly.

Additional Support:
Reteaching, p. 114K

INTERACTIVE LEARNING

TESTED SKILL

Kinds of Sentences

LAB, pp. 38–39

- A **statement** tells something. It ends with a period.
- A **question** asks something. It ends with a question mark.
- A **command** tells someone to do something. It ends with a period.
- An **exclamation** shows strong feeling. It ends with an exclamation point.

Teach/Model Write these quotations from the story on the chalkboard.

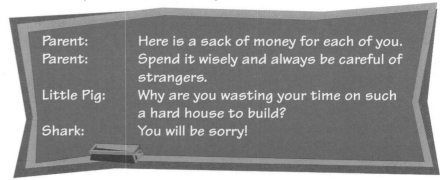

Parent:	Here is a sack of money for each of you.
Parent:	Spend it wisely and always be careful of strangers.
Little Pig:	Why are you wasting your time on such a hard house to build?
Shark:	You will be sorry!

As you ask each pair of questions below, have volunteers go to the chalkboard, point to the appropriate sentence, and name the end mark. Then ask volunteers to read each sentence aloud so as to convey its purpose.

- Which sentence tells someone to do something? What mark does it end with?

- Which sentence asks something? What mark does it end with?

- Which sentence shows strong feeling? What mark does it end with?

- Which sentence tells something? What mark does it end with?

Display Transparency 1–13. Point out the name of each kind of sentence. Review the end mark for each. Read aloud the other sentences. Have volunteers label each sentence and add the end mark. Have students write their own statements, questions, commands, and exclamations.

SKILL FINDER Reading-Writing Workshop, p. 117E

INTERACTIVE LEARNING *(continued)*

More Practice
Houghton Mifflin English Level 3
Workbook Plus, pp. 3–6
Reteaching Workbook, pp. 2–3
Write on Track
Write on Track SourceBook, pp. 3–4, 7–8, 57–58

Practice/Apply   ***Literacy Activity Book*** Page 38 provides practice with statements and questions. Page 39 provides practice with commands and exclamations.

***Cooperative Learning:* A Play** Divide the class into four or more small groups. Assign each group a section of the story to turn into a script. Demonstrate script format, and explain that they will be writing only what the characters say. Students should supplement story dialogue with their own lines and include at least one sentence of each type. When the groups are finished, invite each group to act out its script.

Writing Application: Safety Instructions Suggest that students write a paragraph telling how to play safely at the beach or another place. Ask them to include each of the four types of sentences.

Students' Writing Suggest that students check their work in process to see if they have used correct end marks. Encourage them to use different types of sentences in their writing.

Reteaching

Kinds of Sentences

Prepare four cards, each with the name of a different kind of sentence and its end mark. Review the purpose of each kind of sentence, and pass out the cards to four students.

Write the sentences below on chart paper. Have students read aloud the first sentence. Ask a volunteer to say what the sentence does (tells something, asks something, etc.) and point to the student holding the card that identifies the kind of sentence. The card-holder reads the card aloud as the volunteer writes the end mark.

What did the second pig build with   (question ?)
Show me his house   (command .)
He used driftwood   (statement .)
Here comes the shark   (exclamation !)
Keep the door closed   (command .)
What sharp teeth you have   (exclamation !)
What will the pig do now   (question ?)
He is running to his brother   (statement .)

Daily Language Practice
Focus Skills

Grammar: Kinds of Sentences
Spelling: Long *a* and Long *e*

Every day write one sentence on the chalkboard. Have each student write the sentence correctly on a sheet of paper. Tell students to correct incorrect end marks and misspelled words. Have students correct their own paper as a volunteer corrects the sentence on the chalkboard.

1. Pleeze read us another story?
   Please read us another story**.**

2. Why did the thre little pigs go away!
   Why did the **three** little pigs go away**?**

3. They loved to pley at the beach?
   They loved to **play** at the beach**.**

4. How deap that water looks?
   How **deep** that water looks**!**

5. Could the shark hide his tayl.
   Could the shark hide his **tail?**

3

Instruct and Integrate

Communication Activities

Listening and Speaking

Audio Tape
for Oink, Oink, Oink: *The Three Little Hawaiian Pigs and the Magic Shark*

Literature Discussion Guidelines

1. Listen carefully.

2. Take turns talking.

3. Support your ideas with evidence.

4. Stick to the topic.

5. Be polite!

Invite students to set up guidelines for their Literature Discussion groups.

- Begin by asking them to recall discussions that were especially good—or others that were not so good.

- Brainstorm ideas for good discussions, listing all ideas on the board.

- Encourage students to choose those ideas that are most important and create a chart for display.

Divide the class into small groups to practice guidelines they've set up. Pose this question: Which story in "Oink, Oink, Oink" was the best? Why do you think so?

Hawaiian Music

Multicultural Link Offer students the opportunity to listen to the melodic sounds of the Hawaiian language. Especially recommended is *It's a Small World/Pumehana,* a recording by the youth group Na Mele O Na Opio, which includes a variety of Hawaiian styles.

Resources
It's a Small World/Pumehana by Na Mele O Na Opio
Na Mele O Paniolo by the Hawaii State Foundation of Culture and the Arts

Informal Assessment

Check students' speaking skills, using the *Literature Discussion Guidelines.* For students who need additional support, plan more speaking activities in small groups.

Viewing

A Game of Disguise

Discuss how the pigs were able to identify the shark each time he visited. Then play a game of disguise.

One student acts as the shark, by changing something about his or her appearance. The volunteer might put on a hat or take off glasses—out of the sight of classmates. Observers must study details carefully both before and after the change. The first student to identify the disguise becomes the next shark.

Let's Visit Hawaii

To further appreciate life in our fiftieth state, students may enjoy comparing and contrasting these two National Geographic videos.

Hawaii: Stranger in Paradise

Alaska and Hawaii

Hula Hands

Most hula dances, especially the ancient ones, tell of historical or legendary events. If possible, invite an expert to demonstrate a few of the hand movements. Students may also enjoy making up their own dance form to tell a story.

1 A rippling motion of the hands and arms is used to show water.

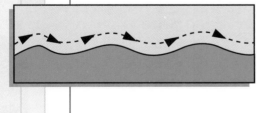

2 Rolling the hands, one over the other, stands for the ocean's roll.

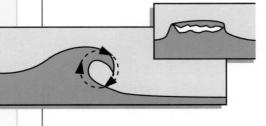

3

Instruct
and
Integrate

Cross-Curricular Activities

Choices for Social Studies

Discovering Tropical Fruits

Challenge Invite students to research Hawaiian fruits. Then have them conduct a poll to see how many classmates have tasted these fruits. They can compile their findings on a chart. If possible, provide tropical fruits for the class to taste. Encourage students to compare these fruits to the ones grown in your region.

Have I tasted it?		
	yes	no
papaya		
guava		
mango		
avocado		
pineapple		
banana		

Making a Relief Map of Hawaii
Cooperative Learning

Students can work together to create a relief map of eight major Hawaiian islands—Hawaii, Maui, Oahu, Kauai, Molokai, Niihau, Lanai, and Kahoolawe. Encourage them to form teams and consult encyclopedias and atlases. Each team collects topographical information about one island and coordinates with the other teams to create one large class map.

To make the dough:
1. Mix the salt and flour in a bowl.
2. Add the water. The dough should look like thick icing.
3. Stir to mix the dough.
4. Use the dough right away.

Materials
- 2 cups salt
- 1 cup flour
- 1 cup water
- heavy cardboard
- pencils and markers
- paint and brushes

1 Draw an outline of the eight main Hawaiian islands on heavy cardboard. Spread the dough inside the outline.

2 Build the mountains a layer at a time. Let each layer dry to prevent cracking.

3 Allow 1-3 days for the map to dry. Then paint the cities, the ocean, and other waterways. Label them.

Choices for Science

Collecting Shark Facts
Cooperative Learning

Have the class list ten types of sharks they want to investigate. Then encourage students to work in research teams. Each team selects a type of shark, illustrates it, and then cuts it out. On the flip side of each cutout, the team writes the type of shark and its characteristics, including physical features and behavior. Each team pins up its shark on a blue "ocean" bulletin board and has others guess which kind it is.

Types of Sharks

tiger	great white
thresher	dogfish
nurse	mako
hammerhead	bull
basking	scalloped

Making a Food Chain Mobile
Cooperative Learning

Invite students to construct a mobile illustrating a shark's food chain. Students can work in small groups. Each group selects a type of shark (perhaps the same one chosen for the activity above) and researches the food chain for that specific shark.

1 **Draw** on construction paper the creatures for your food chain. (Omit the plankton.)

2 **Make** each fish a two-sided figure by holding a blank piece of construction paper behind your drawing. Cut through both layers. Use markers to color both sides.

3 **Staple** the two sides together except for a small "fill" hole. Stuff the fish with shredded paper.

4 **For** plankton, use just a single layer of construction paper and no stuffing.

5 **Use** yarn or tape to attach each part of the food chain to a coat hanger for display.

Materials
- construction paper
- scissors
- markers or crayons
- stapler
- shredded paper
- yarn
- tape
- coat hanger

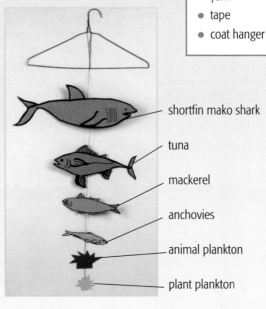

shortfin mako shark

tuna

mackerel

anchovies

animal plankton

plant plankton

Pigs

Activating Prior Knowledge

Invite students to summarize their knowledge about pigs. Map responses.

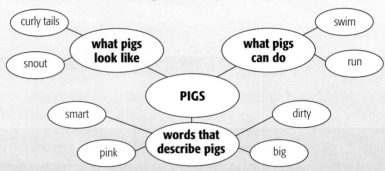

Keep the map on the board to check which of the traits Charles Ghigna explores in his poem.

Building Background

Discuss with students how a reader can tell immediately that "Pigs" is a poem. Here are elements you may wish to bring out in this discussion.

- It is divided into four groups of lines, or stanzas.
- Although each line begins with a capital letter as in a sentence, there is no end punctuation.
- The second and fourth line of each stanza rhyme.
- The poet repeats different sounds, such as the *p* and the *s* in the word *pigs*.

 Challenge

Ask students to read the poem aloud twice—once with no punctuation, and once by inserting punctuation where it would ordinarily be. Discuss how the rhythm of the poem is enhanced by leaving out the punctuation.

Pigs

Pigs are playful
Pigs are pink
Pigs are smarter
Than you think

Pigs are slippery
Pigs are stout
Pigs have noses
Called a snout

Pigs are pudgy
Pigs are plump
Pigs can run
But never jump

Pigs are loyal
Pigs are true
Pigs don't care for
Barbecue

115

Instruct and Integrate

Language Arts

Alliteration Have volunteers copy lines of the poem on the board, read them aloud, and then circle any sounds that are repeated.

Visual Literacy

Symbols Pigs are pervasive! Suggest that students keep their eyes out for how pigs are used as icons in advertising and as decoration for stationery and other writing materials. Perhaps students could bring objects to class that show pigs and discuss

- what trait of a pig is emphasized
- elements of the art that makes the pig humorous, sad, etc.

Music Link

Song Students will enjoy using a familiar tune, such as "The Alphabet Song" or "Twinkle, Twinkle, Little Star," to sing the poem.

Art Link

Class Book Have students work in small groups to create their own illustrations for Pigs. They might copy and illustrate each stanza and then compile the pages into a class book.

Interact with Literature

 ## Students Acquiring English

Expressions Explain that the phrase *don't care for* means "don't like."

 ## Home Connection

Poetry Students may enjoy reciting the poem to family members. Also encourage students to ask family members to share poems they know.

Reading-Writing Workshop

A Story

About the Workshop

This workshop includes story-specific suggestions and ideas to help you guide students as they use the writing process to write a fictional story.

Minilessons focus on characters and setting, plot, and dialogue. These elements form the assessment criteria at the end of the workshop.

Keep in mind these considerations:

- Friends or stereotypic heroes, heroines, and TV characters may still crop up in students' stories.
- Acknowledge and praise students' progress with the emerging skills of dialogue and description.
- Continue to read aloud quality picture books and guide students to discuss them as both writers and readers.

Connecting to Literature

Have students discuss how different authors used characters, setting, and events to write three different stories based on the traditional story of the three little pigs.

Introducing the Student Model

Explain that Kara Johnson, a third-grade student, wove together characters, setting, and events into an enjoyable story of her own. Have students read Kara's story about Mr. Pig's surprise and discuss the questions on page 117.

BE A WRITER

Surprise, Surprise
A story by Kara Johnson

Mr. Pig has a surprise in store for him! Read what happens on his special day.

Surprise, Surprise

It was a sunny day. The birds were singing, the trees and shrubs in full bloom, but Whooper City was a state of confusion. The streets were packed with people bustling all around.

Mr. Reindeer, the Whooper City mail carrier, had a very important letter for Mr. Pig. He could hear the shower running inside Mr. Pig's house. "Mr. Pig, Mr. Pig!" he screamed at the top of his lungs. Mr. Reindeer had a party to go to, so he was finishing his job as fast as possible. Finally, Mr. Pig came out in a towel and got the morning's mail.

A moment later Mr. Pig came down specially dressed because it was his birthday. He sifted through the mail, hoping to find a birthday card, but all he could find was a notice for a meeting at Ms. Rabbit's house. It read:

116

SKILL FINDER

PREWRITING/DRAFTING

Workshop Minilessons	Theme Resources
• Characters and Settings, p. 117A	*Writing*
• Beginning, Middle, End, p. 117B	• Writing a Sentence, p. 60D
• Dialogue, p. 117C	• Setting, p. 85

Dear Mr. Pig,
 We have another council meeting this afternoon. Please attend.

"Uh-oh," thought Mr. Pig, "the meeting starts soon." He moped all the way there, opened the door, and "SURPRISE!" All his friends jumped out, party things all around them. Mr. Pig grinned. "You remembered my birthday!" he cried.
 "Of course we did," they said. "Let's party!" They all danced until midnight.

Kara Johnson
Blake Lower School
Hopkins, Minnesota

Kara wrote this story when she was in the third grade. "When I started the story, I sat at my desk just thinking and thinking," she said. "Then this idea occurred to me to have Mr. Pig and Ms. Rabbit and to have Mr. Pig's birthday in the story. Once I had ideas, it was easy to write the story."
 Kara plays the piano, raises a baby lovebird, and likes water skiing. She would like to become a doctor.

117

Discussing the Model

Reading and Responding

- What did you like best about Kara's story?
- Were you surprised by the end? Why or why not?
- Have you ever been disappointed in some way but later been happily surprised? Tell about it.

Reading As a Writer

- What is the setting? (Whooper City)
- Who are the characters? (Mr. Pig, Mr. Reindeer)
- How does the beginning catch your interest? (creates a sense of excitement; raises interest in the letter)
- What details help you picture Mr. Pig and Mr. Reindeer? (Mr. Reindeer *screams at the top of his lungs;* Mr. Pig *came out in a towel;* Mr. Pig was *specially dressed;* Mr. Pig *moped.*)
- What problem develops for Mr. Pig? (He thought no one remembered his birthday.) Does the ending solve it in a way that makes sense? How else might the story have ended?

Characteristics of Stories

Help students list these story elements:

- *Purpose*: to tell an original story
- Main characters and a setting
- A beginning, a middle, and an end that focus on a problem and how the characters work it out
- Details that make the characters and events "come alive"

SKILL FINDER

PROOFREADING

Theme Resources	**Theme Resources**
Grammar	*Spelling*
• Subjects and Predicates, pp. 60J–60K	• Short Vowels, p. 60I
• Run-on Sentences, pp. 88J–88K	• Vowel-consonant-*e*, p. 88I
• Kinds of Sentences, pp. 114J–114K	• Long *a* and Long *e*, p. 114I
	• Words Often Misspelled, p. 117E

Reading-Writing Workshop (continued)
A Story

Characters and Settings

Resource: Anthology pp. 93–113

- Ask students how the author of *The Three Little Hawaiian Pigs and the Magic Shark* let them know what the shark was like. (by the shark's actions, by mean things the shark says)

- Ask students what they know about the pigs based on what they say and do. (like to play at the beach; are smart enough to recognize the magic shark in his disguises; one pig thinks hard-working pig is foolish)

- Help students write questions to use for developing story characters, such as
  1) What do the characters look like?
  2) How do they act?
  3) What do they say?
  4) What kinds of feelings or ideas do they have?
  5) What are their interests?

- Write the setting for each story in this theme on the chalkboard, and have students discuss how the setting does or does not affect the story.

Students can use the prewriting feature in the Learning Company's new elementary writing center to stimulate ideas for their writing.

Warm-up

Shared Writing

As a class, brainstorm an original story. Keep the brainstorming fast-moving and lively. Ask questions about the characters, where the story takes place, and what happens. Write students' ideas on the chalkboard or chart paper. Then become a storyteller, and have students help tell the story as you write it on chart paper. When finished drafting, encourage them to discuss improvements or changes they could make.

Prewriting

LAB, pp. 40–41

Choose a Story Topic

Students brainstorm and narrow possible story topics and then choose one to write about.

- **Make a List** Have each student list three to five story ideas.

- **Talk and Think About It** Have students tell their ideas to a partner, and narrow their choices by answering these questions about each idea: Can I picture the characters and setting clearly? Do I have enough ideas for the beginning, middle, and end? Do I really want to write about this idea?

Help with Topics

Brainstorm
Cooperative Learning

Draw a chart like the one below on the chalkboard. Have students use the questions to interview each other. Record their responses.

Story Ideas

| What people, animals, or creatures could be story characters? | Where could stories take place? | What problems could stories be about? |

Sources for Ideas

Personal Experiences Invite students to draw pictures of their memorable experiences. Help them see these as story ideas.

Traditional Literature Suggest that students rewrite a traditional story with new plot twists, characters, or settings.

Prewriting *(continued)*

Plan the Story   Students plan their stories before they write their first drafts.

- **Think of Details** Have students make a story map or draw detailed pictures of their characters, setting, and beginning, middle, and end.
- **Audience Check** Have students tell their stories to partners.

Help with Planning

Puppet Walk-through

Have students use their fingers or make simple stick puppets to rehearse story ideas with partners. Prompt listeners to ask questions about parts of the plot that may be unclear or distracting.

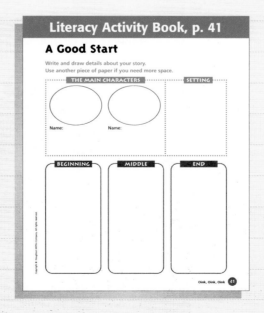

Literacy Activity Book, p. 40

Terrific Topics

Story Ideas Do any of these ideas spark an idea for your story?
- a strange friendship between a wolf and a pig
- a trip in a time machine
- taking a rocket to Jupiter
- finding a lost puppy
- an amazing amusement park
- a talking ant

Can I picture the characters and setting clearly?

My Story Ideas
Write five ideas for your own story here.

Think about each idea you wrote. Then ask yourself the three questions.

Do I have enough ideas for the beginning, middle, and end?

Do I really want to write about this idea?

Oink, Oink, Oink   40

Literacy Activity Book, p. 41

A Good Start

Write and draw details about your story.
Use another piece of paper if you need more space.

| THE MAIN CHARACTERS | | SETTING |

Name: Name:

| BEGINNING | MIDDLE | END |

Oink, Oink, Oink   41

M I N I L E S S O N

Beginning, Middle, End

Resource: Anthology pp. 37–59, 69–87, 93–113

- Review the purposes of the main parts of a story.

  Beginning: to introduce the main characters, setting, and a situation or a problem

  Middle: to show how the characters try to work out the situation

  End: to show how the situation works out

  Tell students that these parts form the *plot* of the story.

- Map the beginning, middle, and end of the stories in this theme. Ask students to compare and contrast the main parts.

- Take a class vote to find out which ending students prefer. Ask volunteers to explain their choice. Elicit that each ending works because it makes sense with that story and makes the story feel finished. Contrast the story endings with a weak ending, such as the evil character gives up after only one try, which would end the story too soon and in a disappointing way.

Reading-Writing Workshop (continued)
A Story

Dialogue

Resource: Anthology pp. 93–113

- Invite students to do a Reader's Theater reading of *The Three Little Hawaiian Pigs and the Magic Shark* from the beginning until the shark destroys the first house.

- Help students determine if the examples of dialogue
  1) show what is happening
  2) show what characters think
  3) show what a character is like

- Help students summarize that writers can use dialogue to help tell the story and bring the characters to life.

- Point out that a speaker's exact words are enclosed in *quotation marks* and the writer began a *new paragraph* each time a different character began to speak.

Self-Assessment

Have students evaluate their stories, using the Revising Checklist.

Drafting

Students write the first drafts of their stories, using any pictures, story maps, or other aids they have prepared.

Help with Drafting

Picture It

Suggest that students close their eyes and picture their stories as movies. Which part of the story can they see most clearly? the beginning? one of the events? Encourage them to write about that "scene" first.

Drafting Strategies

Encourage students to write as much as they can and not to worry about grammar and spelling now. Remind them to skip every other line so that they have room to make changes later on.

TECH TIPS Students can set their document for double spacing to allow extra space for revisions.

Revising

LAB, p. 42

Students revise their stories and discuss them in writing conferences.

Revising Checklist

☐ Does my story have a beginning, middle, and end?

☐ Does it tell about one problem or situation?

☐ Did I use dialogue?

☐ Could my readers picture the characters and events?

Revising (continued)

Writing Conference

Cooperative Learning Encourage students to read their stories aloud to you or to one or more classmates. They can use the Questions for a Writing Conference to guide the discussion.

Questions for a Writing Conference

- Does the story begin in an interesting way?
- Are any parts not clear?
- Do any parts not belong in this story?
- Does the ending make sense? Can it be more interesting?
- What other ways might the story end?

Help with Revising

Author's Chair
Cooperative Learning

Set up a certain time and place each day for students to use an author's chair. Volunteers can use this opportunity to read aloud their drafts and discuss them with the class.

TECH TIPS

Have students record their compliments and suggestions on the computer. They can then print out the notes for the writing conference.

New Ending

Suggest that students write another ending for their stories, present both endings in their writing conference, and choose the one they like better.

Revising Strategies

Demonstrate strategies for revising, such as drawing arrows for moving text, using carets for inserting words or phrases, or taping strips of paper over or beside parts of the story to change or add blocks of text.

Additional Questions for Writing Conferences

These questions may be useful during teacher-student conferences.

- What happened when . . . ?
- Why did this character [do something, say something]?
- Is [this part] really important to the story?
- What did [this scene, this character] look like? Help me picture it.
- What did this character say when . . . ?
- Can you use dialogue to tell some parts of the story?

If your class is using the elementary writing center from The Learning Company, you can add comments to your students' work using the sticky notes feature.

Literacy Activity Book, p. 42

Take Another Look

♦ Revising Checklist ♦

Read your story to yourself. Ask yourself these questions and make changes.

☐ Does it have a beginning, a middle, and an end?
☐ Does it tell about one problem or situation?
☐ Did I use dialogue?
☐ Could my readers picture the characters and the events?

Questions for a Writing Conference
Use these questions to help you discuss your story with a classmate.
- Does the story begin in an interesting way?
- Are any parts not clear?
- Do any parts not belong in this story?
- Does the ending make sense?
- Can it be more interesting?
- What other ways might the story end?

Write notes to remember ideas.
My Notes

42 Oink, Oink, Oink

Reading-Writing Workshop (continued)
A Story

 Students using The Learning Company's **Ultimate Writing & Creativity Center** software can add graphics to their story from the notebook of pictures.

MINILESSON

Spelling

Words Often Misspelled

Write the Spelling Words on the board, say them, and have students repeat them. Work with students to identify the part of each word that is likely to be misspelled.

Spelling Words

and	going	you
said	some	your
goes	something	

Challenge Words

tonight	field
lying	enough

Additional Spelling Words

friend	where
school	myself

> SEE
> **5**-Day Planner
> Spelling Plan p. 114I

Spelling Assessment

Pretest

1. Mr. Pig <u>and</u> Ms. Rabbit are friends.
2. His friends <u>said</u> they wanted to party.
3. Mr. Pig <u>goes</u> to Ms. Rabbit's house.
4. He thought he was <u>going</u> to a meeting.
5. Did they have <u>some</u> cake?
6. I have to tell you <u>something</u>.
7. Did <u>you</u> get our card?
8. When is <u>your</u> birthday?

Test Use the Pretest sentences.

Challenge Words

9. The <u>field</u> is full of mice.
10. Tim is <u>lying</u> in the grass.
11. I have had <u>enough</u> to eat.
12. My friend will sleep over <u>tonight</u>.

Challenge Words Practice Have students write a poem, using the Challenge Words.

Literacy Activity Book

Spelling Practice: pp. 127–128
Take-Home Word Lists: pp. 163–164

Proofreading

Students proofread their stories, using the Proofreading Checklist and the proofreading marks in the Handbook of the *Literacy Activity Book*. Encourage students to make as many corrections as they can by themselves or by consulting with classmates.

Grammar/ Spelling Connections

- **Checking Sentences** Remind students to check that every sentence has a subject and a predicate, that they have used correct end marks, and that they have avoided run-on sentences. *pp. 60J–60K, 88J–88K, 114J–114K*

- **Spelling** Remind students to check the spelling of short and long vowel sounds in the words they used as well as the spelling of any Words Often Misspelled. *pp. 60I, 88I, 114I, 117E*

Publishing and Sharing

Students make neat final copies of their stories and choose a way to share them.

Materials

- construction paper
- scissors
- glue
- magazines for cutting

Ideas for Publishing and Sharing

Make a Pop-up Book

1 For each page, fold a piece of paper in half lengthwise. Cut slits across the fold.

2 Pull out the pop-up tab. Glue a picture to the tab, being careful it does not hang down below the tab.

3 Glue the top half of one page to the bottom half of the next page. Pictures are always inside.

More Ideas for Publishing and Sharing

Writing Buddies

Form writing partnerships between a student in your class and a younger or older student in the school.

Record a Tape

Record students reading their stories on video- or audiotape. Share the tapes with other classes, or send them home.

Reflecting/Self-Assessment

Use the Self-Assessment questions, or others of your own, to help students reflect on and evaluate their experience writing a story. Students can discuss or write their responses.

Evaluating Writing

Use the criteria below to evaluate students' stories.

Criteria for Evaluating Stories

- The story has a beginning, a middle, and an end that focus on one main problem or situation.
- Details are used to develop the characters, setting, and events.
- Dialogue is used to develop characters and to help tell the story.
- The ending shows how the problem or situation works out and makes the story feel finished.

Portfolio Opportunity

- Save students' final copies to show their understanding of writing a story.
- Save students' planning aids and drafts to show their use of the writing process.

Sample Scoring Rubric

1	2	3	4
The story meets the criteria only minimally. The characters, setting, and plot are poorly developed, with little or no detail. Events lack a clear sequence and are confusing.	The story is sketchy or inconsistent in some way. There may be minor gaps in the sequence. More details are needed to make the characters, setting, and events come alive.	The story is coherent and detailed, although some parts could be better developed. Nonessential details do not seriously detract. The story might rate a 4 except for significant errors.	The story meets all the evaluation criteria; is unified, clearly sequenced, sufficiently detailed, and has a minimum of spelling or mechanical errors.

Building Background

Ask students why this play belongs in a theme in which all the stories have pigs or piglike animals as characters. Students might compare the illustration of the boar with the illustrations of the javelinas in *The Three Little Javelinas*.

Explain that a fable often has animal characters that talk and act like humans. It ends with a moral, or lesson.

Students Acquiring English Although this play is short, it will be challenging for students because each line is critical in comprehending the moral. Provide rehearsal time so that students will enjoy acting out the play.

Extra Support Tell students that a play is meant to be read aloud. Ask why it is important to monitor your understanding of the lines before you read them aloud. (It's part of rehearsing for a play.) Then assign each student a partner for oral reading.

The Wild Boar & the Fox
An Aesop's Fable retold by Dr. Albert Cullum

Characters: Boar, Fox
Staging: The story takes place in the middle of a forest. A large table or desk can represent a sturdy tree trunk.

Boar: Now that I have a moment, I think I will sharpen my teeth. Here is a nice sturdy tree that will help me. *(Rubs and rubs his tusks against the very hard tree trunk.)*

Fox: What in the world are you doing, Boar?

Boar: I'm sharpening my tusks.

118

Background: FYI

Aesop A Greek slave who lived during the sixth century B.C., Aesop is the reputed author of hundreds of fables. Ask students if they know any of Aesop's tales, such as "The Tortoise and the Hare" and "The Ant and the Grasshopper."

Fox: That seems like a very silly thing to be doing.

Boar: Really! Why?

Fox: It's silly, for I don't see any danger about. I don't see a hunter and his dogs coming after you!

Boar: I don't see a hunter and his dogs coming after me, either.

Fox: Well, then, why all the nonsense about sharpening your tusks?

Boar: Fox, I don't think you understand. Wouldn't it be foolish of me to wait until the hunter and his dogs attacked before I sharpened my tusks? I think you are silly, not me!

Moral:

Think ahead and be prepared.

119

MINILESSON

Instruct and Integrate

Genre

Plays

Teach/Model

If any students have acted in a play, ask them to discuss how they prepared for it. Then brainstorm with students how reading a play is different from reading a story.

```
              all          stage
            dialogue     directions
                  \       /
                   PLAYS
                  /       \
         colons instead   description
         of quotation     comes from
         marks            dialogue
```

Discuss how plays are often shorter than stories.

Practice/Apply

Ask volunteers to read the script aloud. Encourage them to read their lines with expression.

Interact with Literature

  Extra Support

Point out the boar's tusks. Ask students to name another animal with tusks and to speculate what the tusks are used for. Discuss how rubbing creates friction, which sharpens the tusks. Have students think of tools or equipment that are sharpened by friction.

Interact with Literature

Discussion

Discuss the moral of the fable with students. Do they agree with it? Do they disagree? Ask students to suggest times when they have thought ahead and were thus prepared for some situation.

Theme Assessment Wrap-Up

Time: About 1 hour

Evaluates:

1 **Theme Concept:** Traditional tales can be retold in a variety of humorous altered versions.

2 **Skills:** Story Structure/ Summarizing, Compare and Contrast

This is a brief, informal performance assessment activity. For a more extended reading-writing performance assessment, see the Integrated Theme Test.

Literacy Activity Book, p. 43

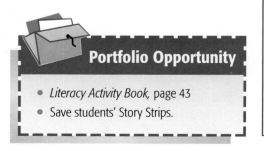

New Pigs on the Block

Read this summary of "The Three Little Pigs."

Three pigs built houses of straw, sticks, and bricks. A wolf blew down the straw and the stick houses and ate the two pigs. The wolf couldn't blow down the brick house, so he jumped down the chimney and fell into a pot of soup on the fire. Then the third pig ate the wolf.

Invent your own version of "The Three Little Pigs." Use the chart to help you. Check whether each part of your story is **alike** or **different** from "The Three Little Pigs."

	Alike	Different
Characters		
Problem		
Events		
1.		
2.		
3.		
Ending		

On a strip of paper, draw your story scenes in order. Use your story strip to tell your version of "The Three Little Pigs."

Checklist Use this list to check your work.
- ❏ My story retells "The Three Little Pigs" in a new way.
- ❏ My story has characters, a problem, events, and an ending.
- ❏ I can use my story strip to tell my story.
- ❏ I can compare my story to "The Three Little Pigs."

Oink, Oink, Oink **43**

Portfolio Opportunity

- *Literacy Activity Book,* page 43
- Save students' Story Strips.

Making Story Strips

LAB, p. 43

Materials
- paper
- glue
- tag board
- scissors
- markers

Introducing

Invite students to make story strips that tell their own version of the traditional story "The Three Little Pigs." Have them use *Literacy Activity Book* page 43 to plan their project. Make a model story strip by following these steps:

1 Cut strips of paper 3" wide and glue them together, forming a strip about 30" long. Mark off 3"x 4" frames. Illustrate the frames in story order, from left to right.

2 Make a viewing screen from a 6"x 6" sheet of tag board by marking and cutting two 3 1/2" vertical slits, spaced 4" apart.

3 Slide the left end of the strip through the right-hand slit of the screen from back to front. Then pass it through the left-hand slit from front to back.

Evaluating

As students slide the strip through the screen, have them summarize their versions of "The Three Little Pigs" for the class. Then have them compare and contrast their version with the traditional story. Evaluate the presentation using the scoring rubric.

Scoring Rubric

Criterion	1	2	3	4
Retells a new version of a traditional tale	Story doesn't resemble traditional tale	Story vaguely resembles traditional tale	Story generally resembles traditional tale	Story is a creative retelling of traditional tale
Shows understanding of story structure	Focuses on single, unconnected elements	Summary is disorganized or incomplete	Summary includes all story elements	Summary is complete and well organized
Compares and contrasts	Does not compare or contrast stories	Gives similarities or differences, but not both	Compares and contrasts tales in a general way	Compares and contrasts several aspects of tales

Choices for Assessment

Informal Assessment

Review the Informal Assessment Checklist and observation notes to determine:

- Did students use the reading strategies?
- Did students' responses during and after reading indicate comprehension?
- How well did students use the Writing Process?

Formal Assessment

Select formal tests that meet your needs:

- Integrated Theme Test for Oink, Oink, Oink
- Theme Skills Test for Oink, Oink, Oink
- Benchmark Progress Test

See the *Teacher's Assessment Handbook* for guidelines for administering and scoring tests.

Portfolio Assessment

Introducing Portfolios to the Class

Explain to students that their portfolios will show samples of their work and how they improve over time.

- Have students create temporary collection folders to keep all their work for the theme.
- Partway through the first theme, have students create their portfolios for special work selected from the collection. Encourage them to decorate their portfolios to reflect their interests.

Selecting Materials for the Portfolio

Meet with students to review the work in their collections. Discuss your criteria as you pick samples that reflect important categories. Also include samples of students' best work and areas of improvement.

Grading Work in Portfolios

You don't need to grade all the work in portfolios. You may wish to grade formal tests, some student writing, and some *Literacy Activity Book* pages. See also the *Teacher's Assessment Handbook*.

Managing Assessment

Testing Options

Question How can I assess students' progress?

Answer *Invitations to Literacy* includes a range of testing options at the end of a theme. Select the options that best meet your needs:

Performance Assessment

The Performance Assessment on page 119A is a hands-on activity that evaluates student understanding of the theme concept and major comprehension skills.

Integrated Theme Test

This test provides a new theme-related reading selection. It uses written and multiple-choice formats to evaluate reading and language skills and strategies.

Theme Skills Test

This test evaluates discrete literacy skills of the theme. Sections of this test can be used to evaluate specific areas of concern.

Benchmark Progress Test

This test can be given two or three times a year to evaluate students' overall progress in reading. It is not theme-related.

See also the *Teacher's Assessment Handbook.*

M I N I L E S S O N   /   A S S E S S M E N T

Spelling Review

Review with students the Spelling Words and, if appropriate, the Challenge Words from the spelling lessons on pages 60I, 88I, 114I, and 117E. Have volunteers summarize each spelling principle and explain how the words in each lesson illustrate the principle.

Pretest/Test

1. Which <u>three</u> stories are <u>your</u> favorites?
2. The pig used its <u>nose</u> to <u>smell</u>.
3. The <u>smoke</u> was <u>black</u>.
4. The water close to the <u>beach</u> is <u>deep</u>.
5. Dad <u>said</u> that we were <u>going</u> to the store.
6. Give the baby <u>something</u> to <u>play</u> with.
7. Please <u>shut</u> the door and fasten the <u>chain</u>.
8. Where should we look <u>next</u> for <u>mice</u>?

Challenge Words

9. It will be <u>easy</u> to see the moon <u>tonight</u>.
10. Please <u>knock</u> on the door when you <u>arrive</u>.
11. The size of the <u>reef</u> will <u>amaze</u> you.
12. There is <u>plenty</u> of corn in that <u>field</u>.

S E E

5-Day Planner

Spelling Plan p. 114I

Challenge

Challenge Words Practice Have students use Challenge Words to write sentences that a little pig might say.

Literacy Activity Book

Spelling Practice: pp. 129–130
Take-Home Word Lists: pp. 163–164

Celebrating the Theme

Safe Houses!

- Aluminum siding protects from wind!
- Small chimney keeps out intruders!
- Solid brick walls prevent fire damage!

See the **Teacher's Resource Disk** for theme-related Teacher Support material.

Choices for Celebrating

Design a Real Estate Ad

Ask students to think about houses and buildings in their community that might serve as a safe haven for characters like the three little pigs. Groups of students could make real estate shopping guides featuring photos or drawings of places in their community along with descriptions that emphasize why the pigs would feel safe there.

Home Connection Invite students to work with family members to find photos of homes in their community, perhaps by scanning newspaper real estate ads or taking pictures themselves.

Make a Wanted Poster

Have students celebrate the villains in this theme by making wanted posters of them. You may want to first review the type of information often found on wanted posters, such as

- a photo of the suspect
- information about the crime and previous convictions
- a reward for information
- where the suspect was last seen

A Class Party

Set aside one day to celebrate what students have accomplished during the theme. Invite parents or other classes to attend. Students may enjoy creating a backdrop for the celebration that reflects the theme, such as a fantasy forest. With students, plan a schedule of activities such as

- readings of student writing projects
- displays of artwork or projects
- a dramatization of "The Three Little Pigs"

Students Acquiring English Students can dramatize a story from their culture in their primary language. Perhaps they can teach the class a refrain to repeat.

Self-Assessment

Have students meet in small groups to compare and discuss their Selection Connections charts (*Literacy Activity Book*, p. 8). Ask groups to share answers to questions such as the following:

- Which story setting did I learn the most about?
- What things did I learn in this theme that I would like to know more about?
- What other folktales would be fun to reverse the way "The Three Little Pigs" was reversed in this theme? Why?

Glossary

Some of the words in this book may have pronunciations or meanings you do not know. This glossary can help you by telling you how to pronounce those words and by telling you the meanings for the words as they are used in this book.

You can find out how to pronounce any glossary word by using the special spelling after the word and the key that runs across the bottom of the glossary pages.

The full pronunciation key on the next page shows how to pronounce each consonant and vowel in a special spelling. The pronunciation key at the bottom of the glossary pages is a shortened form of the full key.

310

Full Pronunciation Key

Consonant Sounds

b	**bib**, ca**bb**age	kw	**ch**oir, **qu**ick	t	**t**ight, s**t**o**pp**ed
ch	**ch**urch, sti**tch**	l	**l**id, need**l**e, ta**ll**	th	ba**th**, **th**in
d	**d**ee**d**, maile**d**,	m	a**m**, **m**an, du**mb**	_th_	ba**th**e, **th**is
	pu**dd**le	n	**n**o, sudde**n**	v	ca**v**e, val**v**e, **v**ine
f	**f**ast, **f**i**f**e, o**ff**,	ng	thi**ng**, i**nk**	w	**w**ith, **w**olf
	phrase, rou**gh**	p	**p**o**p**, ha**pp**y	y	**y**es, **y**olk, on**i**on
g	**g**a**g**, **g**et, fin**g**er	r	**r**oa**r**, **rh**yme	z	**r**o**s**e, **s**i**z**e,
h	**h**at, **wh**o	s	mi**ss**, **s**au**c**e,		**x**ylophone, **z**ebra
hw	**wh**ich, **wh**ere		**sc**ene, **s**ee	zh	gara**g**e, plea**s**ure,
j	**j**ud**g**e, **g**em	sh	di**sh**, **sh**ip, **s**ugar,		vi**s**ion
k	**c**at, **k**i**ck**, s**ch**ool		ti**ss**ue		

Vowel Sounds

ă	r**a**t, l**au**gh	ŏ	h**o**rrible, p**o**t	ŭ	c**u**t, fl**oo**d, r**ou**gh,
ā	**a**pe, **ai**d, p**ay**	ō	g**o**, r**ow**, t**oe**,		s**o**me
â	**ai**r, c**a**re, w**ea**r		th**ou**gh	û	c**i**rcle, f**u**r, h**ea**rd,
ä	f**a**ther, k**o**ala, y**a**rd	ô	**a**ll, c**au**ght, f**o**r,		t**e**rm, t**u**rn, **u**rge,
ĕ	p**e**t, pl**ea**sure, **a**ny		p**aw**		w**o**rd
ē	b**e**, b**ee**, **ea**sy,	oi	b**oy**, n**oi**se, **oi**l	yōō	c**u**re
	pian**o**	ou	c**ow**, **ou**t	yōō	ab**u**se, **u**se
ĭ	**i**f, p**i**t, b**u**sy	ōō	f**u**ll, t**oo**k, w**o**lf	ə	**a**bout, sil**e**nt,
ī	b**y**, p**ie**, h**i**gh	ōō	b**oo**t, fr**ui**t, fl**ew**		penc**i**l, lem**o**n,
î	d**ea**r, d**ee**r, f**ie**rce,				circ**u**s
	m**e**re				

Stress Marks

Primary Stress ´: bi•ol•o•gy [bī ŏl´ ə jē]
Secondary Stress ´: bi•o•log•i•cal [bī´ ə lŏj´ i kəl]

Pronunciation key © 1993 by Houghton Mifflin Company. Adapted and reprinted by permission from _The American Heritage Children's Dictionary._

311

ac•cent (**ăk´** sĕnt´) _noun_ A small detail that looks different than the things around it, usually added for color or decoration: _The bedroom was blue with pink pillows for_ **accent**.

a•do•be (ə **dō´** bē) _noun_ Brick that is made from clay and straw and dried in the sun: _Many houses in the southwestern United States are built with_ **adobe**.

adobe

ADOBE
Adobe is a Spanish word. It goes back to the Arabic word _attoba_ meaning "the brick."

an•xious•ly (**ăngk´** shəs lē´) _adverb_ In a worried way: _The crowd watched_ **anxiously** _as the firefighter carried the child down the ladder._

art•ist (**är´** tĭst) _noun_ **1.** A person who practices an art, such as painting or music: _The_ **artist** _displayed her paintings in the town hall._ **2.** A person who shows great skill in what he or she does: _Mr. Brown's bake shop has the prettiest wedding cakes in town. He is a true_ **artist**.

bar•rel (**băr´** əl) _noun_ A large, round container with a flat top and bottom: _On the ship, fresh water was stored in large wooden_ **barrels**.

barrels

bel•low (**bĕl´** ō) _verb_ To say in a deep, loud voice: _The police officer_ **bellowed** _to the crowd to get away from the burning building._

brace (brās) _verb_ To get ready for something difficult or unpleasant: _As Eric walked toward the lake, he_ **braced** _himself against the shock of the cold water._

312

---

bur•y (**bĕr´** ē) _verb_ To hide or cover by placing under the ground: _The wind blew sand over the beach and_ **buried** _my sandals._

cac•tus (**kăk´** tas) _noun_ A plant with thick, often spiny, leafless stems that grows in hot, dry places.

cactus

crav•ing (**krā´** vĭng) _noun_ A very strong desire for something: _As I passed the bakery, I suddenly had a_ **craving** _for a piece of apple pie._

cus•tom (**kŭs´** təm) _noun_ Something that members of a group usually do: _One birthday_ **custom** _is to blow out the candles on a birthday cake._

des•ert (**dĕz´** ərt) _noun_ A dry area of land that is usually sandy and without trees: _Very few plants grow in the_ **desert** _because it hardly ever rains._

DESERT
Desert comes from a Latin word meaning "to abandon, or leave behind." When a place was abandoned, it was called a _desert_.

de•sign (dĭ **zĭn´**) _noun_ A pleasing pattern of lines and shapes: _The wrapping paper was decorated with colorful flower and leaf_ **designs**.

di•a•mond (**dī´** ə mənd) _noun_ A shape (◊) with four equal sides.

dust storm (dŭst stôrm) _noun_ Strong winds that carry clouds of sand and dust across an area: _During the_ **dust storm**, _Dad had to stop the car because he couldn't see to drive._

e•rupt (ĭ **rŭpt´**) _verb_ To burst out violently: _The moving van knocked over the fire hydrant, and water_ **erupted** _into the air._

313

F

fu•ri•ous (fyŏŏr′ ē əs) *adjective* Full of anger: *Carlos was **furious** when he saw that the puppy had chewed his favorite shoes.*

G

gas (găs) *noun* A poisonous substance that is not liquid or solid and fills the air: *The instructions for the new stove said to call for repairs right away if we smelled **gas**.*

goo•ey (gŏŏ′ ē) *adjective* Very sticky: *The jar of honey fell off the table and broke into a **gooey** mess on the floor.*

GOOEY
Gooey is the adjective form of the noun *goo* which, in turn, may come from the word *burgoo*. *Burgoo* was a thick kind of oatmeal served to sailors long ago.

grunt (grŭnt) *verb* To say or speak in a short, deep, harsh voice: *Grandpa sleepily **grunted** an answer to my question.*

I

in•spire (ĭn spīr′) *verb* To cause someone to think or act in a particular way: *My grandmother, who made all of her own clothes, **inspired** me to learn to sew.*

M

mar•ket (mär′ kĭt) *noun* A place where people buy and sell goods: *Mr. Choy goes to the **market** each morning to buy fresh fish for his restaurant.*

market

---

mo•las•ses (mə lăs′ ĭz) *noun* A thick, sweet syrup: *Marta likes to put **molasses** on her pancakes.*

MOLASSES
Molasses comes from the Portuguese word *melaço*, which means "honey."

O

or•ders (ôr′ dərz) *noun* Certain commands or rules that must be followed: *A soldier must follow the commander's **orders**.*

P

pang (păng) *noun* A short but sharp feeling, as of pain: *Just before dinner, I began having little **pangs** of hunger.*

pas•sen•ger (păs′ ən jər) *noun* A person riding in a vehicle, such as a car, a plane, or a boat: *All the **passengers** in our car must wear their seat belts.*

passengers

pitch•er (pĭch′ ər) *noun* A container, usually with a handle, for holding and pouring liquids: *Mom placed a **pitcher** of cold milk on the table.*

plot (plŏt) *verb* To plan secretly: *Dad will **plot** a way to sneak Mom's birthday present into the house without her seeing it.*

poi•son•ous (poi′ zə nəs) *adjective* Causing sickness or death when swallowed or breathed: *The firefighter had to wear a mask to protect him from the **poisonous** air.*

prowl (proul) *verb* To sneak about as if hunting or looking for something: *The stray dog was **prowling** the streets looking for food.*

---

pyr•a•mid (pĭr′ ə mĭd) *noun* A figure that has a flat bottom and sides shaped like triangles.

pyramid

R

rec•og•nize (rĕk′ əg nīz′) *verb* To see and know from past experience: *Even from far away, Becky could **recognize** her brother in the crowd by his red cowboy hat.*

res•cue (rĕs′ kyŏŏ) *adjective* Being able to save from danger or harm: *The **rescue** team hurried up the mountain to help the hurt hiker.*

S

scene (sēn) *noun* A view of a place: *The photograph showed a **scene** of a cabin by a lake.*

scheme (skēm) *verb* To make up a plan for: *Our team will **scheme** to win the game.*

sur•vi•vor (sər vī′ vər) *noun* Someone who manages to stay alive: *All the **survivors** of the car accident had been wearing seat belts.*

T

tat•tered (tăt′ ərd) *adjective* Torn and ragged looking: *By the time Andy got the stuffed animal away from the puppy, it was torn and **tattered**.*

TATTERED
Tattered comes from the Scandinavian word *tötturr*, which means "rag."

ti•tle (tīt′ l) *noun* A name given to a person to show rank, office, or job: *After finishing medical school, my uncle's new **title** became Doctor.*

ti•tle fight (tīt′ l fīt) *noun* A boxing match to determine the champion: *Joe Louis first won the heavyweight championship in a **title fight** in 1937.*

---

trem•ble (trĕm′ bəl) *verb* **1.** To shake from fear or the cold: *I knew Aunt Shirley was afraid of something when I saw her hands **trembling**.* **2.** To shake: *The earthquake made our house **tremble**.*

tri•an•gle (trī′ ăng′ gəl) A shape (△) with three sides.

tum•ble•weed (tŭm′ bəl wēd′) *noun* A plant that breaks off from its roots when it dies and is blown about in the wind.

tumbleweed

V

vol•ca•no (vŏl kā′ nō) *noun* An opening in the earth through which lava, ash, and hot gases come out.

volcano

VOLCANO
Volcano comes from the Latin word *Vulcanus* and the name of a god in Roman mythology. In these myths, *Vulcan*, "the god of fire," was thought to cause volcanoes.

voy•age (voi′ ĭj) A long trip to a far away place: *The Wu family took a long **voyage** across the Pacific Ocean when they moved to the United States.*

W

whirl (wûrl) *verb* To spin around in circles: *The children **whirled** round and round until they felt dizzy.*

whirl•wind (wûrl′ wĭnd′) *noun* A current of air that spins rapidly around: *The **whirlwind** picked up the pile of leaves and spun them around in circles.*

ACKNOWLEDGMENTS

For each of the selections listed below, grateful acknowledgment is made for permission to excerpt and/or reprint original or copyrighted material, as follows:

Selections

Selection from *Earthwise at school*, by Linda Lowery and Marybeth Lorbiecki. Copyright © 1993 by Linda Lowery and Marybeth Lorbiecki. Reprinted by permission of Carolrhoda Books.

Family Pictures, written and illustrated by Carmen Lomas Garza. Copyright © 1990 by Carmen Lomas Garza. Reprinted by permission of Children's Book Press.

A Fruit & Vegetable Man, by Roni Schotter, illustrated by Jeanette Winter. Text copyright © 1993 by Roni Schotter. Illustrations copyright © 1993 by Jeanette Winter. Reprinted by permission of Little, Brown and Company.

"History Makers," from June/July 1993 *Kids Discover* magazine. Copyright © 1993 by Kids Discover. Reprinted by permission.

"Make Your Own Erupting Volcano," from *Science Wizardry for Kids*, by Margaret Kenda and Phyllis S. Williams. Copyright © 1992 by Margaret Kenda and Phyllis S. Williams. Reprinted by permission of Barrons Educational Series, Inc., Hauppage, NY.

Miss Nelson Is Missing!, by Harry Allard, illustrated by James Marshall. Text copyright © 1977 by Harry Allard. Illustrations copyright © 1977 by James Marshall. Reprinted by permission of Houghton Mifflin Company. All rights reserved.

"Molasses Tank Explosion Injures 50 and Kills 11," from the *Boston Daily Globe*, January 16, 1919. Public domain.

"My Hairy Neighbors," by Susan Lowell, from March 1994 *Ranger Rick* magazine. Copyright © 1994 by the National Wildlife Federation. Reprinted by permission.

Patrick and the Great Molasses Explosion, by Marjorie Stover. Copyright © 1985 by Dillon Press. Reprinted by permission of Silver Burdett Press.

Pompeii . . . Buried Alive! by Edith Kunhardt. Copyright © 1987 by Edith Kunhardt. Reprinted by permission of Random House, Inc.

"Pronunciation Key," from the *American Heritage Children's Dictionary*. Copyright © 1994 by Houghton Mifflin Company. Reprinted by permission. All rights reserved.

"This Little Piggy!" by Linda Granfield, from November 1992 *Owl* magazine. Copyright © 1992 by Linda Granfield. Reprinted by permission of the author and the Young Naturalist Foundation.

The Three Little Hawaiian Pigs and the Magic Shark, by Donivee Martin Laird. Copyright © 1981 by Donivee Martin Laird. Reprinted by permission of Barnaby Books, a Hawaii Partnership.

The Three Little Javelinas, by Susan Lowell. Illustrated by Jim Harris. Text copyright © 1992 by Susan

Lowell. Illustrations copyright © 1992 by Jim Harris. Reprinted by permission of Northland Publishing, Flagstaff, AZ.

The Three Little Wolves and the Big Bad Pig, by Eugene Trivizas, illustrated by Helen Oxenbury. Text copyright © 1993 by Eugene Trivizas. Illustrations copyright © 1993 by Helen Oxenbury. Reprinted by permission of Margaret K. McElderry Books, Simon & Schuster Children's Publishing Division. First published by Heinemann Young Books in Great Britain.

The Titanic, adapted and arranged by Alan Lomax. Copyright © renewed 1964 by Ludlow Music, Inc., New York, NY. Reprinted by permission.

The Titanic: Lost . . . and Found, by Judy Donnelly. Copyright © 1987 by Judy Donnelly. Reprinted by permission of Random House, Inc.

Titanic Trivia, by A.F.J. Marshello. Copyright © 1987 by A.F.J. Marshello. Reprinted by permission of the Titanic Historical Society, Inc., Indian Orchard, MA 01151.

"What's Up, Pup?" by Lyle Prescott, from July 1994 *Ranger Rick* magazine. Copyright © 1994 by the National Wildlife Federation. Reprinted by permission.

"The Wild Boar & the Fox," from *Aesop's Fables: Plays for Young Children*, by Dr. Albert Cullum. Copyright © 1993 by Fearon Teacher Aids, a Paramount Communications Company. Reprinted by permission of Paramount Communications.

When Jo Louis Won the Title, by Belinda Rochelle, illustrated by Larry Johnson. Text copyright © 1994 by Belinda Rochelle. Illustrations copyright © 1994 by Larry Johnson. Reprinted by permission of Houghton Mifflin Company. All rights reserved.

Poetry

"Away from Town," from *Runny Days, Sunny Days*, by Aileen Fisher. Copyright © 1958 by Aileen Fisher. Reprinted by permission of the author.

"City," by Langston Hughes, from *The Langston Hughes Reader*. Copyright © 1958 by Langston Hughes. Copyright renewed 1986 by George Houston Bass. Reprinted by permission of Harold Ober Associates, Inc.

"Pigs," by Charles Ghigna, from January 1993 *Ranger Rick* magazine. Copyright © 1993 by Charles Ghigna. Reprinted by permission of the author.

Additional Acknowledgments

Special thanks to the following teachers whose students' compositions are included in the Be a Writer features in this level.

David Burton, Blake Lower School, Hopkins, Minnesota; Linda Chick, Paloma Elementary School, San Marcos, California; Debora Adam, South Dover Elementary School, Dover, Delaware

CREDITS

Illustration 12–27 James Marshall; 37–59 Helen Oxenbury; Courtesy of Eugene Trivizas and Reed Children's Books; 92–113 Don Stuart; 115 Brian Lies; 118–119 Loretta Lustig; 127–144 Jeanette Winter; 151–179 Carmen Lomas Garza; 181 Pam Rossi; 184 Pam Rossi; 189–210 Larry Johnson; 225–247 John Gamache; 254–274 Robert G. Steele; 285–304 Brad Teare

Photography 28 Courtesy of Harry Allard (tl); Houghton Mifflin Co. 36 Courtesy of Helen Oxenbury; Courtesy of Eugene Trivizas and Reed Children's Books. ©Otto Rogge/The Stock Market (t,bl) 61 Ranger Rick Magazine; Art Wolfe 62 Art Wolfe (t,bl) 63 Art Wolfe (t,b); Ranger Rick Magazine (b) 64 © Andrew Sacks/©Tony Stone Images/Chicago Inc 65 ©David Falconer/DRK Photo (t); John Colwell/Grant Heilman Photography (b) 66 The Bettmann Archive (t); ©Andrew Sacks/Tony Stone Images/Chicago Inc (b) 67 ©Stephen J. Krasemann/DRK Photo (t); ©Phil Dotson/Photo Researchers (b); Alain Compost/Bruce Coleman Inc (t); Robert Barclay/Grant Heilman Photography (b) 68-69 Mark Muench/©Tony Stone Images/Chicago Inc 68 Ross Humphreys/ Courtesy of Susan Lowell; Courtesy of Jim Harris (b) 88 Renee Lynn/Photo Researchers 89 Thomas A. Wiewandt (tr) 90-91 Thomas A. Wiewandt 92 Courtesy of Donivee M. Laird (tl); Courtesy of Don Stuart (br) 117 Courtesy of Kara Johnson 126 Courtesy of Roni Schotter (tl); Courtesy of Jeanette Winter (br) 146 Fred Boyles 182-183 ©Ken Biggs/©Tony Stone Images/Chicago Inc 213 Courtesy of Joyce Hsieh 214 Little, Brown & Co. 215 Francine Seders Gallery 216 Nat. Museum of the American Indian 217 The Cleveland Museum of Art 218-19 Joanna McArthy/The Image Bank 220-21 G. Brad Lewis/©Tony Stone Images/Chicago Inc 222-23 © G. Brad Lewis/©Tony Stone Images/Chicago Inc 224 Courtesy of Judy Donnelly; Courtesy of John Gamache 227 Courtesy of The Mariners Museum, Newport News, Virginia (br); Ken Marshall Collection/The Illustrated London News (bl) 228 Courtesy of The Mariners Museum, Newport News, Virginia; Brown Brothers (tl, tr); Ken Marshall Collection/Harland & Wolfe (br) 231 Brown Brothers (br) 232 Stock Montage, Inc. (br); Brown Brothers (br) 235 Brown Brothers (br) 237 Bruce Dale©/National Geographic Society (b); The Bettmann Archive (ml) 239 The Illustrated London News Picture Library (m) 240 Brown Brothers (bl) 241 Brown Brothers (m); The Bettmann Archive (m); Hulton Deutsch (br) 242 Stock Montage, Inc. (m); Brown Brothers (m) 243 The Bettmann Archive (ml); Brown Brothers (mr) 245 R. Sobol/Sipa Press (b) 246 Emory Kristof/National Geographic Society (tl) 246-7 ©Woods Hole Oceanographic Inst. 248 Courtesy of The Mariners Museum, Newport News, Virginia (m) 250 Courtesy of The Mariners Museum, Newport News, Virginia (tr); Brown Brothers (mr); The Bettmann Archive (bl, bm) 251 Ken Marshall Collection (tr) 254 Courtesy of Edith Kundhardt (t) 254 Courtesy of Robert Steele (b) 271 ©O.L. Mazzatenta/National Geographic Society (tl);

©David Hiser/Photographers/Aspen (b) 272 ©Jonathan Blair/National Geographic Society 273 C M Dixon (tl); (c); David Hiser/Photographers/Aspen (b) 274 ©Roy Rainford/Robert Harding Picture Library 276 ©E.R. Degginger/Allstock (bl); Tony Waltham/Robert Harding Picture Library (br) 277 Reuters/Bettmann/The Bettmann Archive (t); The Bettmann Archive (ml) 278 ©Sipa Press (tr); Ralph Perry/Allstock (br); The Bettmann Archive (bl) 279 ©Robert Fried/Robert Fried Photography (tr); UPI/Bettmann/The Bettmann Archive (bl); ©Gary Braasch (br) 282 Courtesy of Marcus Grant 284 John Stover/ Courtesy of Marjorie Stover (tl); Courtesy of Brad Teare (br) 306 Boston Globe 307-9 Bostonian Society 312 The Image Bank (l) 313 Joe Szkoozinski/The Image Bank (l) 314 M. Dwyer/Stock Boston (r) 315 Charles Allen/The Image Bank (r) 317 Patti Murray/Animals Animals (l); Peter Henorie/The Image Bank (r)

Teacher's Handbook

TABLE OF CONTENTS

Study Skills

Taking Notes

Teach/Model

Explain to students that taking notes as they read will help them remember important information. Stress the following points:

- Use a separate page or index card for each topic.
- Write a main heading (a key word or phrase) for each topic.
- Below the heading, write important details about the topic.

Tell the class that they will be doing research and taking notes on particular animals. Use the Think Aloud to model how to use this skill.

Think Aloud

My research topic is pigs. I can probably find this topic in the P book of the encyclopedia. (Some encyclopedias have the information under "Hogs." If so there will be a cross-reference under "Pigs.") I have several sheets of paper for notes. First I think about what I want to learn about pigs, and write these topics as headings on separate pages. For example, I will write the heading "What Pigs Eat" at the top of one page and "Kinds of Pigs" on another page. *(Write these two headings on the chalkboard.)*

Next I will read the article about pigs in the encyclopedia. As I read, I will write down the details I find on the appropriate pages. For example, I read that farmers feed pigs grains such as corn, wheat, rye, and oats. I will write "Corn, wheat, rye, and oats" under "What Pigs Eat." *(Write this on chalkboard.)* I will write other details on that page telling any other foods that pigs eat as well as how much they eat. I will do the same for other topics about pigs.

As I read, I will probably find other interesting topics, such as "Where Pigs Live." Then I will create a separate page of notes—with a heading and details—for each of those topics. When I am done, I will have the information written in a form I can use to study or to write about pigs.

Practice/Apply

Divide the class into small groups and assign each group an animal topic. Monitor students as they research their assigned topics. When they are done, ask questions such as these:

- What is the importance of taking notes?
- When you take notes, how do you group the information?
- What does each detail have to do with the topic?

SKILL FINDER Minilesson, p. 63

Study Skills
K-W-L

INTERACTIVE LEARNING

Teach/Model

Write the letters *K W L* on the chalkboard. Tell students that *K* stands for *Know, W* stands for *Want to find out,* and *L* stands for *Learned.* Together these three letters represent a strategy, or plan, that students can use before and after reading to help them understand what they read and remember it better.

Choose a chapter in a classroom text. Display Transparency H-1. Demonstrate how to use the K-W-L strategy by using the Think Aloud. Point to the headings and columns on the K-W-L chart as you explain the strategy.

Think Aloud

I will use the K-W-L chart before and after I read this chapter to help me understand and remember the information. The topic of this chapter is *(name the topic)*. Before I begin reading, I will think about what I already know about this topic. I will write these things in the first column, under the "What I Know" heading. Next, I will thumb through the chapter, thinking about what I want to learn or what I expect to learn about the topic. I will list these things in the second column, under "What I Want to Find Out." Then, as I read the chapter, I will keep on thinking about what I want to learn.

After reading the chapter, I will list what I learned in the third column. Then I will compare this list with my "What I Know" list to see if what I thought I knew turned out to be true. Finally, I will check my "What I Want to Find Out" list to see what questions were not answered yet.

Practice/Apply

Have each student make a K-W-L chart by copying the three column headings on a sheet of paper. Assign another short chapter or section from the same classroom text. Have students fill in their K-W-L charts. Then have them take turns reading one entry from each of the columns on their charts.

Have students summarize what they have learned about the K-W-L strategy by answering these questions.

- What do the letters *K-W-L* stand for?
- What does the K-W-L strategy help a student to do?
- Why is K-W-L a good plan to follow for reading and studying?

SKILL FINDER — Minilesson, p. 65

Transparency H–1

K-W-L Chart

What I Know	What I Want to Find Out	What I Learned

TRANSPARENCY H–1
TEACHER'S BOOK PAGE H3

INFORMAL ASSESSMENT CHECKLIST

Record observations of student progress for those areas important to you.

− = **Beginning Understanding**
✔ = **Developing Understanding**
✔+ = **Proficient**

Student Names

The Three Little Wolves and the Big Bad Pig									
Reading									
Responding									
Comprehension: Summarizing: Story Structure									
Writing Skills: Writing a Sentence									
Word Skills: Base Words									
Spelling: Short Vowels									
Grammar: Subjects and Predicates									
Listening and Speaking									

The Three Little Javelinas									
Reading									
Responding									
Comprehension: Compare and Contrast									
Writing: Writing a Book Report									
Word Skills: Inflected Endings -ed, -ing									
Spelling: Vowel-Consonant-e									
Grammar: Correcting Run-on Sentences									
Listening and Speaking									

Reading-Writing Workshop									
Spelling: Words Often Misspelled									

INFORMAL ASSESSMENT CHECKLIST

Record observations of student progress for those areas important to you.

- − = **Beginning Understanding**
- ✔ = **Developing Understanding**
- ✔+ = **Proficient**

Student Names

The Three Little Hawaiian Pigs and the Magic Shark								
Reading								
Responding								
Comprehension: Fantasy/Realism								
Writing Skills: Combining Sentences: Compound Sentences								
Word Skills: Using Context								
Spelling: Long *a* & Long *e*								
Grammar: Kinds of Sentences								
Listening and Speaking								

Performance Assessment								
Spelling Review								

General Observation								
Independent Reading								
Independent Writing								
Work Habits								
Self-Assessment								

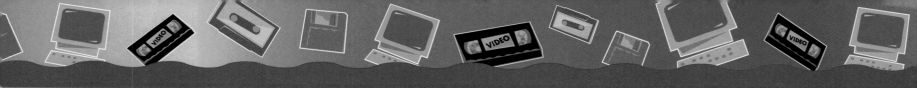

Audio-Visual Resources

Adventure Productions
3404 Terry Lake Road
Ft. Collins, CO 80524
970-493-8776

AIMS Media
9710 DeSoto Avenue
Chatsworth, CA
91311-4409
800-367-2467

Alfred Higgins Productions
6350 Laurel Canyon
Blvd.
N. Hollywood, CA
91606
800-766-5353

Audio Bookshelf
174 Prescott Hill Road
Northport, ME 04849
800-234-1713

Audio Editions
Box 6930
Auburn, CA 95604-6930
800-231-4261

Audio Partners, Inc.
Box 6930
Auburn, CA 95604-6930
800-231-4261

Bantam Doubleday Dell Audio
1540 Broadway
New York, NY 10036
212-782-9489

Bullfrog Films
Box 149
Oley, PA 19547
800-543-3764

Clearvue/EAV
6465 Avondale Ave.
Chicago, IL 60631
800-253-2788

Coronet/MTI
2349 Chaffee Drive
St. Louis, MO 63146
800-777-8100

Dial Books for Young Readers
375 Hudson St.
New York, NY 10014
800-526-0275

Direct Cinema Ltd.
P.O. Box 10003
Santa Monica, CA 90410
800-525-0000

Disney Educational Production
105 Terry Drive,
Suite 120
Newtown, PA 18940
800-295-5010

Encounter Video
14825 NW Ash St.
Portland, OR 97231
800-677-7607

Filmic Archives
The Cinema Center
Botsford, CT 06404
800-366-1920

Films for Humanities and Science
P.O. Box 2053
Princeton, NJ 08543
609-275-1400

Finley-Holiday Film Corp.
12607 E. Philadelphia St.
Whittier, CA 90601
562-945-3325

Fulcrum Publishing
350 Indiana St.
Golden, CO 80401
303-277-1623

HarperAudio
10 East 53rd Street
New York, NY 10022
212-207-6901

Houghton Mifflin/Clarion
181 Ballardvale St.
Wilmington, MA 01887
800-225-3362

Kidvidz
618 Centre St.
Newton, MA 02158
617-965-3345

Kimbo Educational
Box 477
Long Branch, NJ 07740
800-631-2187

Let's Create
50 Cherry Hill Rd.
Parsippany, NJ 07054
973-299-0633

Listening Library
One Park Avenue
Old Greenwich, CT
06870
800-243-4504

Live Oak Media
P.O. Box 652
Pine Plains, NY 12567
518-398-1010

McGraw-Hill
220 East Danieldale Rd.
Desoto, TX 75115
800-843-8855

Media Basics
Lighthouse Square
705 Boston Post Road
Guilford, CT 06437
800-542-2505

MGM/UA Home Video
2500 Broadway St.
Santa Monica, CA
90404-3061
310-449-3000

Milestone Film and Video
275 W. 96th St.
Suite 28C
New York, NY 10025
212-865-7449

Miramar
200 Second Ave.
Seattle, WA 98119
800-245-6472

National Geographic
1145 17th Street NW
Washington, DC 20036
800-368-2728

The Nature Company
P.O. Box 188
Florence, KY 41022
800-227-1114

PBS Video
1320 Braddock Place
Alexandria, VA
22314-1698
800-424-7963

Philomel Books
200 Madison Ave.
New York, NY 10016
212-951-8400

Premiere Home Video
755 N. Highland
Hollywood, CA 90038
213-934-8903

Puffin Books
375 Hudson St.
New York, NY 10014
212-366-2000

Rabbit Ears Books/Simon and Schuster
1230 Avenue of the
Americas
New York, NY 10020
800-223-2336

Rainbow Educational Media
4540 Preslyn Drive
Raleigh, NC 27616
800-331-4047

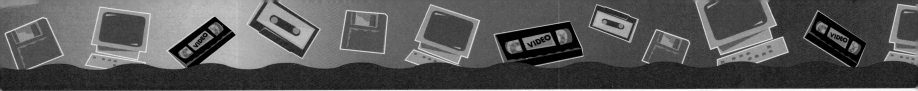

Audio-Visual Resources *(continued)*

Random House Media
400 Hahn Road
Westminster, MD 21157
800-733-3000

Recorded Books
270 Skipjack Road
Prince Frederick, MD
20678
800-638-1304

SelectVideo
5475 Peoria St., Unit 4C
Denver, CO 80239
800-742-1455

Silo/Alcazar
Box 429
Waterbury, VT 05676
802-844-5178

Spoken Arts
8 Lawn Ave.
New Rochelle, NY
10801
914-633-4516

SVE and Churchill Media
6677 N. Northwest
Highway
Chicago, IL 60631
800-334-7830

Time-Life Education
P.O. Box 85026
Richmond, VA
23285-5026
800-449-2010

Video Project
200 Estates Drive
Ben Lomond, CA 95005
800-475-2638

Warner Home Video
4000 Warner Blvd.
Burbank, CA 91522
818-954-6000

Weston Woods
12 Oakwood Ave.
Norwalk, CT 06850
800-243-5020

Wilderness Video
P.O. Box 3150
Ashland, OR 97520
541-488-9363

BOOKS AVAILABLE IN SPANISH
Spanish editions of English titles referred to in the Bibliography are available from the following publishers or distributors.

Bilingual Educational Services, Inc.
2514 South Grand Ave.
Los Angeles, CA
90007-9979
800-448-6032

Charlesbridge
85 Main Street
Watertown, MA 02172
617-926-0329

Children's Book Press
246 First St., Suite 101
San Francisco, CA 94105
415-995-2200

Econo-Clad Books
P.O. Box 1777
Topeka, KS 66601
785-233-4252

Farrar, Straus & Giroux
19 Union Square West
New York, NY 10003
212-741-6900

Grolier Publishing Co.
P.O. Box 1796
Danbury, CT 06816
800-621-1115

Harcourt Brace
6277 Sea Harbor Drive
Orlando, FL 32887
800-225-5425

HarperCollins
10 E. 53rd Street
New York, NY 10022
717-941-1500

Holiday House
425 Madison Ave.
New York, NY 10017
212-688-0085

Kane Press
48 W. 25th St.
New York, NY 10010
800-528-8273

Alfred A. Knopf
201 E. 50th St.
New York, NY 10022
800-726-0600

Lectorum
111 Eighth Ave.
New York, NY 10011
800-345-5946

Santillana
2105 NW 86th Ave.
Miami, FL 33122
800-245-8584

Simon and Schuster
1230 Avenue of the
Americas
New York, NY 10020
800-223-2336

Viking
357 Hudson Street
New York, NY 10014
212-366-2000

Index

Boldface page references indicate formal strategy and skill instruction.

188–189F, 219, 219A, 219B, 219F, 225; *TB6:* 230E, 237, 241, 255A, 255B, 255F, 255I, 255M, 255O, 257A, 258, 259, 277, 280, 287A, 293, 293C, 293D, 321A, 321B, 321F, 323C

Creative writing. *See* Writing, creative.

Critical thinking, *TB1:* 42, 46, 47, 52, 58, 74, 78, 86, 96, 106, 111, 112; *TB2:* 124E, 132, 138, 144, 160, 170, 178, 194, 202, 206, 210; *TB3:* 222E, 230, 238, 242, 248M, 260, 266, 274, 294, 300, 304; *TB4:* 18, 20, 22, 28, 34, 37C, 46, 47, 52, 56, 58B, 58D, 67, 68, 71, 74, 77, 80, 84D, 84F, 84H, 84O, 85, 88, 91A, 94, 99, 100, 106, 112, 114, 120, 121G, 121H, 121J, 121K; *TB5:* 128E, 140, 148, 166, 186, 202, 208, 218; *TB6:* 230E, 232, 238, 240, 244, 246, 248, 252, 255E, 255I, 255N, 257A, 266, 270, 272, 274, 275, 276, 280, 282, 284, 287N, 293C, 296, 298, 300, 302, 303, 304, 308, 310, 313, 316, 320, 321A, 321B, 322, 323

Cross-cultural connections. *See* Multicultural activities.

Cross-curricular activities

art, *TB1:* 5A, 6A, 29A, 34H, 54, 55, 60C, 60N, 67C, 86, 88A, 88E, 88N, 88O, 113, 114C, 114O, 117A; *TB2:* 145B, 149, 154, 180O, 183, 195, 214, 215, 216, 217, 217C; *TB3:* 222G, 248, 248M, 251, 271, 275P, 305A, 309C; *TB4:* 16G, 16H, 37A, 37B, 37D, 37F, 37N, 38, 58E, 58M, 84A, 84M, 89, 91E, 91F, 96, 104, 106, 121B, 121I, 121O, 121P, 123A, 123C; *TB5:* 149A, 149B, 155C, 187N, 223, 225, 225C; *TB6:* 230G, 255A, 255B, 255F, 255I, 255L, 257F, 263, 263C, 287A, 287B, 287F, 287P, 289, 321B, 323C

careers, *TB1:* 60N; *TB2:* 145; *TB5:* 149O, 149P, 219A, 219P; *TB6:* 255P, 284, 287F, 312, 321L, 321O

dance, *TB1:* 60O

health, *TB1:* 58, 67; *TB2:* 140, 145P; *TB3:* 240, 246, 305O; *TB4:* 16H, 30, 37O, 37P, 58N, 59, 61, 67, 79, 84N, 87, 89, 97, 105, 123, 123C; *TB5:* 187P, 197; *TB6:* 244, 253, 280, 302, 305, 306, 310, 312, 315, 321O

language arts, *TB2:* 183; *TB4:* 20, 22, 23, 26, 27, 28, 34, 35, 44, 48, 50, 52, 54, 56, 58L, 69, 78, 80, 95, 108, 121M

math, *TB1:* 6A, 34A, 38, 60O, 71, 88O, 91; *TB2:* 130, 145I, 145P, 149, 165, 172, 198; *TB3:* 223D, 229, 231, 233, 244, 248O, 249, 251, 265, 305P, 307; *TB4:* 19, 30, 31, 58O, 84N, 84O, 88, 98, 112, 121P, 122, 123; *TB5:* 138, 141, 149P, 167, 191, 199; *TB6:* 247, 249, 297, 255P, 287O

media literacy, *TB1:* 61, 89; *TB2:* 124G; *TB3:* 222G, 242, 244, 306, 309; *TB4:* 37A, 37F, 64, 85; *TB5:* 151; *TB6:* 255, 255F, 255I, 255N, 321B

multicultural, *TB1:* 15, 40, 41, 50, 74, 76, 88L, 91C, 94, 99, 106; *TB2:* 124A, 124B, 129, 134, 143, 144, 151, 154, 156, 161, 168, 170, 180N, 200, 206; *TB3:* 231, 246, 286, 298; *TB4:* 24, 37M, 44, 50, 51, 52, 54, 58E, 58L, 58M, 61, 65, 95, 97, 99, 109, 110, 121, 121M; *TB5:* 128A, 132, 179, 187P, 196; *TB6:* 260, 275, 302, 322

music, *TB1:* 34B, 57, 71, 107; *TB2:* 180L, 180N, 200, 202, 211O; *TB3:* 239, 252, 253, 309; *TB4:* 37F, 84L, 116, 121M; *TB5:* 187B, 219M; *TB6:* 237

science, *TB1:* 6A, 34A, 35A, 35F, 60N, 62, 67, 67D, 69, 73, 80, 87, 88N, 91, 97, 99, 100, 114O; *TB2:* 124A, 124E, 136, 142, 145O, 163, 164; *TB3:* 233, 237, 248N, 253D, 256, 258, 263, 264, 269, 270, 275N, 277, 278, 280, 283J, 305N, 309; *TB4:* 31, 37P, 71, 72, 84O, 88, 89, 121P; *TB5:* 128A, 128B, 128H, 129D, 136, 137, 139, 140, 143, 144, 148, 149O, 151, 154, 155, 155D, 168, 187O,

193D, 198, 201, 207, 213, 219O, 221, 223; *TB6:* 238, 243, 247, 255N, 263, 266, 267, 274, 277, 284, 287O, 289, 292, 293D, 300, 302, 303, 310, 316

social studies, *TB1:* 6A, 39, 62, 67, 81, 96, 114N; *TB2:* 124A, 125D, 149, 149D, 152, 164, 180N, 183, 186, 187D, 190, 201, 211P; *TB3:* 226, 230, 235, 243, 248O, 250, 261, 262, 275O, 275P, 279, 288, 291, 298, 305O, 309; *TB4:* 19, 25, 29, 34, 37P, 39, 41P, 44, 54, 55, 58O, 61D, 75, 85, 100, 107, 115, 121O, 123C, 128A; *TB5:* 134, 164, 187P, 214, 221; *TB6:* 231D, 235, 263D, 274, 287A, 287I, 287K, 287O, 287P, 291, 293, 321O

sports, *TB5:* 219O

technology, *TB1:* 6A, 50; *TB2:* 198, 199, 205; *TB3:* 235, 246, 248M, 272; *TB4:* 63; *TB5:* 142, 149I; *TB6:* 245, 282, 300

visual literacy, *TB1:* 43, 66, 69, 73, 77, 86, 89, 100; *TB2:* 131, 132, 137, 147, 153, 154, 175, 177; *TB3:* 257, 271, 288, 290, 305A; *TB4:* 18, 19, 25, 29, 32, 45, 57, 73, 93, 94, 103; *TB5:* 135, 158, 174, 186, 192, 215; *TB6:* 251, 270, 291, 298, 308

Cue systems. *See* Decoding, context clues; Think About Words.

Cultural diversity. *See* Multicultural activities.

D

Decoding skills

dictionary, *TB3:* **248G;** *TB4:* 37I, 84G; *TB6:* **321H**

See also Context; Phonics; Structural analysis; Think About Words; Vocabulary, selection; Word roots.

Details, noting, *TB1:* 29A, 52, 58, 59, 86, 88B, 88C, 90, 95, 103, 106, 114B, 117; *TB2:* 132, **133,** 134, 144, **145C–145D,** 145N, 153, **157,** 170, 171, 180B, 180M, 187C, 211B, 213, 213B, 214; *TB3:* 230, **231,** 238,

239, 242, 246, 248, **267,** 274, 283B, 290, 291, 300, 304, 305B; *TB4:* 21, 31, 33, 35, 53, 57, 58C, 67, 77, 91B, 97, 117; *TB5:* 136, 140, 148, 149B, 166, **167,** 186, 218; *TB6:* **243,** 245, 246, 252, 257, 257B, 257C, 281, 293, 296, 300, 301, 303, 316, 321A. *See also* Main idea and supporting details.

Diagrams, reading. See Graphic information, interpreting; Graphic organizers.

Dialogue. *See* Literary devices.

Diaries and journals. *See* Journal.

Dictionary
  accent marks, *TB2:* 149H
  alphabetical order, *TB1:* 114G
  base words, *TB5:* **219H**
  bilingual, *TB2:* 211A; *TB6:* 321
  definitions, *TB2:* 180G, 211A; *TB3:* **248G;** *TB4:* 37I
  guide words, *TB2:* 187B, **211H**
  inflected forms, *TB5:* **219H**
  multilingual, *TB3:* 248
  pictionary, *TB2:* 180I; *TB4:* 58A; *TB6:* 321A
  sample sentences, *TB3:* **248G**
  stress/syllables, *TB2:* **149H;** *TB3:* **321H**
  unfamiliar words, *TB1:* 88H; *TB2:* 180L, 186; *TB4:* 84G, 84H
  using, *TB6:* 255H
  word patterns, *TB6:* 241

Directions, following, *TB1:* 60E; *TB2:* **171,** 180N, 187; *TB3:* 248M, 248O, 275N, 280, **281,** 305O, **H6;** *TB4:* **31, 37C–37D, 69,** 121E, 123A; *TB5:* 149A, 191

Drafting. *See* Reading-Writing Workshop.

Drama. *See* Creative dramatics.

Drawing conclusions. *See* Conclusions, drawing.

323A. *See also* Writing conferences.

Evaluation. *See* Assessment options, choosing.

Expanding literacy. *See* Literacy, expanding.

Expository text, *TB1:* 60P–63, 64–67, 88P–91; *TB2:* 146–148, 184–187, 214–217; *TB3:* 223A–248O, 248P–251, 253A–275, 276–279, 280–281, 282–283, 306, 307–309; *TB4:* 38–40, 122–123; *TB5:* 129A–149, 152–155, 188–189, 190–192; *TB6:* 258–263, 293A–321

211E; *TB3:* **248D–248E;** *TB4:* 37L; *TB6:* 255L
    subject, *TB1:* **60J–60K;** *TB2:* **211E–211F;** *TB3:* 248D; *TB6:* 255L, 287K
  sentences
    fragments, *TB1:* 60D, 60K
    run-on sentences, *TB1:* **88J–88K**
  sentences, types of, *TB1:* **114J–114K**
  spelling connection, *TB1:* 117E; *TB2:* 213E; *TB3:* 283E; *TB4:* 91E; *TB5:* 189E; *TB6:* 257E
  usage
    subject/verb agreement, *TB3:* 248J, 248K; *TB6:* 255K, 255L
    verb tenses, *TB3:* **248J,** 248K, **275K,** 275L, 305K, 305L; *TB4:* 58J–58K

Graphic information, interpreting
  bar graphs, *TB6:* **307, H4**
  captions, *TB2:* 185; *TB5:* 190, 192
  charts, *TB2:* 185; *TB3:* 231, 248A; *TB4:* 58A, **87,** 88, **H4;** *TB5:* 143
  diagrams, *TB1:* 88N; *TB2:* 125C, 145P; *TB3:* **223C, 229,** 248, 251, **H2;** *TB4:* 88; *TB5:* 132, 137, 149C, 149D; *TB6:* 293, 305, 308
  globes, *TB4:* **39,** 58O, **H2**
  graphs, *TB1:* 88O; *TB4:* 84O, 91E
  headings, *TB2:* 185; *TB5:* 149C, 149D
  maps, *TB1:* 62, 67, 91C, 99, 114N; *TB2:* 145A, 149C, 149D, 152, 164, 197, 198, 211L; *TB3:* 222G, 226, 243, **245,** 248O, 253C, 275, 276, 279, 305A, **H3;** *TB4:* 19, 37P, 39, 107, 121N, 121O; *TB5:* 134, 135, 137, 149C, 149N, 149P, 155, 219L, 221; *TB6:* 263C, 274, 287N, 291, 321N
  nutrition labels, *TB4:* 37P
  photographs, *TB1:* 60M, 62, 88C, 89, 272
  scale models, *TB5:* 149P
  schedules, *TB2:* **129, H2;** *TB4:* 55; *TB6:* 263D, 287B, 287N, 287O
  tables, *TB2:* 153, 168
  time lines, *TB3:* 222H, 248O, 253C, 275P, **277,** 305O, **H5**
  Venn diagrams, *TB2:* **163, H3;** *TB4:* 47; *TB5:* 187E; *TB6:* 263C, 293C

Graphic organizers

calendar, *TB2:* 148; *TB3:* 309C; *TB6:* 258, **259,** 260–263, **H2**

character web, *TB2:* 207; *TB6:* 231C

chart, *TB1:* 10A, 41, 47, 57, 59, 63, 65, 67C, 79, 85, 88C, 88M, 91C, 95, 103, 114B, 114N, 117A; *TB2:* 135, 141, 145C, 145D, 145G, 145L, 149, 153, 157, 161, 169, 180B, 187C, 180H, 193, 194, 195, 205, 211C, 211N, 213A, 217C; *TB3:* 231, 232, 233, 239, 248B, 248P, 252, 253, 253C, 253D, 265, 267, 269, 275C, 275D, 283J, 295, 299, 303, 305C; *TB4:* 33, 37P, 39, 41D, 53, 55, 58B, 58H, 58P, 65, 67, 84P, 87, 88, 91A, 91E, 99, 117, 121C, 123C; *TB5:* 141, 147, 149C, 149D, 158, 178, 185, 187C, 187L, 189B, 190, 192, 193D, 196, 199, 205, 211, 219D; *TB6:* 231C, 241, 255C, 255D, 255G, 255N, 257A, 259, 281, 285, 287C, 287G, 301, 303, 305, 311, 313, 321A, 321O, 323A

clusters, *TB1:* 29D; *TB4:* 62

cross-section, *TB3:* 229

diagrams, *TB4:* 77, 88

flowchart, *TB2:* 137, 213B

graphs. *See* Graphic information, interpreting.

idea circle, *TB5:* 189A

K-W-L charts. *See* K-W-L strategy.

lists, *TB1:* 29D, 49, 60, 62, 65, 96, 114O; *TB2:* 124G, 125C, 145K, 145O; *TB3:* 248C, 248P, 275D, 275F; *TB4:* 21, 37D, 37N, 37P, 67, 71, 84E, 84H, 84O, 91A, 121H, 121I; *TB5:* 167, 189A; *TB6:* 257A, 281, 287I, 293

maps, *TB1:* 62, 67, 91C, 99, 114N; *TB4:* 37P, 39, 91E, 123C; *TB6:* 263C, 287A, 287K

research logs, *TB4:* 91B

schedules, *TB1:* 129; *TB5:* 187B

semantic chart, *TB1:* 35E, 223D, 253C; *TB4:* 41C; *TB6:* 263D

semantic map, *TB1:* 35E

semantic web, *TB2:* 125C, 223C; *TB3:* 261, 283J; *TB4:* 61C; *TB6:* 258, 263C, 293C

sentence strips, *TB1:* 88K

steps, *TB1:* 31

story map, *TB1:* 117B, 117C; *TB2:* 157; *TB3:* 299; *TB4:* 80; *TB6:* 255A

storyboards, *TB2:* 187C; *TB3:* 253C; *TB4:* 41C

table, *TB3:* 265; *TB4:* 37P, 58O, 121P; *TB6:* 255P, 321O

time lines, *TB2:* 149C; *TB4:* 33; *TB5:* 149I; *TB6:* 287P, 321F

Venn diagram, *TB1:* 60, 75, 88B; *TB2:* 125C, **163,** 187C, 191, **H3;** *TB4:* 47; *TB5:* 187E; *TB6:* 263C, 293C

web, *TB2:* 133, 145P, 207, 211D, 211N; *TB3:* 275E, 283I; *TB4:* 41C; *TB5:* 149L, 189A; *TB6:* 243, 263C

word map, *TB2:* 125D, 207; *TB4:* 121F

word walls, *TB4:* 61C

word web. *See* Word webs.

Guided reading. *See* Reading modes, guided reading.

H

High-utility words. *See* Spelling; Words, automatic recognition of.

Home/Community Connections, *TB1:* 34H; *TB2:* 124H; *TB3:* 222H; *TB4:* 16H; *TB5:* 128H; *TB6:* 230H *See also Home/Community Connections* booklet.

Home Connection, *TB1:* 29, 29H, 44, 52, 60, 66, 88, 89, 91, 113, 114, 119C; *TB2:* 131, 144, 145, 145M, 149C, 155, 171, 172, 180, 180H, 183, 186, 211, 211M, 211O; *TB3:* 248, 251, 275, 281, 283D, 290, 305, 309C; *TB4:* 16G, 16H, 37, 40, 55, 58, 58A, 62, 81, 84, 84M, 89, 90, 100, 121; *TB5:* 149, 155, 187, 219; *TB6:* 255, 255N, 255P, 284, 287, 287F, 287M, 312, 321, 321B, 321N

Home-school communication. *See* Home Connection.

Homework. *See* Home Connection.

I

Idioms/expressions, *TB1:* 39, 42, 64, 65, 70, 91, 94, 105; *TB2:* 137, 178, 184; *TB3:* 232, 233, 256, 266, 289, 293, 294; *TB4:* 22, 27, 31, 33, 37, 62, 89, 85, 95, 100, 102, 108, 120; *TB5:* 141, 145, 181, 198, 211; *TB6:* 235, 236, 238, 251, 258, 267, 270, 280

Illustrate original writing, *TB1:* 29D, 60K, 88E, 88H, 88N, 114; *TB2:* 145B, 149, 172, 180, 180E, 180I, 211, 211A; *TB3:* 305A, 305B; *TB4:* 37F, 84N, 91E; *TB5:* 187A, 187O, 187P, 189D, 189E, 219P; *TB6:* 231F

Illustrators of selections in Anthology. *See* Selections in Anthology.

Independent reading

promoting, *TB1:* 7A, 34H; *TB2:* 124E; *TB3:* 222E, 222H; *TB6:* 230H, 323B

suggestions for, *TB1:* 34A–34B, 34E, 60G, 60H, 60N, 74, 88G, 88H, 88M, 114G, 114H; *TB2:* 124A–124B, 124E, 124H, 145H, 145I, 145O, 167, 180G, 180H, 180N, 211H, 211I, 211O; *TB3:* 222A–222B, 222E, 222H, 248G, 248H, 248N, 275H, 275I, 305H, 305I, 305O; *TB4:* 16A, 16B, 16E, 16H, 35, 37H, 37I, 37O, 58G, 58H, 58N, 61A, 84G, 84H, 84N, 121B, 121H, 121I, 121N, 121O; *TB5:* 128A–128B, 128E, 128H, 149H, 149I, 149O, 187H, 187I, 187O, 219H, 219I, 219O; *TB6:* 230A–230B, 230E, 230H, 231A, 255H, 255I, 255P, 287H, 287I, 287O, 293A, 321H, 321I, 321O

See also Paperback Plus books.

Independent reading option. *See* Reading modes, independent reading.

Independent writing

promoting, *TB3:* 222H; *TB6:* 230H

suggestions for, *TB1:* 7A, 34H, 60E, 88E, 114E; *TB2:* 124H, 145F, 180E, 211F; *TB3:* 275F,

305F; *TB4:* 16F, 16H, 37, 37E, 58, 58E, 84, 84E, 121F; *TB5:* 128H, 149E, 187E, 219E; *TB6:* 230H, 255F, 256, 287, 287F, 293C, 321F, 321

Individual needs, meeting
challenge, *TB1:* 29, 35E, 47, 51, 54, 57, 60I, 60N, 62, 76, 81, 88I, 88N, 91C, 103, 114I; *TB2:* 124E, 125C, 137, 145B, 145J, 149C, 162, 180I, 180M, 185, 197, 204, 211A, 211J, 211O; *TB3:* 222E, 223C, 242, 248M, 248O, 250, 253C, 259, 275J, 279, 283I, 292, 305A, 305J, 305N, 309; *TB4:* 16E, 19, 37B, 37J, 37M, 37P, 41C, 53, 58H, 58I, 58O, 59, 71, 78, 84H, 84N, 84O, 98, 121J, 121P; *TB5:* 128E, 129C, 144, 146, 149B, 149I, 149J, 155C, 169, 175, 187A, 187J, 193C, 212, 217, 219A, 219J, 219P; *TB6:* 230E, 231C, 241, 255J, 255L, 255O, 255P, 263C, 287J, 287O, 293, 293C, 300, 305, 321J, 321O, 321P
extra support, *TB1:* 38, 40, 48, 56, 59, 60F, 62, 65, 73, 74, 78, 83, 87, 88F, 89, 100, 111, 113, 118, 119; *TB2:* 124E, 125C, 128, 133, 137, 141, 144, 145G, 148, 156, 179, 180F, 180N, 187C, 192, 194, 196, 209, 211G; *TB3:* 222E, 223D, 243, 247, 253C, 268, 273, 274, 276, 279, 297, 301, 304; *TB4:* 16E, 20, 39, 41D, 47, 52, 61C, 66, 70, 75, 81, 94, 106; *TB5:* 128E, 138, 141, 145, 148, 154, 155C, 159, 160, 181, 182, 185, 186, 187A, 193C, 197, 198, 201, 202, 208, 211, 215, 218, 221, 222; *TB6:* 230E, 231C, 234, 235, 263C, 267, 280, 287A, 287B, 291, 293, 293C, 296, 306, 320, 323
guided reading. *See* Reading modes.
reteaching, *TB1:* 60C, 60G, 60K, 88C, 88G, 88K, 114C, 114G, 114K; *TB2:* 145D, 145H, 145L, 180C, 180G, 180K, 211D, 211H, 211L; *TB3:* 248C, 248K,

275D, 275L, 305D, 305H; *TB4:* 37D, 37L, 58C, 58G, 58K, 84C, 84G, 84K, 121D, 121H, 121L; *TB5:* 149D, 149H, 149L, 187D, 187H, 187L, 219D, 219H, 219L; *TB6:* 255D, 255H, 255L, 287D, 287H, 287L, 321D, 321H, 321L
students acquiring English. *See* Students acquiring English.
support in advance, *TB1:* 35E, 67C, 91C; *TB2:* 125C, 149C, 187C; *TB3:* 223C, 253C, 283I; *TB4:* 41C, 61C; *TB5:* 129C, 155C, 193C; *TB6:* 231C, 263C, 293C

Inferences, making
about characters' actions and feelings, *TB2:* 136, 204, 205; *TB3:* 246, 290, 294, **303;** *TB4:* 50, 62, 64; *TB5:* 162, **179, 187C–187D, 205,** 225A; *TB6:* 238, 244, 246, 248, 252, 255A, 255B, 255C, 257A, 257B, 269, 270, 272, 280, 284, 287B, 287D, 287E, 291
from illustrations, *TB2:* 204; *TB3:* 272; *TB4:* 44; *TB6:* 251, 287D
by predicting, *TB2:* 204; *TB3:* 286, 290, 294; *TB4:* 44, 50, 62, 64, 106; *TB5:* 196, 206; *TB6:* 232, 238, 244
See also Cause-effect relationships; Conclusions, drawing; Generalizations, making.

Inferencing, *TB1:* **13, 38, 50, 64, 70, 72;** *TB2:* **204;** *TB3:* **238, 242, 246, 286, 290, 303;** *TB5:* **179, 187C–187D, 196, 205, 206.** *See also* Strategies, reading: Predict/Infer.

Information activities, *TB1:* 62, 63, 65, 114N, H2; *TB2:* 145O, 185, 187, 211D, H4, H5; *TB3:* 248, 265, 279; *TB4:* 19, 37I, 37N, 37P, 38, 39, 58D, 58O, 60, 67, 79, 84G, 84O, 87, 107, H2, H3, H4, 134; *TB5:* 135, 141, 149M, 149N, 205; *TB6:* 230H, 241, 255N, 255O, 255P, 259, 261, 263, 274, 287B, 287I, 287N, 287O, 287P, 289, 293, 300, 303, 305, 307, 310, 311, 321A, 321B, 321C, 321E, 321N, 321O, H2, H3, H4, H5

Interactive Learning
building background, *TB1:* **10A, 33E, 67C, 91C;** *TB2:* **125C, 149C, 187C;** *TB3:* **223C, 253C, 283I;** *TB4:* **17C, 41C, 61C, 91I;** *TB5:* **129C, 155C, 193C;** *TB6:* **231C, 263C, 293C**
comprehension, *TB1:* **60B, 88B, 114B;** *TB2:* **145C–145D, 180B–180C, 211C–211D;** *TB3:* **248B, 275C, 305C;** *TB4:* **37C, 58B, 84B, 121C;** *TB5:* **149C, 187C, 219C;** *TB6:* **255C, 287C, 321C**
grammar, *TB1:* **60J–60K, 88J–88K, 114J–114K;** *TB2:* **145K–145L, 180J–180K, 211K–211L;** *TB3:* **275K, 305K, 305L;** *TB4:* **37K–37L, 58J–58K, 84J–84K, 121K–121L;** *TB5:* **149K, 187K–187L;** *TB6:* **255K, 287K–287L, 321K**
prior knowledge. *See* Interactive learning, building background.
program, launching the, *TB1:* **4A**
selection vocabulary. *See* Vocabulary, selection.
theme, launching the, *TB1:* **34G;** *TB2:* **124G;** *TB3:* **222G;** *TB4:* **16G;** *TB5:* **128G;** *TB6:* **230G**
word skills and activities, *TB1:* **60F, 88F, 114F;** *TB2:* **145G, 180F, 211G;** *TB3:* **248F, 275G, 305G;** *TB4:* **37G, 58F, 84F, 121G;** *TB5:* **149G, 187G, 219G;** *TB6:* **255G, 287G, 321G**
writing skills and activities, *TB1:* **60D, 88D, 114D;** *TB2:* **145E, 180D, 211E;** *TB3:* **248D, 248K, 275E, 275L;** *TB4:* **37E, 58D, 84D, 121E;** *TB5:* **149E, 187E, 219E;** *TB6:* **255E, 287E, 321E**

Intervention, Soar to SUCCESS level 3 books, *TB1:* 33A, 34E; *TB2:* 123A, 124E; *TB3:* 221A, 222E; *TB4:* 15A, 16E; *TB5:* 127A, 128E, *TB6:* 229A, 230E

Interviewing. *See* Speaking activities.

Introductory selection
Miss Nelson Is Missing! by Harry Allard, *TB1:* 8A–29A

116, 121J; *TB6:* 255E, 277, 287G, 287M, 289, 321M

for enjoyment, *TB1:* 38, 60C, 60L, 67, 113, 117A, 117B; *TB2:* 180L, 180N; *TB3:* 248L, 275M, 283H, 305M; *TB4:* 37B, 37F, 37M, 56, 58L, 73, 121M; *TB5:* 187M, 219M; *TB6:* 255I, 287M

to follow directions, *TB2:* 171, 180N, 187; *TB3:* 281; *TB4:* 31, 37D, 69; *TB5:* 149M; *TB6:* 255M, 321F, 321M

to gain information, *TB1:* 60A, 60K, 88L, 88M; *TB2:* 145M, 180L; *TB3:* 248L, 275M, 283H, 305M; *TB4:* 27, 33, 37E, 39, 46, 49, 58D, 58F, 58M, 75, 79, 84H, 84M, 84P, 88, 121K, 121O, 123; *TB5:* 149M, 149P, 187M; *TB6:* 231C, 243, 245, 255B, 255C, 255I, 255K, 255P, 256, 257B, 258, 266, 274, 284, 285, 287B, 287G, 287N, 291, 292, 303, 311, 312, 321I, 321M, 321O, 321P, 322

to generate questions. *See* Questions, generating.

to recall information and details, *TB1:* 88L. *See* Main idea and supporting details.

to reread. *See* Rereading.

for sharing. *See* Sharing.

to think aloud. *See* Think aloud.

to visualize. *See* Visualizing.

Literacy, expanding, *TB1:* 60P–63, 64–67, 118–119; *TB2:* 146–149, 181, 182–183, 184–187, 214–217; *TB3:* 249P–251, 252–253, 276–279, 280–281, 306, 307–309; *TB4:* 38–40, 58P–61, 84P–89, 122–123; *TB5:* 150–151, 152–155, 190–192, 220–223, 224–225; *TB6:* 258–263, 288–289, 290–293, 322, 323

Literary appreciation, *TB1:* 34G–34H, 60, 60A, 88, 88A, 88B, 114A, 114B, 119C; *TB2:* 125C–125D, 128, 145, 145B, 149C–149D, 152, 180–180A, 187C–187D, 190, 211–211A; *TB3:* 222A–222B, 222C–222D,

223C–223D, 248, 248A, 253C–253D, 275, 275A–275B, 283I–283J, 305, 305A–305B, 309C; *TB4:* 37A–37B, 58, 58A, 84A, 121, 121B; *TB5:* 149, 149A–149B, 187, 187A–187B, 219, 219A–219B, 225C; *TB6:* 230G–230H, 255, 255A–255B, 287, 287A–287B, 321, 321A–321B. *See also* Literary devices; Literary genres; Literature.

Literary devices

alliteration, *TB2:* **131,** 145F, 145M; *TB4:* 59; *TB5:* 187F

author's craft, *TB6:* 230E, 255B

author's purpose, *TB2:* 161, 162, 169; *TB3:* 233; *TB5:* 160, 164, 184, 186, 196

author's viewpoint, *TB2:* **153, 180B–180C, 205,** 212; *TB4:* 94, **97**

descriptive language. *See* Language concepts and skills.

detail, use of. *See* Details, noting and using. *See also* Main idea and supporting details.

dialogue, *TB1:* 63, 69, 74, 78, 83, 109, **117C;** *TB2:* 133, 180A, 196, 204, 211C; *TB3:* 239, 305B; *TB4:* 37E, 48, 65, 84H, **84J,** 84K; *TB5:* **173,** 187F, 216, 219B; *TB6:* 255M, 281, 321A

exact words, *TB5:* 189, 189A, 189B, 219I

figurative language, *TB3:* 232; *TB5:* 159, 189B, 201. *See also* Language concepts and skills.

humor, *TB1:* 57, 74, 78, 82, 86, 97, 114B; *TB2:* 145M; *TB3:* 296, 305A; *TB5:* 174; *TB6:* 245

idioms. *See* Idioms.

imagery, *TB2:* 182, 213B; *TB6:* 277, 322

metaphors, *TB2:* **191;** *TB6:* 287A

mood, *TB1:* 57; *TB3:* 275M; *TB5:* 158, 164, 167, 187M

onomatopoeia, *TB3:* **293,** 305F

personification, *TB4:* 95; *TB5:* **201,** 202, 219F

poetic devices. *See* Poetic devices.

point of view, *TB2:* 204; *TB3:* 248E, 275B; *TB4:* 94; *TB5:* 189C, 219M

repetition, *TB1:* 110; *TB2:* 182; *TB3:* 248E, **261,** 275F; *TB4:* 21, 35, 37F, 95

rhyme, *TB1:* 64, 74, 88, 88H, 114E; *TB2:* 204; *TB4:* 37F, 59, 61; *TB5:* 151

rhythm, *TB1:* 74; *TB5:* 219M

similes, *TB2:* **191;** *TB3:* 256; *TB4:* **95;** *TB5:* 189B

sound words, *TB1:* 110; *TB3:* 288, 295; *TB5:* 155D, 166, 167, 187I, 208

suspense, *TB1:* 102, 110; *TB3:* 261, 275F

word play, *TB1:* 114A; *TB5:* 225

Literary genres

biography/autobiography, *TB2:* **167**

content area reading, *TB6:* **305**

fantasy, *TB1:* **41**

fantasy/realism, *TB1:* **57, 95, 114B–114C;** *TB5:* **211**

folktales, *TB4:* **21**

historical fiction, *TB3:* **295**

narrative nonfiction, *TB3:* **233**

nonfiction, *TB2:* **147**

plays, *TB1:* **119**

realistic fiction, *TB4:* **71**

song, *TB3:* **253**

See also Selections in Anthology.

Literary skills. *See* Literary devices and skills; Poetic devices; Story elements/story structure.

Literature

analyzing, *TB1:* 64, 66, 88B, 88L, 102, 110; *TB2:* 153, 161, 166, 182, 213; *TB4:* 27, 33, 37, 49, 53, 55, 77, 97, 117; *TB5:* 187L, 204, 214; *TB6:* 241, 243, 245, 258, 266, 277, 305, 322, 323. *See also* Literary devices; Story elements.

celebrating. *See* Theme, celebrating the.

comparing, *TB1:* 34H, 42, 60, 60M, 66, 74, 75, 85, 88, 88B, 103, 118, 119; *TB2:* 182; *TB3:* 221G, 248A, 275B, 305B; *TB4:* 35, 47, 120; *TB5:* 187L, 204, 214; *TB6:* 255A, 255B, 287B, 291, 292, 305, 321B. *See also* Connections, between selections.

school in other countries, *TB1:* 15; *TB6:* 302

sound words in other languages, *TB1:* 110

Spanish pictionary, *TB1:* 88H

storytelling, *TB5:* 179, 155C

weather and climate, *TB5:* 187P

wolves in Sarcee and other cultures, *TB1:* 41

Multigenerational activities, *TB2:* 131, 144, 145M, 211M, 211O; *TB3:* 290; *TB4:* 16G, 40, 58L, 62, 81, 95, 119, 121F; *TB6:* 255P, 323C

Music. *See* Cross-curricular activities.

N

Narrative text. *See* Literary genres.

Newsletter. *See* Home Connection.

Newspaper, *TB3:* 228G, 306, 309

Nonfiction. *See* Literary genres; Selections in Anthology.

Notes

making, *TB5:* 136, 142, 187M, 189A

O

Oral

composition. *See* Speaking activities.

language. *See* Speaking activities.

presentation, *TB1:* 60K, 88L, 88M; *TB2:* 129, 145M, 180L, 213F, 217A; *TB5:* 187A, 225, 225A; *TB6:* 263

reading. *See* Reading modes; Rereading.

summary. *See* Summarizing.

P

Paired learning, *TB1:* 7A, 10A, 11A, 17, 20, 21, 27, 35F, 48, 59, 60K, 60L, 60N, 87, 88L, 91C, 95, 96, 100, 101, 117A, 117F, 118; *TB2:* 125D, 141, 145G, 149D, 179, 180, 180G, 180K, 180L, 184, 187D, 209, 211P, 213A; *TB3:* 235, 248, 248K, 253C, 274, 276, 277, 281, 283A, 283B, 304, 305B, 307; *TB4:* 37A, 37B, 41C, 60, 84L, 84N, 97,

117, 121A; *TB5:* 148, 149M, 160, 179, 187C, 187F, 187H, 189A, 189B, 189D; *TB6:* 231D, 245, 255E, 255F, 255H, 255M, 257A, 257B, 257C, 257D, 257E, 287G, 320, 321A, 321C, 321I, 321M, 321N

Paperback Plus books

Anna, Grandpa, and the Big Storm by Carla Stevens, *TB3:* 221A, 222E, 222H

The Bravest Dog Ever: The True Story of Balto by Natalie Standiford, *TB3:* 221A, 222E, 222H

Cam Jansen and the Mystery of the Babe Ruth Baseball by David A. Adler, *TB2:* 123A, 124E

Everybody Cooks Rice by Norah Dooley, *TB4:* 15A, 16E

Julian, Dream Doctor by Ann Cameron, *TB6:* 229A, 230E, 230H

Kate Shelley and the Midnight Express by Margaret K. Wetterer, *TB5:* 127A, 128E, 128H

My Buddy by Audrey Osofsky, *TB2:* 123A, 124E

Sidney Rella and the Glass Sneaker by Bernice Myers, *TB1:* 33A, 34E

Sleeping Ugly by Jane Yolen, *TB1:* 33A, 34E

Who Put the Pepper in the Pot? by Joanna Cole, *TB4:* 15A, 16E

Will and Orv by Walter A. Schulz, *TB6:* 229A, 230E, 230H

Yagua Days by Cruz Martel, *TB5:* 127A, 128E, 128H

Parent involvement. *See* Home Connection.

Parts of a book, *TB3:* **265,** 307, **H4**

Peer conferences. *See* Writing conferences.

Peer evaluation, *TB1:* 117A, 117B, 117C, 117D; *TB2:* 180M, 213B, 213D; *TB3:* 283A, 283B, 283D; *TB4:* 121L; *TB5:* 189A, 189B, 189D, 225B; *TB6:* 257A, 257B, 257C, 257D, 257E. *See also*

Cooperative learning activities; Writing conferences.

Peer interaction. *See* Cooperative learning activities; Paired learning.

Performance assessment. *See* Assessment options.

Personal narrative. *See* Literary genre.

Personal response. *See* Responding to literature.

Phonics. *See* Decoding skills.

consonants

beginning, *city* and *just, TB4:* **37J,** 37L

clusters, *TB3:* **275H**

digraphs, *TB3:* **305H**

silent, *TB1:* 46; *TB5:* **187H**

soft *c* and *g, TB6:* **287H**

phonograms, *TB4:* **121H**

vowels

changing final *y* to *i, TB5:* **219J,** 219L

final sound in *funny, TB5:* **187J,** 187L

in *cook* and *knew, TB2:* **145H,** **180I,** 180K

in *saw, TB3:* **248I,** 248K

in *town* and *boy, TB2:* **145H,** **211J,** 211L

long, *TB1:* **88G, 114I,** 114K; *TB2:* **145J,** 145L

plus *-r, TB3:* **275J,** 275L, **305J,** 305L; *TB4:* **58G**

short, *TB1:* **60G, 60I,** 60K

vowel pairs, *TB2:* **145H**

See also Decoding skills; Think About Words.

Pluralism. *See* Multicultural activities.

Poems in Anthology

"Away from Town" by Aileen Fisher, *TB2:* 181

"Celebration" by Alonzo Lopez, *TB6:* 322

"City" by Langston Hughes, *TB2:* 182–183

"I'd Never Eat a Beet" by Jack Prelutsky, *TB4:* 60–61

"Pigs" by Charles Ghigna, *TB1:* 114P–115

"Snowflakes" by Suk-Joong Yoon, *TB5:* 224

"Spaghetti! Spaghetti!" by Jack

Prelutsky, *TB4:* 59
"Sunflakes" by Frank Asch, *TB5:* 225
"That Kind of Day" by Eloise Greenfield, *TB6:* 288–289
"Who Has Seen the Wind?" by Christina Rossetti, *TB5:* 150–151

Poems in Teacher's Edition
"August" by Sandra Liatsos, *TB1:* 88L

Poetic devices, *TB1:* 88L; *TB2:* 181, 182; *TB4:* **59, 95,** 121E, 121F; *TB5:* 151, 224; *TB6:* 277, 287A, 322

Poetry
discussion, *TB2:* 181; *TB4:* 58P, 61, 121E; *TB5:* 150–151, 224–225; *TB6:* 288, 322
introducing, reading, responding to, *TB1:* **88L,** 114P–115; *TB2:* 181, 182–183; *TB4:* 58P–61, 121E; *TB5:* 150–151, 224–225; *TB6:* 287A, 288, 289, 322
writing, *TB1:* 114E; *TB2:* 145F, 183, 211F; *TB4:* 16H, 61, 121H; *TB5:* 155, 187F, 225; *TB6:* 287A

Poets in Anthology. *See* Poems in Anthology.

Portfolio Opportunity. *See* Assessment options, choosing.

Predicting outcomes. *See* Reading strategies, predict/infer.

Predictions, making
from previewing, *TB1:* 12, 64, 70, 94, 230, 256, 286, 307; *TB4:* 18, 22, 44, 46, 61C, 94; *TB5:* 132, 158, 196; *TB6:* 232, 266
while reading, *TB1:* 12, 13, 38, 42, 46, 50, 52, 72, 74, 78, 96, 102, 106; *TB2:* 128, 132, 138, 152, 160, 170, 190, 194, 202, **204,** 206; *TB3:* 226, 238, 242, 260, 266, 290, 294, 300; *TB4:* 28, 34, 50, 52, **53, 58B,** 58C, 62, 63, **67,** 68, 74, 99, 106; *TB5:* 140, 166, 172, 202, 208; *TB6:* 232, 238, 244, 246, 272, 280, 296, 302, 308
See also Skills, major.

Previewing
captions, *TB3:* 276
illustrations, *TB1:* 12, 61, 67C, 91C, 94; *TB2:* 125C, 128, 151, 152; *TB3:* 256, 280, 283I, 286; *TB4:* 41C, 44, 45, 47, 48, 58P, 60, 61C, 62, 69, 84P; *TB5:* 129C, 155C, 193C; *TB6:* 231C, 232, 288, 293C
photos, *TB2:* 146, 184; *TB3:* 276; *TB4:* 84P; *TB5:* 150, 190
section headings, *TB3:* 253C, 256, 260, 266, 306; *TB4:* 84P; *TB6:* 232
text, *TB1:* 64, 94; *TB2:* 187C; *TB3:* 230, 248P, 253C, 256, 280, 306; *TB4:* 38, 69, 122; *TB5:* 158, 193C, 196; *TB6:* 232, 258, 266, 293C, 322
title, *TB1:* 61, 64; *TB3:* 222G, 230, 286; *TB4:* 58P; *TB5:* 150

Prewriting. *See* Reading-Writing Workshop.

Prior knowledge. *See* Background building.

Problem solving, *TB2:* **141,** 149; *TB4:* **49, 99, 121C–121D,** 123A; *TB5:* 186, 187

Process writing. *See* Reading-Writing Workshop.

Pronouns. *See* Speech, parts of.

Proofreading. *See* Reading-Writing Workshop.

Publications, student-produced, *TB1:* 29H, 88E, 114E, 114O, 117E, 119C; *TB2:* 145L, 145O, 180E, 211A, 213D, 213E–213F; *TB3:* 222E, 222H, 283A, 283E, 283F, 305A; *TB4:* 16H, 91E; *TB5:* 189F, 219P; *TB6:* 257E

Punctuation. *See* Mechanics, language.

Purpose setting for reading, *TB1:* 12, 38, 42, 46, 52, 70, 74, 78, 94, 96, 102, 106; *TB2:* 128, 132, 138, 152, 160, 170, 190, 194, 202, 206; *TB3:* 226, 230, 242, 256, 260, 266, 286, 294, 300; *TB4:* 18, 22, 28, 44, 46, 52, 60, 62, 68, 74, 94, 99, 106, 122; *TB5:* 132, 140, 152, 158, 166, 172, 196, 202, 208; *TB6:* 238, 246, 266, 272, 280, 296, 302, 308

Q

Questions, generating, *TB1:* 19, 29F, 60L, 60N, 65, 88A, 88C, 94, 108, 117B; *TB2:* 124G, 132, 138, 145M, 184, 185, 211A, 213E; *TB3:* 248D, 251, 256, 260, 266, 268, 276, 305K; *TB4:* 37B, 39, 40, 44, 54, 91A–91B, 94, 100; *TB5:* 136, 149P, 152, 190; *TB6:* 266, 270, 282, 293C, 302, 307, 310, 321P

Quotations, interpreting, *TB1:* 89

R

Reading across the curriculum. *See* Cross-curricular activities.

Reading fluency. *See* Fluency.

Reading modes
cooperative reading, *TB1:* 12, 20, 38, 42, 70, 74, 94; *TB2:* 128, 132, 152, 190, 194; *TB3:* 226, 230, 256, 260, 286, 294; *TB4:* 22, 46, 58P, 60, 68, 81, 104, 121A, 121G; *TB5:* 132, 136, 158, 166, 196, 202, 218; *TB6:* 238, 272, 302
guided reading, *TB1:* 38, 42, 46, 52, 58, 70, 94; *TB2:* 128, 132, 138, 144, 152, 160, 170, 178, 194, 202, 206, 210; *TB3:* 230, 238, 242, 246, 256, 260, 266, 274, 294, 300, 304; *TB4:* 18, 22, 28, 34, 44, 46, 52, 56, 62, 68, 74, 80, 84, 94, 100, 106, 120, 121A; *TB5:* 132, 136, 140, 148, 158, 166, 172, 186, 196, 202, 208, 218; *TB6:* 238, 246, 252, 272, 280, 284, 302, 308, 320
independent reading, *TB1:* 12, 38, 42, 70, 74, 94, 96; *TB2:* 128, 132, 152, 190, 194; *TB3:* 222E, 222H, 226, 230, 256, 260, 286, 294; *TB4:* 16H, 22, 37F, 46, 58E, 60, 68, 74, 100, 121F; *TB5:* 132, 136, 158, 196, 202; *TB6:* 238, 250, 266, 272, 291, 292, 302
oral reading, *TB1:* 44, 48, 78, 82,

114A; *TB2:* 145, 182, 211, 211A, 211B; *TB3:* 248, 248A, 275, 275A, 305, 305B; *TB4:* 37, 37B, 58, 58A, 84, 84A, 121, 121B; *TB5:* 149, 187, 187A, 187B, 219, 219A, 219B; *TB6:* 255, 255A, 255B, 287, 287A, 287B, 321, 321A

Reteaching. *See* Individual needs.

Revising. *See* Grammar and usage; Reading-Writing Workshop; Spelling.

Rhyme, rhythm. *See* Literary devices.

Root words. *See* Word roots.

S

Science activities. *See* Cross-curricular activities.

Selecting books. *See* Independent reading.

Selections in Anthology
autobiography
Chicken Sunday by Patricia Polacco, *TB4:* 91G–121A
Family Pictures/Cuadros de familia, written and illustrated by Carmen Lomas Garza, *TB2:* 149A–180
calendar
"A Calendar for Kids" by Margo McLoone-Basta and Alice Siegel, *TB6:* 258–263
comic strip
"Peanuts" by Charles M. Schulz, *TB6:* 323
description
"Be a Writer: Snowy Winter Days" by Annie Holstein, *TB5:* 188–189
ecology guide
"Earthwise," from *Earthwise at School,* by Linda Lowery and Marybeth Lorbiecki, *TB2:* 184–186
fantasy
The Three Little Wolves and the Big Bad Pig by Eugene Trivizas, illustrated by Helen Oxenbury, *TB1:* 35C–60A

fiction
Brave Irene written and illustrated by William Steig, *TB5:* 193A–219
Chicken Sunday written and illustrated by Patricia Polacco, *TB4:* 91G–121P
A Fruit & Vegetable Man by Roni Schoter, illustrated by Jeanette Winter, *TB2:* 125A–145
Halmoni and the Picnic by Sook Nyul Choi, illustrated by Karen M. Dugan, *TB4:* 41A–58
Henry and Beezus by Beverly Cleary, illustrated by Alan Tiegreen, *TB4:* 61A–84
Mac & Marie & the Train Toss Surprise by Elizabeth Fitzgerald Howard, illustrated by Gail Gordon Carter, *TB6:* 263A–287
Miss Nelson Is Missing! by Henry Allard, *TB1:* 8A–29A
Ramona and Her Mother by Beverly Cleary, illustrated by Alan Tiegreen, *TB6:* 231A–255
Storm in the Night by Mary Stolz, illustrated by Pat Cummings, *TB5:* 155A–187
When Jo Louis Won the Title by Belinda Rochelle, illustrated by Larry Johnson, *TB2:* 187A–211
fine art
Painting the Town, TB2: 214–217
folktale
The Three Little Hawaiian Pigs and the Magic Shark by Donivee Martin Laird, illustrated by Don Stuart, *TB1:* 91A–114A
The Three Little Javelinas by Susan Lowell, illustrated by Jim Harris, *TB1:* 67A–88A
Tony's Bread written and illustrated by Tomie dePaola, *TB4:* 17A–37
historical account
"It Really Happened" from *Patrick and the Great*

Molasses Explosion by Marjorie Stover, *TB3:* 307–309
historical facts
"Titanic Trivia" from *Titanic Trivia* by A.F.J. Marshello, *TB3:* 248P–251
historical fiction
Patrick and the Great Molasses Explosion by Marjorie Stover, illustrated by Brad Teare, *TB3:* 283G–305
instructions
"Be a Writer: How to Take Care of a Cut" by Marcus Grant, *TB3:* 282–283
legend
"How Snowmaker was taught a lesson" from *How we saw the world* by C.J. Taylor, *TB5:* 220–223
musical score
"The Titanic," *TB3:* 252–253
newspaper article
"Molasses Tank Explosion Injures 50 and Kills 11" from the *Boston Daily Globe, TB3:* 306
nonfiction
Pompeii . . . Buried Alive! by Edith Kunhardt, illustrated by Robert G. Steele, *TB3:* 253A–275
Say Woof! The Day of a Country Veterinarian written and illustrated by Gail Gibbons, *TB6:* 293A–321
The Titanic: *Lost . . . and Found* by Judy Donnelly, illustrated by John Gamache, *TB3:* 223A–248O
Tornado Alert by Franklyn M. Branley, illustrated by George Guzzi, *TB5:* 129A–149
nutrition article
"Fun Food Facts" from *Crayola Kids* magazine, *TB4:* 122–123
"Get the Facts on Fast Food" from *Current Health Magazine, TB4:* 85–89
personal narrative
"Be a Writer: The Pool Somersault" by Joyce Hsieh,

dramatics. *See* Creative dramatics.

explanation, *TB1:* 55, 67, 88H; *TB2:* 211I; *TB3:* 275E, 278, 281, 298; *TB4:* 31, 58M, 84D, 84H; *TB5:* 145, 213, 225A, 225B; *TB6:* 255E, 255K, 255N, 258, 285, 303, 321N

interview, *TB1:* 29, 60L, 60N, 88A, 117A; *TB2:* 145M, 180N, 211M, 211O; *TB3:* 248L, 290; *TB4:* 37B

oral presentation. *See* Oral presentation.

press conference, *TB3:* 248L

retelling, *TB1:* 29, 60L, 88, 113; *TB3:* 305B; *TB5:* 187M, 219, 219M, 225B; *TB6:* 255A, 316

speech, *TB3:* 305M

storytelling, *TB1:* 13, 38, 60L, 67, 113, 117A, 117B; *TB2:* 145M, 180L; *TB3:* 283I, 305, 305F; *TB4:* 21, 37F; *TB5:* 155C, 186, 196, 219B; *TB6:* 323C

summary. *See* Summarizing.

guidelines, *TB1:* 60L; *TB2:* 145M; *TB3:* 283B, 305M; *TB4:* 37M; *TB5:* 149M; *TB6:* 255M, 321M

purpose

analyzing/evaluating literature. *See* Literature, analyzing; Literature, evaluating.

contributing information, *TB1:* 5A, 15, 60K, 60N, 65, 67, 88H, 88N, 114N, 114O; *TB2:* 127, 131, 145; *TB3:* 293; *TB4:* 18, 20, 28, 41C, 50, 58D, 58M, 69, 70, 71, 79, 84H, 84M, 84P, 85, 87, 88, 99, 111, 119, 121H, 121O; *TB5:* 140, 145, 164, 212; *TB6:* 230G, 232, 243, 255D, 255E, 255K, 257A, 257B, 257C, 257D, 257E, 263, 266, 270, 281, 282, 287C, 287G, 287N, 291, 303, 311, 321N, 321O

enjoyment, *TB1:* 60E; *TB4:* 21, 58L; *TB6:* 287M

evaluation, *TB1:* 64, 117B, 117F

explanation. *See* Literature, evaluating.

giving opinions, *TB1:* 23, 26, 60,

61, 78, 106, 117; *TB2:* 147, 148, 182; *TB3:* 248A, 275D; *TB4:* 60, 84D, 85, 123; *TB5:* 148, 166, 184, 192; *TB6:* 231C, 245, 255C, 255N, 256, 257A, 257B, 257C, 277, 285, 287B, 292, 321A, 322

role-play. *See* Creative dramatics.

self-expression, *TB1:* 60, 61, 78, 106, 117; *TB2:* 145M, 213B; *TB3:* 251; *TB5:* 155C, 166; *TB6:* 256, 260, 262, 323C

sharing experiences. *See* Sharing.

See also Fluency, speaking; Reading modes.

Speech, parts of

adjectives, *TB2:* **125C,** 193; *TB5:* **149E,** 149F, **149K–149L, 187K–187L,** 189E; *TB6:* 287A

adverbs, *TB5:* **219K–219L**

conjunction, *TB1:* 114D

nouns, *TB1:* 48; *TB2:* 145G–145H, **145K–145L, 180J–180K,** 211G, **211K–211L, 213E;** *TB3:* 248J, 248K; *TB4:* 32; *TB5:* 204; *TB6:* 255E, **255G–255H,** 255K, 255L, 287A, 287K, 287L

pronouns, *TB6:* **255E, 255K–255L, 257E, 287K–287L, 321K–321L**

verbs, *TB3:* 228, **248J–248K, 275K–275L, 305K–305L;** *TB4:* **37K–37L, 58J–58K;** *TB5:* 189B; *TB6:* 279, 287A

Spelling

assessment, *TB1:* 35F, 60I, 67D, 88I, 91D, 114I; *TB2:* 125D, 145J, 149D, 187D, 211J; *TB3:* 223D, 248I, 253D, 275J, 283J, 305J; *TB4:* 37I, 58I, 84I, 84J, 121J; *TB5:* 129D, 149J, 155D, 187J, 193D, 219J; *TB6:* 255J, 287J, 321J

integrating grammar and spelling, *TB1:* 29G, 117E; *TB2:* 213E; *TB3:* 283E; *TB4:* 91E; *TB5:* 189E; *TB6:* 257E

integrating spelling and reading consonants in *city* and *just,* *TB4:* **37J,** 37L

contractions, *TB6:* **321J,** 321L

endings, *TB4:* **58I,** 58K; *TB5:* **149J,** 149L, 189E, **219J,** 219L

homophones, *TB4:* **121J,** 121L

prefixes, *TB6:* **255J,** 255L, 257E

rules, *TB4:* 32

spelling review, *TB1:* **119B;** *TB2:* **217B;** *TB3:* **309B;** *TB4:* **123B;** *TB5:* **225B;** *TB6:* **323B**

suffixes, *TB6:* **255J,** 255L, 257E, **287J,** 287L

VCCV pattern, *TB4:* **84I,** 84K

vowels

consonant *-e, TB1:* **88I,** 88K, 117E

final *y, TB5:* **187J,** 187L, **219J,** 219L

in *cook* and *knew, TB2:* **180I,** 180K, 213E

long *a* and long *e, TB1:* **114I,** 114K, 117E

long *i* and long *o, TB2:* **145J,** 145L, 213E

plus *-r, TB3:* **275J,** 275L, 283E, **305J,** 305L

in *saw, TB3:* **248I,** 248K, 283E

short vowels, *TB1:* **60I,** 60K, 117E

in *town* and *boy, TB2:* **211J,** 211L, 213E

words often misspelled, *TB1:* **117E;** *TB2:* **213E;** *TB3:* **283E;** *TB4:* **91E;** *TB5:* **189E;** *TB6:* **257E**

See also additional spelling lists with practice on pages 139–148 of the level 3.1 *Literacy Activity Book* and on pages 149–158 of the level 3.2 *Literacy Activity Book;* Decoding skills.

Spelling, personal word lists for, *TB1:* 60I, 88I, 114I, 117E, 119B; *TB2:* 145J, 180I, 211J, 213E, 217B; *TB3:* 248I, 275J, 283E, 305J, 309B; *TB4:* 37J, 84I, 91E, 121J, 123B; *TB5:* 149J, 187J, 189E, 219J, 225B; *TB6:* 255J, 257E, 287J, 321J, 323B

Story elements/story structure

character, *TB1:* 27, **45, 60B, 60C, 83,** 116, 117, 117A, **117B,** 119A; *TB2:* 152, **207;** *TB3:* 233, 296;

189B, 216; *TB6:* 256, 263C, 281, 321B

Study skills

graphic organizers and sources. *See* Graphic information, interpreting; Graphic organizers.

information skills

library, using, *TB4:* **79, H3**; *TB6:* **317, H5**

locating, *TB3:* 222G, 251, 253C, 261, 275M; *TB4:* 19, 39, 79, 84H, 84O, 87, 121O, H2, H3, H4; *TB6:* 230H, 241, 255O, 255P, 261, 263, 274, 287I, 287O, 293, 305, 310, 321B, 321N, 321O, H2, H3, H4, H5

See also Information activities.

reference sources

calendars, *TB6:* **259, H2**

dictionary, using the pronunciation key, *TB6:* **321H**

encyclopedias, using, *TB1:* 88N, 114N; *TB6:* **261, H3**

globes, *TB4:* **39, H2**

parts of a book, *TB3:* **265, H4**

study strategies

adjusting reading rate. *See* Adjusting reading rate.

directions, following, *TB3:* **281, H6**

K-W-L, *TB1:* **65, H3**

SQRR, *TB2:* **185, H4**

taking notes, *TB1:* **63, H2**; *TB4:* **H5**

test taking, *TB5:* **191, H2**

See also Graphic information; Graphic organizers; Information skills; Research activities.

Study strategies. *See* Skills, major; Strategies, reading; Study skills.

Suffixes. See Structural Analysis; Think About Words.

Summarizing

oral summaries, *TB1:* 12, 27, 45, 60B–60C, 70, 78, **80, 83,** 88, 96, 102, 107, 114, 117C, 119A; *TB3:* 226, 232, 240, 246, 260, 266, 283A, 296; *TB4:* 37M, 80, 102, 112; *TB5:* 132, 142, 162, 184; *TB6:* 257C, 296, 304, 316

written summaries, *TB5:* 132, **143,** 148, 158, 176, 178, 186

Syllabication, *TB3:* **275G–275H**

Symbols, *TB4:* 18, 58M

Syntax, *TB1:* 60J–60K

T

Teacher-guided reading. *See* Reading modes, guided reading.

Teaching across the curriculum. *See* Content areas, reading in the; Cross-curricular activities.

Teaching and management

grouping students flexibly, *TB1:* 34D; *TB2:* 124D; *TB3:* 222D, 275L, 275O, 292; *TB4:* 41C, 61C; *TB5:* 128D; *TB6:* 230C–230D, 230E, 231B, 231C, 263B, 263C, 293B, 293C

managing assessment, *TB1:* 5A, 30B, 34F, 119B; *TB2:* 124F, 217B; *TB3:* 222F, 309B; *TB4:* 16F, 123B; *TB5:* 128F, 225B; *TB6:* 230F, 323B

managing instruction, *TB1:* 4A, 7A, 10A, 91C; *TB2:* 124E, 125C, 149C, 187C; *TB3:* 222D, 222E, 248B, 248E, 253C, 283I; *TB4:* 16C–16D, 41B, 61B, 90; *TB5:* 129C, 155C, 193C, 225B; *TB6:* 230C–230D, 230E, 230F, 256, 263B, 293B

managing program materials, *TB1:* 9A, 34C–34D, 35D, 67B, 91B; *TB2:* 124C–124D, 125B, 149B, 187B; *TB3:* 222C–222D, 223B, 253B; *TB4:* 16C–16D, 41B, 61B, 90, 123B; *TB5:* 128C–128D, 129B, 155B, 193B; *TB6:* 230C–230D, 230E, 230F, 256, 263B, 293B

special needs of students, meeting. *See* Individual needs, meeting.

Technology resources

Channel R.E.A.D., *TB1:* 34B, 34E, 60C, 114C; *TB2:* 124B, 124E, 125B, 145D, 149B, 180C; *TB3:* 222B, 222E, 248C, 253B, 275D, 283H, 305D; *TB4:* 16B, 16E, 61B, 84C; *TB5:* 128B, 128E, 155B, 187D, 193B, 219D; *TB6:* 230B, 230E, 231B, 263B, 287D, 293B, 321D

Great Start CD-ROM, *TB1:* 34B, 34E, 35D, 35E, 67B, 67C, 91B, 91C; *TB2:* 124B, 124E, 125B, 125C, 149B, 149C, 187B, 187C; *TB3:* 222B, 222E, 223B, 223C, 253B, 253C, 283I; *TB4:* 16B, 16E, 41B, 41C, 61B, 61C; *TB5:* 128B, 128E, 129B, 155B, 155C, 193B, 193C; *TB6:* 230B, 230E, 231B, 231C, 263B, 263C, 293B, 293C

Internet: Education Place, *TB1:* 34B, 34E, 34G; *TB2:* 124B, 124E, 124G; *TB3:* 222E, 222G; *TB4:* 16B, 16E, 16G; *TB5:* 128B, 128E, 128G; *TB6:* 230B, 230E, 230G

Spelling Spree CD-ROM, *TB1:* 34B, 34E, 35D, 60I, 67B, 88I, 91B, 114I; *TB2:* 124B, 124E, 125B, 145J, 149B, 180I, 187B, 211J; *TB3:* 222B, 222E, 223B, 248I, 253B, 275J, 283H, 305J; *TB4:* 16B, 16E, 17B, 37J, 41B, 58I, 61B, 84I, 91H, 121J; *TB5:* 128B, 128E, 129B, 149J, 155B, 187J, 193B, 219J; *TB6:* 230B, 230E, 231B, 255J, 263B, 287J, 293B, 321J

Teacher's Resource Disk, *TB1:* 34B, 34G, 119C; *TB2:* 124B, 124G; *TB3:* 222G; *TB4:* 16B, 16G; *TB5:* 128B, 128G; *TB6:* 230B, 230G

Tech Tips, *TB1:* 29F, 117C, 117D; *TB2:* 213C; *TB3:* 283D; *TB4:* 91D; *TB5:* 189C; *TB6:* 257E

Ultimate Writing & Creativity Center software, *TB1:* 29C, 34B, 35B, 60E, 67B, 88E, 91B, 114E, 117A, 117D, 117E; *TB2:* 124B, 124E, 125B, 145F, 149B, 180E, 187B, 211F, 213D, 213E; *TB3:* 222E, 223B, 253B, 275F, 283D, 283E, 283H; *TB4:* 16E, 37F, 41B, 58E, 61B, 84E, 91D, 91E, 121F; *TB5:* 128B, 128E, 129B, 149F, 155B, 187F, 189D, 189E, 193B, 219F; *TB6:* 230B, 230E, 231B, 255F, 257D, 257E, 263B, 287F, 283B, 321F

Text organization, *TB2:* 147, 185; *TB3:* 248C, 253C; *TB5:* **137,**